SCHOOLING AND LANGUAGE MINORITY STUDENTS: A THEORETICAL FRAMEWORK

Second Edition

Edited by
Charles F. Leyba

Published by

Evaluation, Dissemination and Assessment Center
School of Education
California State University, Los Angeles
Los Angeles, California

Developed in cooperation with

California State Department of Education
Bilingual Education Office
Sacramento, California

ISBN: 0-89755-030-7

Library of Congress Catalog Card Number: 94-61644

This publication was funded in whole or in part by a contract (G007902844) between the California State Department of Education and the United States Education Department. The opinions expressed herein do not, however, necessarily
reflect the positions or policy of the United States Education Department; no official endorsement by the United States Education Department should be
inferred.

Published and Disseminated by

EVALUATION, DISSEMINATION AND ASSESSMENT CENTER
California State University, Los Angeles
5300 Paseo Rancho Castilla, #2105
Box 2-019
Los Angeles, California 90032

Developed in cooperation with

BILINGUAL EDUCATION OFFICE
California State Department of Education
Sacramento, California

First Edition Published 1981
Second Edition Published 1994
Printed in USA

ACKNOWLEDGMENTS

Sincere appreciation, in the first instance, must be extended to three pioneering authors whose work appeared in the first edition of this volume and appears in this second edition as well: James Cummins, Stephen Krashen, and Eleanor Thonis.

We welcome and extend equally sincere appreciation to two new authors, Marguerite Ann Snow and Alan Crawford, whose excellent contributions to this second edition replace those of Dorothy Legarreta-Marcaida and Tracy Terrell who have passed away since publication of the first edition.

Particular gratitude is extended to two administrators: Allen Mori, Dean, School of Education, California State University, Los Angeles, and David Dolson, Consultant, Bilingual Education Office, California State Department of Education.

Dr. Mori has continually lent strong support to all our efforts in serving language minority students and in preparing and training their teachers to serve in multicultural/multilingual settings. His good judgment generously lent to our efforts has invariably endowed them with excellence.

Dr. Dolson, Project Team Leader in developing the first edition, has contributed an Introduction and a revised Appendix for the second edition. He also reviewed the contributions of our five authors. This was done despite the many and diverse activities required by his office.

In short, the high quality found in the current edition is due to, and fully merited by, the persons mentioned.

Charles F. Leyba, Ph.D.
Director
Bilingual Training Center

BIOGRAPHICAL SKETCHES

ALAN N. CRAWFORD is Professor of Education and Chair of the Division of Curriculum and Instruction at California State University, Los Angeles. During the United Nations-sponsored International Literacy Year, 1990, he served as a senior literacy specialist at UNESCO in Paris. He is the author of many articles and publications on second language acquisition and reading for Spanish-speaking children. He is also the co-author of several reading/language arts programs in both English and Spanish.

* * *

JIM CUMMINS (Ph.D. University of Alberta, 1974) is currently a professor in the Modern Language Centre and Curriculum Department of the Ontario Institute for Studies in Education. He has published several books related to bilingual education and minority student achievement including **Bilingualism and Special Education: Issues in Assessment and Pedagogy** (Multilingual Matters, 1984), **Bilingualism in Education: Aspects of Theory, Research and Policy** (Longman, 1986, with Merrill Swain), **Minority Education: From Shame to Struggle** (Multilingual Matters, 1988, with Tove Skutnabb-Kangas) and **Empowering Minority Students** (California Association for Bilingual Education, 1989).

* * *

STEPHEN KRASHEN is Professor of Linguistics at the University of Southern California. He has published extensively on second language acquisition theory, second language teaching, and neurolinguistics. He is the author of **Second Language Acquisition and Second Language Learning** (Pergamon Press, 1981), co-author of **The Human Brain** (Prentice-Hall, 1977), and co-editor of **Research in Second Language Acquisition** (Newbury House, 1980).

MARGUERITE ANN SNOW is Associate Professor at California State University, Los Angeles, where she teaches in the Teaching English to Speakers of Other Languages (TESOL) M.A. program and co-directs Project LEAP: Learning English for Academic Purposes, a U.S. Department of Education grant to improve instruction for language minority students. She is co-author of **Content-Based Second-Language Instruction** (Newbury House, 1989), and co-editor of **The Multicultural Classroom: Readings for Content-Area Teachers** (Longman, 1992). She has published in **TESOL Quarterly, The Modern Language Journal,** and **Applied Linguistics.** In 1985, she was awarded a Fulbright fellowship to teach in Hong Kong and more recently, she has trained teachers in Brazil, the Czech Republic, Hungary, Japan, Latvia, Russia, Morocco, and Pakistan.

*　　　*　　　*

ELEANOR WALL THONIS is the district psychologist for Wheatland Elementary School District; a part-time instructor, University of California, Berkeley; and the consultant for bilingual education in the Marysville Unified School District. She has served as the director of the area Reading Center and is the author of several publications on reading for language minority students.

INTRODUCTION

The purpose of the first edition of the **Theoretical Framework** was to collect, organize, and present to educators a comprehensive and understandable review of research on language minority education. It was thought that such information would improve the ability of educators to predict individual and group outcomes for specific types of students, given certain types of instructional treatments, under different types of background conditions. The articles contained in the first volume were viewed as an initial step in the promotion of effective programs and practices for schooling language minority students. The status of the volume was described in the following manner:

> This publication is a progress report, not a collection of proven answers. The theoretical framework implied in this volume is, however, based on the best information that science can provide at this time. The research herein reported does not lead to perfect programs with perfect outcomes, nor does it answer all the questions regarding language development, language acquisition, and cognitive/academic development in bilingual contexts. But, taken collectively, these articles form the beginning of a research-based theoretical framework for planning and improving bilingual education programs. (p. iii)

Now, more than a decade later, this new edition represents a second progress report. Those involved in this revision have reviewed the five papers making up the 1981 volume and attempted to (1) refine and clarify basic concepts, (2) update the supporting evidence for the primary hypotheses and postulates, and (3) identify and further explain the major implications of the research. Most importantly, the authors have expanded upon the original research base and added new and increasingly important information on various cultural, social, and political ramifications of language minority education. What has not been changed in this edition is the persistent focus on the potential practical applications of the research—a feature that makes this publication particularly useful to educators.

When the first edition of the **Theoretical Framework** was published in 1981, California's schools had an enrollment of 810,000 language minority students, 375,000 of which were classified, on the basis of objective assessment, as students of limited English proficiency (LEP). In 1993, these numbers have nearly doubled, with schools reporting enrollments of 1,700,000 language minority and 1,200,000 LEP students, respectively. California has more than half of all the language minority students enrolled in kindergarten through grade twelve in the United States. These demographic trends suggest that racial and ethnic minorities, including language minority students, may soon become the new numerical majority in the state. From a demographic perspective, the issue of language minority education is more important than ever.

The contributors to the first volume clearly promoted the establishment of rigorous language and academic programs in which participants would become successful students and proficient bilinguals. Many educators, succumbing to fierce social, political, and economic opposition to bilingual education, decided instead to implement early-exit transitional bilingual programs in which the primary language of the language minority students was more likely to be used to support structured English immersion (a.k.a. sheltered, specially designed academic instruction in English—SDAIE) instruction rather than as a vehicle to develop high levels of literacy and provide full access to the core curriculum. These educators speculated that such programs would be sufficient to provide language minority students with equal educational opportunities. Recent studies have provided clear evidence that most early-exit bilingual and structured immersion programs fail to close the academic gap between language minority and native speakers of English. This finding has sparked renewed interest in developing comprehensive bilingual program designs that elude the inherent flaws of compensatory models. The articles in this volume address the theoretical underpinnings, the programmatic structures, and the essential instructional elements associated with these more effective and powerful approaches.

The underlying theme of the first edition of the **Theoretical Framework** was that educators of language minority students must become knowledgeable of a myriad of linguistic, academic, and sociocultural factors in order to be thoroughly competent providers of formal schooling for this at-risk group of children and youth. Now, in addition, we realize that the provision of adequate educational programs for non-English background students is a very significant part of the much larger struggle for social justice for minority groups. Under this scenario, educators must decide on the role they will play in challenging those aspects of our educational system which work against rather than facilitate the establishment of authentic bilingual and crosscultural programs which empower minority groups and enlighten the majority group. As formidable as this sounds, our success in advocating for these fundamental changes in our educational system may well determine the degree to which future generations of Americans from all racial, ethnic, and language groups are able to live together in harmony.

David P. Dolson
Project Team Leader
Bilingual Education Office

CONTENTS

Part One
Theoretical Foundations

Primary Language Instruction and the Education of Language Minority Students

Jim Cummins

As diversity increases, school systems throughout California are coming to grips with the fact that culturally diverse students are the mainstream population in many urban and rural districts. The persistent academic difficulties experienced by a significant proportion of these students have implications for the prosperity of the entire state as we enter an era in which knowledge and intellectual resources are key to growth in a highly competitive global economy. In past generations, racist ideologies that resulted in grossly inferior educational opportunities for culturally diverse groups such as African-Americans, Latinos/Latinas, and Native Americans served to maintain the economic and social status quo (i.e., the power structure) in the society. There was no shortage of menial work that undereducated individuals could perform. By contrast, today the economic performance of a nation depends on its intellectual and informational resources which are directly determined by the success of its schools in educating all its citizens. Employment opportunities are increasingly limited for undereducated individuals, and the costs of undereducation to the society are enormous. For example, research suggests that for every dollar invested in preschool Head Start programs, taxpayers will save seven dollars in reduced costs for later social services that these children or adults will not need (e.g., special education, welfare, incarceration) (Schweinhart, Weikart, & Larney, 1986). Despite the fact that education is a far better public investment than incarceration, the level of K-12 educational expenditures of the U.S. is considerably lower than that of other industrialized countries (in 1985, 4.1% of gross domestic product compared with a non-U.S. average of 4.6%) (Hodgkinson, 1991).

In short, discrimination in educational provision is not only repugnant from the perspective of social justice (and the ideals of the U.S. Constitution), it directly jeopardizes the economic and social prospects of *all* citizens. In view of this reality, everybody has a vested interest in reversing the legacy of educational failure that culturally diverse students have experienced historically.

This chapter attempts to present a framework for understanding the causes of minority students' underachievement and proposes directions for reversing this pattern. I argue that the causes of underachievement are rooted in the continuation of historical patterns of coercive relations of power between dominant and subordinated groups. These relations of power find expression in educational structures that limit students' possibilities for learning and for developing a strong sense of cultural identity. They also find expression in the ways educators define their roles in relation to minority students and communities. Both the educational structures and educator role definitions affect the interactions that minority students experience in the school system. Reversal of educational failure requires that the interactions that occur in school between educators and students be empowering for both; in other words, power must be generated in these interactions for both educators and students. This chapter will examine the kinds of educational structures and educator role definitions that will challenge coercive relations of power and promote collaborative relations of power in the school system.

Before analyzing how power is negotiated in educational settings, I will review the research on the development of second language proficiency, bilingualism, and bilingual education in the context of the debate on the education of language minority students during the past 25 years. I will suggest that the research data support three theoretical principles that are central to program planning for language minority students. These principles are: (a) the conversational/academic language proficiency principle, (b) the linguistic interdependence principle, and (c) the additive bilingualism enrichment principle. The research data will be reviewed under these headings.

The Conversational/Academic Language Proficiency Principle

Appropriate ways of conceptualizing the nature of language proficiency and its relationship to other constructs (e.g., "intelligence") have been debated by philosophers and psychologists since ancient times. However, the issue is not just an abstract theoretical question but one that is central to the resolution of a variety of applied educational issues. Educational policies are frequently based on assumptions about the nature of "language proficiency" and how long it takes to attain. For example, funding for English as a second language (ESL) and bilingual education classes in North America is based (at least in part) on assumptions about how long it takes language minority students to acquire sufficient English proficiency to follow instruction in the regular classroom. Yet what exactly constitutes "English proficiency" is rarely analyzed by policy makers or researchers.

Misconceptions about the Nature of Language Proficiency

Two major misconceptions regarding the nature of language proficiency remain common among educators in North America. These misconceptions have important *practical* implications for the way educators interact with culturally diverse students. Both involve a confusion between the surface or conversational aspects of children's language and deeper aspects of proficiency that are more closely related to conceptual and academic development.

The first misconception entails drawing inferences about children's ability to think logically on the basis of their familiarity with and command of standard English. Children who speak a non-standard variety of English (or their first language [L1]) are frequently thought to be handicapped educationally and less capable of logical thinking. This assumption derives from the fact that these children's language is viewed as inherently deficient as a tool for expressing logical relations. Since Labov's (1970) refutation of this position with respect to the language of African-American inner-city children, it has found few adherents among applied linguists, although it is still a common misconception among some educators and academics who have little background in sociolinguistics.

A recent example of how persistent some of these linguistic prejudices are among academics who know little about language comes from a monograph on Latino/Latina children written by Lloyd Dunn (1987), the primary author of the Peabody Picture Vocabulary Test. In expressing his concerns that bilingual education could result in "at least the partial disintegration of the United States of America" (pp. 66-67), Dunn argues that Latino/Latina children and adults "speak inferior Spanish" and that "Latin pupils on the U.S. mainland, as a group, are inadequate bilinguals. They simply don't understand either English or Spanish well enough to function adequately in school" (p. 49). He goes on to argue that this is due to the fact that these children "do not have the scholastic aptitude or linguistic ability to master two languages well, or to handle switching from one to the other, at school, as the language of instruction" (p. 71). He attributes the causes of this lower scholastic ability approximately equally to environmental factors and "to genes that influence scholastic aptitude" (p. 64). (See the special issue of the *Hispanic Journal of Behavioral Science,* vol. 10, 1988, for critical discussion of Dunn's views.)

The second misconception is in many respects the converse of the first. In this case, children's adequate control over the surface features of English (i.e., their ability to converse fluently in English) is taken as an indication that all aspects of their "English proficiency" have been mastered to the same extent as native speakers of the language. In other words, conversational skills are interpreted as a valid index of overall proficiency in the language.

This implicit assumption has had a major impact on the organization of bilingual education programs in the United States. The rationale for bilingual education, as it is understood by most policy makers and practitioners, can be stated as follows:

> Lack of English proficiency is the major reason for language minority students' academic failure. Bilingual education is intended to ensure that students do not fall behind in subject matter content while they are learning English, as they would likely do in an all-English program. However, when students have become proficient in English, then they can be exited to an all-English program, since limited English proficiency will no longer impede their academic progress.

Despite its intuitive appeal, there are serious problems with this rationale. First, it ignores the social and historical determinants of language minority students' school failure which, it will be argued, are more fundamental than linguistic factors. Second, an inadequate understanding of what is meant by "English proficiency" is likely to result in the creation of academic deficits in language minority students.

Some concrete examples will help illustrate how this process operates. These examples are taken from a study conducted in western Canada in which the teacher referral forms and psychological assessments of over 400 language minority students were analyzed (Cummins, 1984). Throughout the teacher referral forms and psychological assessment reports there are references to the fact that children's English communicative skills appeared considerably better developed than their academic language skills. The following examples illustrate this point:

> *PS (094)*. Referred for reading and arithmetic difficulties in second grade, teacher commented that "since PS attended grade one in Italy, I think his main problem is language, although he understands and speaks English quite well."
>
> *GG (184)*. Although he had been in Canada for less than a year, in November of the grade one year, the teacher commented that "he speaks Italian fluently and English as well." However, she also referred him for psychological assessment because "he is having a great deal of difficulty with the grade one program" and she wondered if he had "specific learning disabilities or if he is just a very long way behind children in his age group."
>
> *DM (105)*. Arrived from Portugal at age 10 and was placed in a second grade class; three years later in fifth grade, her teacher commented that "her oral answering and comprehension is so much better than her written work that we feel a severe learning problem is involved, not just her non-English background."

These examples illustrate the influence of the environment in developing English conversational skills. In many instances immigrant students were considered to have sufficient English proficiency to take a verbal IQ test within about one year of arrival in Canada. Similarly, in the United States, language minority students are often considered to have developed sufficient English proficiency to cope with the demands of an all-English classroom after a relatively short time in a bilingual or ESL program.

There is little doubt that many language minority students can develop a relatively high degree of English conversational skills within about two years of exposure to English-speaking peers, television, and schooling. However, we cannot logically extrapolate from the considerable English proficiency that students may display in face-to-face communication to their overall proficiency in English. If we do, we risk contributing to students' academic difficulties.

Consider the following example:

> *PR (289).* PR was referred in first grade by the school prin-
> cipal who noted that "PR is experiencing considerable dif-
> ficulty with grade one work. An intellectual assessment
> would help her teacher to set realistic learning expectations
> for her and might provide some clues as to remedial assistance
> that might be offered."

No mention was made of the child's ESL background; this only
emerged when the child was referred by the second grade teacher in the
following year. Thus, the psychologist does not consider this as a possible factor in accounting for the discrepancy between a verbal IQ of 64
and a performance IQ of 108. The assessment report reads as follows:

> Although overall ability level appears to be within the low
> average range, note the significant difference between verbal
> and nonverbal scores....It would appear that PR's develop-
> ment has not progressed at a normal rate and consequently
> she is, and will continue to experience much difficulty in
> school. Teacher's expectations at this time should be set
> accordingly.

What is interesting in this example is that the child's English communicative skills are presumably sufficiently well developed that the
psychologist (and possibly the teacher) is not alerted to the child's ESL
background. This leads the psychologist to infer from her low verbal IQ
score that "her development has not progressed at a normal rate" and to
advise the teacher to set low academic expectations for the child since she
"will continue to experience much difficulty in school." There is ample
evidence from many contexts of how the attribution of deficient
cognitive skills to language minority students can become self-fulfilling.
Ortiz and Yates (1983), for example, report that more than three times as
many Latino/Latina students were classified as "learning disabled" in
Texas than would be expected based on their proportion in the school
population. These classifications usually resulted in a one-way ticket
into special education classes where students fell even further behind
academically.

In many of the referral forms and psychological assessments analyzed in the Cummins (1984) study, the following line of reasoning was invoked:

> Because language minority students are fluent in English, their poor academic performance and/or test scores cannot be attributed to lack of proficiency in English. Therefore, these students must either have deficient cognitive abilities or be poorly motivated.

The trend to exit students to all-English programs as quickly as possible in many bilingual programs inevitably gives rise to a similar line of reasoning. It is commonly observed that students classified as "English proficient" after a relatively short stay in a bilingual program and then exited to an all-English program often fall progressively further behind grade norms in the development of English academic skills. Because these students appear to be fluent in English, their poor academic performance can no longer be explained by the fact that their English language abilities are still in the process of development. Policy makers and educators are also reluctant to blame the school for minority students' poor performance because the school has accommodated the students by providing a bilingual program (albeit usually one with minimal first language [L1] instruction). Thus, the academic deficiency is typically attributed to factors within the child or his or her community, as in Dunn's (1987) argument outlined above.

In both of the misconceptions outlined here, a close relationship is assumed between the two faces of language proficiency, the conversational and the academic. In order to address these misconceptions and clarify the relationship between language proficiency and minority students' academic progress, I have suggested that it is necessary to make a fundamental distinction between conversational and academic aspects of language proficiency (Cummins, 1981a, 1984). This distinction is similar to that proposed by a number of other investigators (e.g., Bruner, 1975; Donaldson, 1978; Olson, 1977; Snow et al., 1991).

These investigators have pointed to a distinction between *contextualized* and *decontextualized* language as fundamental to understanding the nature of children's language and literacy development. The terms used by different investigators have varied but the essential distinction refers to the extent to which the meaning being communicated is supported by contextual or interpersonal cues (such as gestures, facial expressions, and intonation present in face-to-face interaction) or dependent largely on linguistic cues that are largely independent of the immediate communicative context. To illustrate the nature of linguistic cues, a cohesive device such as *however* coming at the beginning of a sentence tells the proficient reader (or listener) to expect some qualification to the immediately preceding statement. Lack of experience with or sensitivity to such linguistic cues will reduce students' ability to interpret meaning in decontextualized settings where interpersonal or non-linguistic cues are lacking.

In discussing this distinction between contextualized and decontextualized language, I originally used the terms *basic interpersonal communicative skills* (BICS) and *cognitive academic language proficiency* (CALP) and later (e.g., Cummins, 1981a, 1984) elaborated the distinction into a framework that distinguished the cognitive and contextual demands made by particular forms of communication.

Cognitive and Contextual Demands

The framework outlined in Figure 1 is designed to identify the extent to which students are able to cope successfully with the cognitive and linguistic demands made on them by the social and educational environment in which they are obliged to function. These dimensions are conceptualized within a framework made up of the intersection of two continua, one relating to the range of contextual support available for expressing or receiving meaning and the other relating to the amount of information that must be processed simultaneously or in close succession by the student in order to carry out the activity.

Figure 1

**RANGE OF CONTEXTUAL SUPPORT AND DEGREE
OF COGNITIVE INVOLVEMENT IN
COMMUNICATIVE ACTIVITIES**

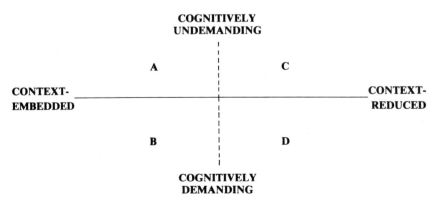

The extremes of the context-embedded/context-reduced continuum are distinguished by the fact that in context-embedded communication the participants can actively negotiate meaning (e.g., by providing feedback that the message has not been understood) and the language is supported by a wide range of meaningful interpersonal and situational cues. Context-reduced communication, on the other hand, relies primarily (or, at the extreme of the continuum, exclusively) on linguistic cues to meaning, and thus successful interpretation of the message depends heavily on knowledge of the language itself. In general, context-embedded communication is more typical of the everyday world outside the classroom, whereas many of the linguistic demands of the classroom (e.g., manipulating text) reflect communicative activities that are close to the context-reduced end of the continuum.

The upper parts of the vertical continuum consist of communicative tasks and activities in which the linguistic tools have become largely automatized and thus require little active cognitive involvement for appropriate performance. At the lower end of the continuum are tasks and activities in which the linguistic tools have not become automatized and thus require active cognitive involvement. Persuading another individual that your point of view is correct, and writing an essay, are examples of quadrant C and D skills, respectively.

The framework elaborates on the conversational/academic (or BICS/CALP) distinction by highlighting important underlying dimensions of conversational and academic communication. Thus, conversational abilities (quadrant A) often develop relatively quickly among language minority students because these forms of communication are supported by interpersonal and contextual cues and make relatively few cognitive demands on the individual. Mastery of the academic functions of language (quadrant D), on the other hand, is a more formidable task because such uses require high levels of cognitive involvement and are only minimally supported by contextual or interpersonal cues.

It is important to stress that the distinction between conversational and academic aspects of language proficiency is not one between oral and written language. Performing an oral cloze task may be far more context-reduced than sending an electronic mail message to a good friend, an activity that in many respects is highly context-embedded.

How Long Does It Take Language Minority Students to Master Different Aspects of Proficiency?

One application of the framework considered in Figure 1 is in the interpretation of data regarding the time required for bilingual students to develop proficiency in different aspects of English. Two large-scale studies have reported that, on the average, at least five years is required for ESL students to attain grade norms on academic (context-reduced, cognitively demanding) aspects of English proficiency (Collier, 1987, 1989; Cummins, 1981b). Collier's data are particularly interesting in that most students studied were from relatively affluent backgrounds attending a district school (Fairfax County, Virginia) that was regarded as having an exemplary ESL program (and no bilingual education). She reports that children who arrived in the United States between ages 8 and 12 with several years of L1 schooling required five to seven years to reach national norms in reading, social studies, and science. Those who arrived before age 8 required seven to ten years to attain national norms, while those who arrived after age 12 often ran out of time before they could catch up academically in language-based areas of the curriculum. A considerably shorter period of time was usually required to catch up in math.

Cummins (1981b) also reported that five to seven years were required for immigrant students from non-English-speaking backgrounds to catch up academically in English proficiency. Students who had been in Canada for three years were approximately one standard deviation (the equivalent of 15 IQ points) behind grade norms despite the fact that after three years most would have become relatively fluent in English conversational skills.

Students who arrive after developing literacy in their L1 have a second advantage in that they are less likely to lose their L1 than students who arrive at younger ages (see, e.g., Cummins et al., 1984). Language minority students typically experience rapid loss of L1 in the first few years of learning English in preschool or in the early grades (Cummins, 1991; Wong Fillmore, 1991a). In short, students who arrive between ages 8 and 12 have the best prospect for developing proficient bilingual and biliterate abilities, a conclusion that agrees with the data of Skutnabb-Kangas and Toukomaa (1976).

Other research suggests that a much shorter period (less than two years) is usually required for immigrant students to attain peer-appropriate levels of proficiency in conversational (context-embedded, cognitively undemanding) aspects of their second language (e.g., Gonzalez, 1986; Snow and Hoefnagel-Hohle, 1978). These patterns are depicted in Figure 2.

There are two reasons why such major differences are found in the length of time required to attain peer-appropriate levels of conversational and academic skills. First, as outlined above, considerably less knowledge of language *per se* is usually required to function appropriately in interpersonal communicative situations than is required in academic situations. The social expectations of the learner and sensitivity to contextual cues greatly facilitate communication of meaning. These cues are largely absent in most academic situations that depend on literacy skills and manipulation of language for successful task completion.

The second reason is that English L1 speakers are not standing still waiting for ESL students to catch up. A major goal of schooling for all children is to expand their ability to manipulate language in increasingly decontextualized situations, and every year English L1 speaking students

Figure 2

LENGTH OF TIME REQUIRED TO ACHIEVE AGE-APPROPRIATE LEVELS OF CONTEXT-EMBEDDED AND CONTEXT-REDUCED COMMUNICATIVE PROFICIENCY

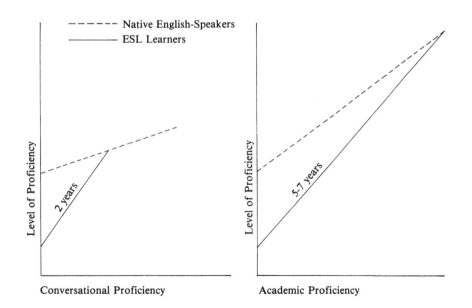

gain more sophisticated vocabulary and grammatical knowledge and increase their literacy skills. Thus, ESL students must catch up with a moving target. It is not surprising that this formidable task is seldom complete in one or two years. By contrast, in the area of conversational skills, most native speakers have reached a plateau relatively early in schooling in the sense that a typical six-year-old can express herself as adequately as an older child on most topics she is likely to speak on and understand most of what is likely to be addressed to her. While some increase in conversational sophistication can be expected with increasing age, the differences are not particularly salient in comparison with the differences in literacy-related skills (compare, for example, the differences in literacy between a twelve and a six-year-old student in contrast to differences in their conversational skills).

The preceding discussion of the nature of language proficiency and the length of time required to develop peer-appropriate levels of conversational and academic skills have immediate relevance for two practical issues. First, support for language and academic development is still beneficial (and frequently necessary) even after students have attained conversational fluency in English. Exiting of children prematurely from bilingual or ESL support programs may jeopardize their academic development, particularly if the mainstream classroom does not provide an environment that is supportive of language and content development.

It is also clear that psychological assessment of language minority students conducted in English is likely to underestimate students' academic potential to a significant extent if any credence is placed in the test norms which are derived predominantly from native English-speaking students. It is clear that as the numbers of language minority students increase in school systems across North America, a radical restructuring of special education placement and assessment procedures will be required (Rueda, 1989).

The Linguistic Interdependence Principle

Arguments Opposing Bilingual Education

Opponents of bilingual education have consistently argued that bilingual programs not only threaten the unity of the United States, but are also spurious in their educational rationale. It is illogical, they claim, to argue that less English instruction will result in greater English achievement (e.g., Bethell, 1979; Dunn, 1987; Porter, 1990; Schlesinger, 1991).

Consider, for example, the view expressed by Bethell (1979) in the early days of this debate:

> Bilingual education is an idea that appeals to teachers of Spanish and other tongues, but also to those who never did think that another idea, the United States of America, was a particularly good one to begin with, and that the sooner it is restored to its component "ethnic" parts the better off we shall all be. Such people have been welcomed with open arms into the upper reaches of the federal government in recent years, giving rise to the suspicion of a death wish. (p. 30)

He goes on to quote approvingly Congressman John Ashbrook's opposition to bilingual education:

> The program is actually preventing children from learning English. Someday somebody is going to have to teach those young people to speak English or else they are going to become public charges. Our educational system is finding it increasingly difficult today to teach English-speaking children to read their own language. When children come out of the Spanish-language schools or Choctaw-language schools which call themselves bilingual, how is our educational system going to make them literate in what will still be a completely alien tongue...? (pp. 32-33)

The same arguments have been rehashed repeatedly in more recent years. Rosalie Pedalino Porter (1990) clearly articulates what she terms the "time-on-task" principle in stating:

> My personal experience and professional investigations together impel me to conclude that the two overriding conditions that promote the best learning of a second language are (1) starting at an early age, say at five, and (2) having as much exposure and carefully planned instruction in the language as possible. Effective time on task — the amount of time spent learning — is, as educators know, the single greatest predictor of educational achievement; this is at least as true, if not more so, for low-socioeconomic-level, limited-English students. Children learn what they are taught, and if they are taught

mainly in Spanish for several years, their Spanish-language skills will be far better than their English-language ones. (pp. 63-64)

A final example of the neo-conservative position on bilingualism and bilingual education comes from Arthur Schlesinger, Jr. (1991) in his book *The Disuniting of America:*

In recent years the combination of the ethnicity cult with a flood of immigration from Spanish-speaking countries has given bilingualism new impetus....Alas, bilingualism has not worked out as planned: rather the contrary. Testimony is mixed, but indications are that bilingual education retards rather than expedites the movement of Hispanic children into the English-speaking world and that it promotes segregation rather than it does integration. Bilingualism shuts doors. It nourishes self-ghettoization, and ghettoization nourishes racial antagonism....Using some language other than English dooms people to second-class citizenship in American society....Monolingual education opens doors to the larger world....Institutionalized bilingualism remains another source of the fragmentation of America, another threat to the dream of "one people." (pp. 108-109)

Leaving aside for the moment the extraordinary claims that "bilingualism shuts doors" and "monolingual education opens doors to the wider world," it is clear that opponents share some common psychoeducational assumptions about the effects of instruction through two languages. Their argument that deficiencies in English should be remediated by intensive instruction in English appears at first sight much more intuitively appealing than the alternative argument that instruction in L1 will be more effective in promoting English skills. This latter argument appears to invoke a "less equals more" type of logic that is unlikely to convince skeptics. In order to evaluate these alternative positions, it is necessary to make their propositions more explicit and make empirical evidence rather than "common sense" the criterion of validity. The issues revolve around two alternative conceptions of bilingual proficiency, termed the Separate Underlying Proficiency (SUP) and Common Underlying Proficiency (CUP) models.

The SUP and CUP Models of Bilingual Proficiency

The argument that if minority children are deficient in English, then
they need instruction in English, not in their L1, implies: (a) that proficiency in L1 is separate from proficiency in English, and (b) that there is
a direct relationship between exposure to a language (in home or school)
and achievement in that language. The SUP model is illustrated in
Figure 3.

Figure 3

**THE SEPARATE UNDERLYING PROFICIENCY (SUP) MODEL
OF BILINGUAL PROFICIENCY**

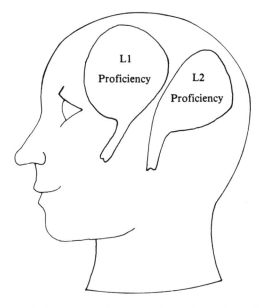

The second implication of the SUP model follows from the first: If L1
and L2 proficiency are separate, then content and skills learned through
L1 cannot transfer to L2 and vice versa. In terms of the balloon
metaphor illustrated in Figure 3, blowing into the L1 balloon will succeed
in inflating L1 but not L2. When bilingual education is approached with
these "common-sense" assumptions about bilingual proficiency, it is not
at all surprising that it appears illogical to argue that L2 proficiency can
be more effectively developed through L1 instruction.

However, despite its intuitive appeal, the empirical evidence clearly
refutes the SUP model by showing significant transfer of conceptual

knowledge and skills across languages.   To account for the evidence
(reviewed below), we must posit a common underlying proficiency
(CUP) model in which the literacy-related aspects of a bilingual's proficiency in L1 and L2 are seen as common or interdependent across
languages.   Two ways of illustrating the CUP model (the linguistic
interdependence principle) are shown in Figures 4 and 5.

Figure 4

THE COMMON UNDERLYING PROFICIENCY MODEL (CUP)
OF BILINGUAL PROFICIENCY

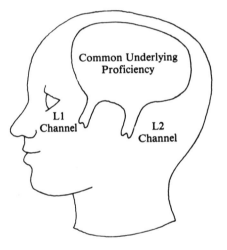

Figure 5

THE "DUAL-ICEBERG" REPRESENTATION OF
BILINGUAL PROFICIENCY

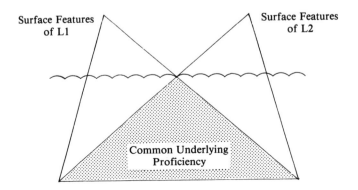

Figure 4 expresses the point that experience with either language can promote development of the proficiency underlying both languages, given adequate motivation and exposure to both either in school or in the wider environment. In Figure 5 bilingual proficiency is represented by means of a "dual iceberg" in which common cross-lingual proficiencies underlie the obviously different surface manifestations of each language. In general, the surface features of L1 and L2 are those that have become relatively automatized or less cognitively demanding whereas the underlying proficiency is that involved in cognitively demanding tasks.

The linguistic interdependence principle can be formally stated as follows:

> To the extent that instruction in Lx is effective in promoting proficiency in Lx, transfer of this proficiency to Ly will occur provided there is adequate exposure to Ly (either in school or in the environment) and adequate motivation to learn Ly.

In concrete terms, what this principle means is that in, for example, a Spanish-English bilingual program, Spanish instruction that develops Spanish reading and writing skills (for either Spanish L1 or L2 speakers) is not just developing *Spanish* skills, it is also developing a deeper conceptual and linguistic proficiency that is strongly related to the development of literacy in the majority language (English). In other words, although the surface aspects (e.g., pronunciation, fluency) of different languages are clearly separate, there is an underlying cognitive/academic proficiency which is common across languages. This "common underlying proficiency" makes possible the transfer of cognitive/academic or literacy-related skills across languages. Transfer is much more likely to occur from minority to majority language because of the greater exposure to literacy in the majority language outside of school and the strong social pressure to learn it.

Evidence Supporting the Interdependence Principle

The results of virtually all evaluations of bilingual programs for both majority and minority students are consistent with predictions derived from the interdependence principle (see Cummins, 1981a, 1984, 1989; Ramirez, Yuen, & Ramey, 1991). The interdependence principle can also account for data on immigrant students' L2 acquisition (e.g. Cummins, 1981b; Skutnabb-Kangas and Toukomaa, 1976) as well as for studies of bilingual language use in the home (e.g., Bhatnagar, 1980; Dolson, 1985). Correlational studies also consistently reveal a moderate degree of cognitive/academic interdependence across languages.

Many studies conducted in the past decade support the interdependence principle. Kemp (1984), for example, reported that the level of Hebrew (L1) cognitive/academic abilities strongly predicted English (L2) academic skills among 196 seventh-grade Israeli students. In a three-year longitudinal study conducted in Newark, New Jersey, Ramirez (1985) followed 75 Latino/Latina elementary school students enrolled in bilingual programs. He reported that Spanish and English academic language scores were so strongly related that they represented the same underlying dimension over the three years of data collection. Hakuta and Diaz (1985) with a similar sample of Latino/Latina students found an increasing correlation between English and Spanish academic skills over time. Between kindergarten and third grade the correlation between English and Spanish went from 0 to .68 (representing close to 50% of shared variance). The low cross-lingual relationship at the kindergarten level is likely due to the varied length of residence of the students and their parents in the United States which would result in varying levels of English proficiency at the start of school.

A case study of five schools attempting to implement the theoretical framework for the education of language minority students developed by the California State Department of Education showed consistently higher correlations between English and Spanish reading skills (range $r = .60-.74$) than between English reading and oral language skills (range $r = .36-.59$) (California State Department of Education, 1985). It was also found that the relation between L1 and L2 reading became stronger as English oral communicative skills grew stronger ($r = .71$, $N = 190$ for students in the highest category of English oral skills).

A study of Italian-English bilinguals in Australia and Italy (Ricciardelli, 1989) reported significant relationships between Italian and English proficiency among both the Australian and Italian samples. In the Italian data, for example, Ricciardelli reported:

> ... there is a large degree of overlap between the standard cognitive measures which were given in the two languages.... These [findings] suggest that bilinguals' linguistic abilities are interdependent and are not separate, and therefore any

instruction which bilingual children receive in either language is capable of promoting academic skills in both languages. (p. 137)

Finally, Verhoeven (1991) has reported the results of two small-scale experiments in transitional L1 literacy instruction with Turkish-background students in The Netherlands. He summarizes the results as follows:

> With respect to linguistic measures, it was found that a strong emphasis on instruction in L1 does lead to better literacy results in L1 with no retardation of literacy results in L2. On the contrary, there was a tendency of L2 literacy results in the transitional classes being better than in the regular submersion classes. Moreover, it was found that the transitional approach tended to develop a more positive orientation toward literacy in both L1 and L2....Finally, there was positive evidence for ... [the] interdependence hypothesis. From the study on biliteracy development it was found that literacy skills being developed in one language strongly predict corresponding skills in another language acquired later in time. (p. 72)

All of the data reviewed above refute Porter's (1990) "time-on-task" hypothesis. The data suggest that the development of academic skills in English depend not just on exposure to English (as "time-on-task" advocates argue) but equally on the knowledge and concepts that children have inside their heads that help them make sense of English. Thus, instruction that builds up Latino/Latina children's reading and writing in Spanish is creating a conceptual foundation upon which academic skills in English can be built; a child who knows how to write sentences and paragraphs in Spanish doesn't have to learn what sentences and paragraphs are all over again in English.

In conclusion, the research evidence shows consistent support for the principle of linguistic interdependence in studies investigating L1-L2 relationships and in evaluations of bilingual education for both majority and minority students. It is worth noting that this research has been carried out in a wide variety of sociopolitical contexts. The consistency and strength of support indicates that highly reliable policy predictions can be made on the basis of this principle.

One evaluation of different types of programs for language minority students (Ramirez et al., 1991) will be reviewed in more detail because of its direct relevance to both theoretical and policy issues.

The Ramirez Report

The Ramirez report (so called after its principal investigator, J. David Ramirez) was released on February 11, 1991, by the U.S. Department of Education and speaks directly to the opposing positions in the public debate on bilingual education. The study compared the academic progress of Latino/Latina elementary school children in three program types: (a) English immersion, involving almost exclusive use of English throughout elementary school, (b) early-exit bilingual in which Spanish was used for about one-third of the time in kindergarten and first grade, with a rapid phase-out thereafter, and (c) late-exit bilingual that used primarily Spanish instruction in kindergarten, with English used for about one-third of the time in grades 1 and 2, half the time in grade 3, and about sixty percent of the time thereafter. One of the three late-exit programs in the study (site G) was an exception to this pattern in that students were abruptly transitioned into primarily English instruction at the end of grade 2, and English was used almost exclusively in grades five and six. In other words, this "late-exit" program is similar in its implementation to early-exit. Students were followed through to the point at which each program model assumed they would be ready for mainstreaming into the regular program; in the case of the early-exit and immersion students this was grade 3, while late-exit students were followed to the end of grade 6.

It was possible to directly compare the progress of children in the English immersion and early-exit bilingual programs, while only indirect comparisons could be made between these programs and the late-exit program because these latter programs were offered in different districts and schools from the former. The comparison of immersion and early-exit programs showed that by the end of grade 3, students were performing at comparable levels in English language and reading skills as well as in mathematics. Slightly more of the early-exit students were reclassified as fully English proficient by the end of grade 3 than was the case for immersion program students (72% vs. 67%). Students in each of these program types progressed academically at about the same rate as students in the general population but the gap between their performance and that of the general population remained large. In other words, they tended not to fall further behind academically between first and third grade but neither did they bridge the gap in any significant way.

While these results do not demonstrate the superiority of early-exit bilingual over English immersion, they clearly do refute the argument that there is a direct relation between the amount of time spent through English instruction and academic development in English. If the "time-on-task" notion were valid, the early-exit bilingual students should have performed at a considerably lower level than the English immersion students, which they did not.

The "time-on-task" notion suffers even further indignity from the late-exit bilingual program results. In contrast to students in the immersion and early-exit programs, the late-exit students in the two sites that continued primary language instruction for at least 40 percent of the time were catching up academically to students in the general population. This is despite the fact that the these students received considerably less instruction in English than students in early-exit and immersion programs and proportionately more of their families came from the lowest income levels than was the case for students in the other two programs. It was also found that parental involvement (e.g., help with homework) was greater in the late-exit sites, presumably because teachers were fluent in Spanish and students were bringing work home in Spanish.

Differences were observed among the three late-exit sites with respect to mathematics, English language (i.e., skills such as punctuation, capitalization, etc.) and English reading. Specifically, according to the report:

> As in mathematics and English language, it seems that those students in site E, who received the strongest opportunity to develop their primary language skills, realized a growth in their English reading skills that was greater than that of the norming population used in this study. If sustained, in time these students would be expected to catch up and approximate the average achievement level of this norming population. (Ramirez et al., 1991, p. 35)

By contrast, students in site G who were abruptly transitioned into almost all-English instruction in the early grades (in a similar fashion to early-exit students) seemed to lose ground in relation to the general population between grades 3 and 6 in mathematics, English language, and reading.

The report concludes that:

> Students who were provided with a substantial and consistent primary language development program learned mathematics, English language, and English reading skills as fast or faster than the norming population used in this study. As their growth in these academic skills is atypical of disadvantaged youth, it provides support for the efficacy of primary language development in facilitating the acquisition of English language skills. (p. 36)

These findings are entirely consistent with the results of other bilingual programs and show clearly, as predicted by the interdependence principle, that there is no direct relationship between the instructional time spent through the medium of a majority language and academic achievement in that language. On the contrary, there appears to be an inverse relation between exposure to English instruction and English achievement for Latino/Latina students in this study. It is also worth noting that the findings are consistent with the data suggesting that at least five years is required for language minority students to approach grade norms in English language arts, since students in the late-exit bilingual programs only began to close the gap between themselves and the norming group in the later grades of elementary school.

The Additive Bilingualism Enrichment Principle

In the past many students from language minority backgrounds have experienced difficulties in school and have performed more poorly than monolingual children on verbal IQ tests and on measures of literacy development. These findings led researchers in the period between 1920 and 1960 to speculate that bilingualism caused language handicaps and cognitive confusion among children. Some research studies also reported that bilingual children suffered emotional conflicts more frequently than did monolingual children. Thus, in the early part of this century bilingualism acquired a doubtful reputation among educators, and many schools redoubled their efforts to eradicate children's L1 on the grounds that this language was the source of children's academic difficulties.

However, virtually all of the early research involved language minority students in both Europe (e.g., Wales) and North America who were in the process of replacing their L1 with the majority language, usually with strong encouragement from the school. Many students were physically punished for speaking their L1 in school. It appears more reasonable to attribute the academic difficulties of bilingual students to the treatment they received in schools rather than to their bilingualism.

Consistent with this interpretation are the results of more recent studies which suggest that bilingualism can positively affect both intellectual and linguistic progress. A large number of studies have reported that bilingual children exhibit a greater sensitivity to linguistic meanings and may be more flexible in their thinking than are monolingual children (Cummins and Swain, 1986; Diaz, 1986; Hakuta and Diaz, 1985; Ricciardelli, 1989). Most of these studies have investigated aspects of children's metalinguistic development, that is, children's explicit knowledge about the structure and functions of language itself.

In general, it is not surprising that bilingual children should be more adept at certain aspects of linguistic processing. In gaining control over two language systems, the bilingual child has had to decipher much more language input than the monolingual child who has been exposed to only one language system. Thus, the bilingual child has had considerably more practice in analyzing meanings than the monolingual child.

The evidence is not conclusive as to whether this linguistic advantage transfers to more general cognitive skills. McLaughlin's review of the literature, for example, concludes that:

> It seems clear that the child who has mastered two languages has a linguistic advantage over the monolingual child. Bilingual children become aware that there are two ways of saying the same thing. But does this sensitivity to the lexical and formal aspects of language generalize to cognitive functioning? There is no conclusive answer to this question— mainly because it has proven so difficult to apply the necessary controls in research. (1984, p. 44)

An important characteristic of bilingual children in the more recent studies (conducted since the early 1960s) is that, for the most part, they were developing what has been termed an *additive* form of bilingualism (Lambert, 1975); in other words, they were adding a second language to their repertoire of skills at no cost to the development of their first language. Consequently, these children were in the process of attaining a relatively high level of both fluency and literacy in their two languages.

The children in these studies tended to come either from majority language groups whose L1 was strongly reinforced in the society (e.g., English-speakers in French immersion programs) or from minority groups whose L1 was reinforced by bilingual programs in the school. This is in contrast to a *subtractive* form of bilingualism, in which L1 skills are *replaced* by L2, frequently developed in bilingual children who lack educational support for literacy development in L1.

This pattern of findings suggests that the level of proficiency attained by bilingual students in their two languages may be an important influence on their academic and intellectual development (Cummins, 1981a). Specifically, there may be a threshold level of proficiency in both languages which students must attain in order to avoid any negative academic consequences and a second, higher, threshold necessary to reap the linguistic and intellectual benefits of bilingualism and biliteracy.

Diaz (1986) has questioned the threshold hypothesis on the grounds that the effects of bilingualism on cognitive abilities in his data were stronger for children of relatively low L2 proficiency (non-balanced bilinguals). This suggests that the positive effects are related to the initial struggles and experiences of the beginning second-language learner. This interpretation does not appear to be incompatible with the threshold hypothesis since the major point of this hypothesis is that for positive effects to become manifest, children must be in an additive situation where both languages are developing. If beginning L2 learners do not continue to develop both their languages, any initial positive effects are likely to be counteracted by the negative consequences of subtractive bilingualism. Thus, positive effects will not be sustained unless high levels of bilingual proficiency are attained.

The findings of the Australian study briefly reviewed above (Ricciardelli, 1989) are consistent with the threshold hypothesis and illustrate the types of advantage that bilingual information processing might confer on the developing child. Ricciardelli conducted two studies to investigate the influence of bilingualism on children's cognitive abilities and creativity. The first involved 57 Italian-English bilingual and 55 English monolingual children aged 5 or 6 at the time of the study. Using analysis of covariance to statistically control for background differences, Ricciardelli reported that children who were proficient in both Italian and English performed significantly better than children who were proficient in English only (the high English monolingual group) and bilinguals who were proficient in English but less proficient in Italian, on several measures reflecting creative thinking (the Torrance Fluency and

Imagination measures), metalinguistic awareness (Word Order Correction), and verbal and non-verbal abilities.

The second study was conducted in Rome with 35 Italian-English bilingual and 35 Italian monolingual 5- and 6-year-old children. Again, those children who were proficiently bilingual in Italian and English performed significantly better than the other groups on the Torrance Fluency and Imagination measures as well as on Word Order Correction and Word Reading. Ricciardelli concludes that these data are consistent with the threshold hypothesis:

> On the whole, the results from this experiment provide additional support for the Threshold Theory, and they are broadly consistent with those found in [the previous study], in that, an overall bilingual superiority on the cognitive measures was found only for those children who had obtained a high degree of bilingualism. (1989, p. 151)

In summary, the following conclusion emerges from the research on the academic, linguistic, and intellectual effects of bilingualism:

> The development of additive bilingual and biliteracy skills entails no negative consequences for children's academic, linguistic, or intellectual development. On the contrary, although not conclusive, the evidence points in the direction of subtle metalinguistic, academic, and intellectual benefits for bilingual children.

Implications of Psychoeducational Principles

This review of psychoeducational data regarding bilingual academic development shows that a theoretical basis for at least some policy decisions regarding minority students' education does exist. In other words, policy makers can predict with considerable confidence the probable effects of bilingual programs for majority and minority students implemented in very different sociopolitical contexts.

First, they can predict that language minority students are likely to take considerably longer to develop grade-appropriate levels of L2 academic or conceptual skills in comparison with the time it takes to acquire peer-appropriate levels of L2 conversational skills, at least in situations where students have access to the target language in the environment.

Second, they can be confident that for students from both majority and minority language backgrounds, spending instructional time through the minority language will not result in lower levels of academic performance in the majority language, provided of course the instructional program is effective in developing academic skills in the minority language. This is because at deeper levels of conceptual and academic functioning, there is considerable overlap or interdependence across languages. Conceptual knowledge developed in one language helps to make input in the other language comprehensible.

Third, they can be confident that if the program is effective in continuing to develop students' academic skills in both languages, no cognitive confusion or handicap will result; in fact, students may benefit in subtle ways from access to two linguistic systems.

In short, there is a substantial psychoeducational knowledge base available to guide policy and practice in the education of bilingual students. These principles by themselves provide a reliable basis for the prediction of program outcomes in situations that are not characterized by unequal power relations between dominant and subordinated groups (e.g., L2 immersion programs for students from majority language backgrounds). However, they do not explain the variation in the achievement of minority groups, nor do they tell us why some groups have experienced persistent school failure over generations. The next section addresses these issues and elaborates a framework that combines a causal analysis of minority student school failure with an intervention framework for reversing this pattern of failure. The focus is on how unequal power relations are played out and can be challenged in the interactions between educators and students in the school context.

A Framework for Reversing School Failure

Macro-Interactions, Structures, and Role Definitions

When patterns of school success and failure among culturally diverse students are examined within an international perspective, it becomes evident that power and status relations between dominant and subordinated groups exert a major influence. Several theorists (e.g., Cummins, 1989; Ogbu, 1978, 1992) have pointed to the fact that subordinated groups that fail academically tend to be characterized by a sense of ambivalence about the value of their cultural identity and powerlessness in relation to the dominant group. This is what Ogbu refers to as "castelike" status, and its educational effects are strikingly evident in many situations where formerly subjugated or colonized groups are still in a subordinated relationship to the dominant group.

The phenomenon of what Blauner (1969) called "internal colonies" is exemplified by the fact that the three groups in the United States context that experience the most pronounced educational difficulty (African-American, Latino/Latina, and Native American students) have each been subordinated for centuries by the dominant group. Similar patterns exist in Scandinavia where Finnish minority students in Sweden are reported to experience severe academic difficulties, a phenomenon not unrelated to the fact that Finland was colonized by Sweden for several hundred years (Skutnabb-Kangas, 1984).

I will term these relations of power and status between societal groups *macro-interactions*. These macro-interactions give rise to particular forms of educational structures that are designed to reproduce the relations of power in the broader society. Educational structures refer to the organization of schooling in a broad sense that includes policies, programs, curriculum, and assessment. This organization is established to achieve the goals of education as defined by the dominant group in the society. For example, the historical patterns of educational apartheid in the United States, Canada, South Africa, and many other countries were designed to limit the opportunities that subordinated groups might have for educational and social advancement. As documented by Kozol (1991) for African-American students and by Berman et al. (1992) for recent immigrants in California, similar patterns of segregation still characterize the education of many subordinated groups (see Skutnabb-Kangas, 1984, for a discussion of similar phenomena in the European context).

Examples of educational structures that reflect coercive relations of power are:

- English submersion programs for bilingual students which actively suppress children's L1 and cultural identity;

- exclusion of culturally diverse parents from participation in their children's schooling;

- tracking practices that place subordinated group students disproportionately in lower-level tracks;

- use of biased standardized tests for both achievement monitoring and special education placement;

- curriculum content reflecting dominant group notions of "cultural literacy" (Hirsch, 1987).

These educational structures constitute a frame that sets limits on the kinds of interactions that are likely to occur between educators and students. As one illustration of the impact of these structures, Jeanie Oakes (1985) has shown that tracking results in major differences in the quality of instruction that students receive; those in lower tracks receive instruction that is less challenging and motivating than those in higher tracks. She concludes that when schools are structured according to tracks, the academic progress of those in average and low groups is retarded. Tracking also lowers educational aspirations, fosters low self-esteem, and promotes dropping out.

Societal macro-interactions also influence the ways in which educators define their roles in relation to culturally diverse students and communities. In other words, they influence the mind-set of assumptions, expectations, and goals that educators bring to the task of educating students. The notion of *educator role definitions* is proposed as a central explanantory construct in the present framework. This framework argues that culturally diverse students

> ... are "empowered" or "disabled" as a direct result of their interactions with educators in the schools. These interactions are mediated by the implicit or explicit role definitions that educators assume in relation to four institutional characteristics of schools. These characteristics reflect the extent to which:

> 1. minority students' language and culture are incorporated into the school program;

> 2. minority community participation is encouraged as an integral component of children's education;

> 3. the pedagogy promotes intrinsic motivation on the part of students to use language actively in order to generate their own knowledge; and

4. professionals involved in assessment become advocates for minority students by focusing primarily on the ways in which students' academic difficulty is a function of interactions within the school context rather than legitimizing the location of the "problem" within students. (Cummins, 1989, p. 58).

These four dimensions, namely, language/culture incorporation, community participation, pedagogy, and assessment, represent sets of educational structures that will affect, but can also be influenced by, educators' role definitions.

Micro-Interactions as Reflections of Coercive or Collaborative Relations of Power

A central tenet of the present framework is that the negotiation of identity in the interactions between educators and students is central to students' academic success or failure. The interactions between educators and students are termed *micro-interactions* (to distinguish them from the macro-interactions between societal groups). These micro-interactions form an interpersonal or an interactional space within which the acquisition of knowledge and formation of identity are negotiated between educators and students.

In the past, dominant group institutions (e.g., schools) have required that subordinated groups deny their cultural identity as a necessary condition for success in the "mainstream" society. The historical pattern of dominant-subordinated group interactions has been one in which educators have constricted the interactional space in an attempt to sanitize deviant cultural identities. For educators to become partners in the transmission of knowledge, culturally diverse students were required to acquiesce in the subordination of their identities and to celebrate as "truth" the "cultural literacy" of the dominant group (e.g., the "truth" that Columbus "discovered" America). The constriction of the interactional space by educators reflected a process whereby they defined their role as "civilizing," "saving," "assimilating," or "educating" students whose culture and values they viewed as inherently deficient. Through these micro-interactions they reproduced the pattern of societal macro-interactions and limited students' possibilities to define and interpret their own realities and identities. In short, the coercive power of the dominant group historically has been used to define the "other" as inferior, thereby justifying their confinement, either physically (e.g., slavery) or psychologically (e.g., through internalization of dominant group attributions resulting in ambivalence in regard to their identities).

It is important to note that students (and communities) do not passively accept dominant group attributions of their inferiority. Frequently, they actively resist the operation of the societal power structure as it is manifested in educational settings (see, e.g., Skutnabb-Kangas, 1988). While for some students, resistance may contribute to academic development (see Zanger, 1994), in many situations resistance has severe costs with respect to academic success and upward mobility (e.g., Fordham, 1990).

What this implies is that the micro-interactions between educators and students script an image of the envisaged relations of culture and power in the society. These micro-interactions either reinforce or challenge particular educational structures within the school or school system and, by implication, the power structure in the wider society. Educational equity requires that educators define their roles and attempt to orchestrate the pattern of micro-interactions in such a way that these interactions actively challenge coercive relations of power in the wider society. Empowerment of both students and educators is an outcome of this process.

In order to better define the nature of empowerment, it is necessary to distinguish between coercive and collaborative relations of power.

Coercive relations of power refer to the exercise of power by a dominant group (or individual or country) to the detriment of a subordinated group (or individual or country). The assumption is that there is a fixed quantity of power that operates according to a balance effect; the more power one group has, the less is left for other groups. Coercive relations of power usually involve a definitional process that legitimates the inferior or deviant status accorded to the subordinated group (or individual or country). In other words, the dominant group defines the subordinated group as inferior (or evil), thereby automatically defining itself as superior (or virtuous).

This process of identity negotiation is interwoven into all educator-student interactions and is usually non-problematic when there is a cultural and class match between educator and student but can be highly problematic when there is a cultural and class mismatch (see, e.g., Fordham, 1990). In these cases, coercive relations of power will operate to define the subordinated group in ways that purport to explain its poor academic performance (e.g., attributing the school failure of bilingual children to cognitive confusion caused by two languages).

Collaborative relations of power, on the other hand, operate on the assumption that power is not a fixed, predetermined quantity but rather can be *generated* in interpersonal and intergroup relations, thereby becoming "additive" rather than "subtractive." In other words, participants in the relationship are *empowered* through their collaboration such that each is more affirmed in her or his identity and has a greater sense of efficacy to create change in his or her life or social situation. Thus, power is created in the relationship and shared among participants.

In educational contexts, the empowerment that results from collaborative relations of power has been documented in the outcomes of cooperative learning activities (Kagan, 1986) and in the global sister class networks described by Sayers (1991). They are also evident in the family literacy projects documented by Ada (1988); McCaleb (1994); and Tizard, Schofield, and Hewison (1982). A central characteristic of these projects is that they challenge assumptions and definitions of minority students and communities that have operated to reinforce coercive relations of power (e.g., the assumption that certain groups of minority parents don't care about their children's education).

Students whose schooling experiences reflect collaborative relations of power develop the ability, confidence, and motivation to succeed academically. They participate competently in instruction as a result of having developed a confident cultural identity as well as appropriate school-based knowledge and interactional structures. Students who are disempowered or "disabled" by their school experiences do not develop this type of cognitive/academic and social/emotional foundation.

For each of the four dimensions of school organization outlined in Figure 6, the role definitions of educators can be described in terms of a continuum, with one end of the continuum promoting the empowerment of students while the other contributes to the disabling of students.

Cultural/Linguistic Incorporation

Considerable research data suggest that for subordinated minorities, the extent to which students' language and culture is incorporated into the school program constitutes a significant predictor of academic success (see, e.g., Campos & Keatinge, 1988; Cummins, 1989, Ramirez et al. 1991). Students' school success appears to reflect both the more solid

Figure 6

INTERVENTION FOR
COLLABORATIVE EMPOWERMENT

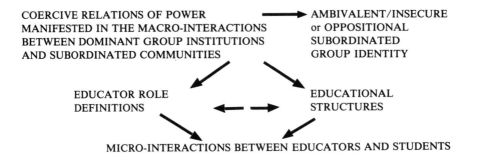

COERCIVE RELATIONS OF POWER ⟶ AMBIVALENT/INSECURE
MANIFESTED IN THE MACRO-INTERACTIONS   or OPPOSITIONAL
BETWEEN DOMINANT GROUP INSTITUTIONS   SUBORDINATED
AND SUBORDINATED COMMUNITIES   GROUP IDENTITY

EDUCATOR ROLE   EDUCATIONAL
DEFINITIONS ⟷ STRUCTURES

MICRO-INTERACTIONS BETWEEN EDUCATORS AND STUDENTS

reflecting an

	INTERCULTURAL ORIENTATION		ASSIMILATIONIST ORIENTATION
Cultural/Linguistic Incorporation	Additive	_____	Subtractive
Community Participation	Participatory	_____	Exclusionary
Pedagogy	Transformative	_____	"Banking"
Assessment	Advocacy	_____	Legitimization
	Academically and Personally Empowered Students		Academically Disabled or Resistant Students

cognitive/academic foundation developed through intensive L1 instruction and the reinforcement of their cultural identity.

Included under incorporation of minority group cultural features is the adjustment of instructional patterns to take account of culturally conditioned learning styles. The Kamehameha Early Education Program in Hawaii provides strong evidence of the importance of this type of cultural incorporation (see, e.g., Au & Jordan, 1981).

With respect to the incorporation of minority students' language and culture, educators' role definitions can be characterized along an "additive-subtractive" dimension. Educators who see their role as adding a second language and cultural affiliation to students' repertoire are more likely to create interactional conditions of empowerment than those who see their role as replacing or subtracting students' primary language and culture in the process of assimilating them to the dominant culture.

It should be noted that an additive orientation is not always dependent upon actual teaching of the minority language. In many cases this may not be possible for a variety of reasons (e.g., low concentration of particular groups of minority students). However, educators communicate to students and parents in a variety of ways the extent to which students' language and culture are valued within the context of the school. Even within a monolingual school context, powerful messages can be communicated to students regarding the validity and advantages of first language development.

Community Participation

Students from subordinated communities will be empowered in the school context to the extent that the communities themselves are empowered through their interactions with the school. When educators and parents develop partnerships to promote their children's education, parents appear to develop a sense of efficacy that communicates itself to children with positive academic consequences (e.g., Ada, 1988; McCaleb, 1994; Tizard et al., 1982).

The teacher role definitions associated with community participation can be characterized along a *collaborative-exclusionary* dimension. Teachers operating at the collaborative end of the continuum actively encourage parents to participate in promoting their children's academic progress both in the home and through involvement in classroom activities. A collaborative orientation may require a willingness on the part of the teacher to work closely with classroom assistants or community volunteers in order to communicate effectively and in a non-condescending way with parents. Teachers with an exclusionary orientation, on the other hand, tend to regard teaching as *their* job and are likely to view collaboration with minority parents as either irrelevant or actually detrimental to children's progress.

Clearly, initiatives for collaboration or for a shared decision-making process can come from the community as well as from the school. Under these conditions, maintenance of an exclusionary orientation by the school can lead communities to directly challenge the institutional power structure. This was the case with the school strike organized by Finnish parents and their children at Bredby school in Rinkeby, Sweden. In response to a plan by the headmistress to reduce the amount of Finnish instruction, the Finnish community withdrew their children from the school. Eventually (after eight weeks) most of their demands were met. According to Skutnabb-Kangas (1988), the strike had the effect of generating a new sense of efficacy among the community and making them more aware of the role of dominant-group controlled (i.e., exclusionary) education in reproducing the powerless status of minority groups. A hypothesis that the present framework generates is that this renewed sense of efficacy will lead to higher levels of academic achievement among minority students in this type of situation.

Pedagogy

Several investigators have suggested that the learning difficulties of culturally diverse students are often pedagogically induced in that children designated "at risk" frequently receive intensive instruction that confines them to a passive role and induces a form of "learned helplessness" (see Cummins, 1984, for a review). Instruction that creates conditions of empowerment, on the other hand, will aim to liberate students from dependence on instruction in the sense of encouraging them to become active generators of their own knowledge.

Two major orientations can be distinguished with respect to pedagogy. These differ in the extent to which the teacher retains exclusive control over classroom interaction as opposed to sharing some of this control with students. The dominant instructional model in most western industrial societies has been termed a *banking* model (Freire, 1983; Freire & Macedo, 1987); this can be contrasted with a *transformative* model of pedagogy.

The basic premise of the banking or transformative model is that the teacher's task is to impart knowledge or skills that he or she possesses to students who do not yet have these skills, that is, to deposit knowledge in the students' memory bank. This implies that the teacher initiates and controls the interaction, constantly orienting it toward the achievement of instructional objectives. The instructional content in this type of program derives primarily from the internal structure of the language or subject matter; consequently, it frequently involves a predominant focus on surface features of language or literacy (e.g., handwriting, spelling, decoding) and emphasizes correct recall of content taught. Content is frequently transmitted by means of highly structured drills and workbook exercises, although in many cases the drills are disguised in order to make them more attractive and motivating to students.

The major problems with "banking" education are:

- It reinforces the cultural ambivalence of subordinated group students by providing no opportunity for students to express and share their experience with peers and teachers; in other words, students are silenced or rendered "voiceless" in the classroom (Giroux, 1991).

- It contravenes central principles of language and literacy acquisition in that it is impossible to learn language or develop literacy in the absence of ample opportunities for communicative interaction in both oral and written modes (Krashen, 1981, 1993; Wong-Fillmore, 1991b).

Encouragement by the teacher of active use of both written and oral language allows students' experience to be expressed and shared within the classroom context. This expression and sharing of experience has the effect of validating students' identity. By contrast, "banking" approaches usually employ textbooks that reflect the values and priorities of the majority group, thereby effectively suppressing the experience of culturally diverse students.

Transformative approaches to pedagogy have three essential characteristics. First, they encourage two-way interaction and active written and oral language use by students; students' language proficiency is developed by providing ample opportunities for students to use language to pursue projects to which they are committed. It is important to note that this in no way implies that explicit instruction of some aspects of language or content is inappropriate. As Delpit (1988) points out, it is important for culturally diverse students to get access to "the rules of the game" or the "codes of power" with respect to how language is used in a wide variety of social contexts. Teachers must learn not only how to "help students to establish their own voices, but to coach those voices to produce notes that will be heard clearly in the larger society" (1988, p. 296). Kalantzis et al. (1990) similarly make the point that explicit teaching of "culturally powerful knowledge and culturally powerful ways of knowing" is central to the promotion of critical thinking in a diverse society undergoing rapid change (p. 246).

A second characteristic of transformative approaches is that they build on students' experience, thereby validating students' cultural identity. In describing the "personal interpretive" phase of her literacy framework, Ada (1988) points out that this process helps develop students' self-esteem by showing that their experiences and feelings are valued by the teacher and classmates. It also helps students understand that "true learning occurs only when the information received is analyzed in the light of one's own experiences and emotions" (p. 104). An atmosphere of acceptance and trust in the classroom is a prerequisite for students (and teachers) to risk sharing their feelings, emotions, and experiences. It is clear how this process of sharing and critically reflecting on their own and other students' experiencess opens up identity options for culturally diverse students. These identity options are typically suppressed within a "banking" approach to pedagogy where the interpretation of texts is non-negotiable and reflective of the dominant group's notions of cultural literacy. The personal interpretive phase deepens students' comprehension of the text or issues by grounding the knowledge in the personal and collective narratives that make up students' histories. It is also developing a genuine cultural literacy in that it is integrating students' own experience with "mainstream" curricular content.

The third characteristic of transformative pedagogy is that it promotes critical thinking about historical and current social realities. In her literacy framework, Ada (1988) terms this the *critical phase.* She emphasizes that school children of all ages can engage in critical thinking, although the analysis will always reflect children's experiences and level of maturity. Critical dialogue further extends students' comprehension of the text or issues by encouraging them to examine both the internal logical coherence of the information or propositions and their consistency with other knowledge or perspectives. When students pursue guided research and critical reflection, they are clearly engaged in a process of knowledge generation. However, they are equally engaged in a process of self-definition. As they gain the power to think through issues that affect their lives, they simultaneously gain the power to resist external definitions of who they are and to deconstruct the sociopolitical purposes of such external definitions.

Pedagogy that is interactive, experiential, and critical will frequently result in concrete projects designed to further promote comprehension of the issues or discover what changes individuals can make to improve their lives or resolve the problem that has been presented (Ada's *action* phase). Let us suppose that students have been researching problems relating to environmental pollution (in the local newspaper or in periodicals such as *National Geographic*). After relating the issues to their own experience, critically analyzing causes and possible solutions, they might decide to write letters to congressional representatives, highlight the issue in their class/school newsletter in order to sensitize other students, write and circulate a petition in the neighborhood, write and perform a play that analyzes the issue, and so on. Once again, this action phase can be seen as extending the process of comprehension insofar as when we act to transform aspects of our social realities, we gain a deeper understanding of those realities.

In short, a transformative pedagogy will aim to go beyond the sanitized curriculum that is still the norm in most schools. It will attempt to promote students' ability to analyze and understand the social realities of their own lives and of their communities. This inevitably means that educators must be willing to expose and challenge the ways in which dominant groups have historically maintained their power. Macedo (1993) clearly highlights the challenge of confronting coercive relations of power when he argues:

> What we have in the United States is not a system to encourage independent thought and critical thinking. Our colonial literacy model is designed to domesticate so as to enable "the manufacture of consent." (p. 204).

Assessment

Historically, assessment has played the role of legitimizing the disabling of minority students. In some cases, assessment itself may have played the primary role but usually its role has been to locate the "problem" within the student, thereby screening from critical scrutiny the subtractive nature of the school program, the exclusionary orientation of teachers toward subordinated communities, and the "banking" models of teaching that inhibit students from active participation in learning.

This process is virtually inevitable when the conceptual base for the assessment process is purely psychoeducational. If the psychologist's task (or role definition) is to discover the causes of a minority student's academic difficulties, and the only tools at her disposal are psychological tests (in either L1 or L2), then it is hardly surprising that the child's difficulties will be attributed to psychological dysfunctions. The myth of bilingual handicaps that still influences educational policy was generated in exactly this way during the 1920s and 1930s.

Recent studies suggest that despite the appearance of change with respect to nondiscriminatory assessment, the underlying structure has remained essentially intact. It was reported that psychologists continued to test children until they "found" the disability that could be invoked to "explain" the student's apparent academic difficulties. A similar conclusion emerged from the analysis of more than 400 psychological assessments of minority students conducted by Cummins (1984). Although no diagnostic conclusions were logically possible in the majority of assessments, psychologists were most reluctant to admit this fact to teachers and parents. In short, the data suggest that the structure within which psychological assessment takes place orients the psychologist to locate the cause of the academic problem within the culturally diverse students themselves.

The alternative role definition that is required to reverse the traditional *legitimizing* function of assessment can be termed an *advocacy* role. Educators must be prepared to become advocates for the child in critically scrutinizing the societal and educational context within which the child has developed. This involves locating the pathology within the societal power relations between dominant and subordinated groups, in the reflection of these power relations between school and communities, and in the mental and cultural disabling of subordinated group students that takes place in classrooms.

In most industrialized countries the training of psychologists and special educators does not prepare them for this advocacy role since advocating for minority students in this way frequently will involve a challenge to the societal and educational power structure. Thus, typically, rather than challenging a socioeducational system that tends to disable minority students, educators accept a role definition and an educational structure that makes discriminatory assessment virtually inevitable.

Conclusion

I have suggested that although there is a psychoeducational basis for policy in the area of bilingual education, psychoeducational factors alone do not address all the questions of policy makers concerned with the educational difficulties of some language minority groups. For example, they do not account for the variability in academic performance among different groups, nor do they adequately explain why certain forms of bilingual education appear particularly effective in reversing these difficulties.

In order to address these issues, a theoretical framework was proposed for analyzing culturally diverse students' academic difficulties and for predicting the effects of educational interventions. It was proposed that the pattern of micro-interactions that culturally diverse students experience in the educational system are a function of the power relations operating in the macro-interactions between dominant and subordinated groups in the wider society. The power structure in the wider society will determine the types of educational structures implemented in the school system and the ways in which educators define their roles with respect to culturally diverse students and communities.

Thus, underachievement among culturally diverse students was analyzed as a function of the extent to which schools reflect, or alternatively, challenge the power relations that exist within the broader society. Specifically, students' educational progress will be strongly influenced by the extent to which individual educators become advocates for the promotion of students' linguistic talents, actively encourage parental participation in developing students' academic and cultural resources, and implement pedagogical approaches that encourage students to use oral and written language to reflect critically on and amplify their experience. When educators define their roles in terms of promoting social justice and equality of opportunity, then their interactions with culturally diverse students will embody a transformative potential by challenging coercive relations of power as they are manifested in the school context.

By contrast, when educators define their roles in such a way that the division of resources and power in the society is not problematized or called into question in any way, then their interactions with students will simply reflect and reproduce the coercive relations of power in the broader society. The educator-student interactions characteristic of the disabling end of the proposed continua reflect the typical patterns of interaction that subordinated societal groups have experienced historically in relation to dominant groups. Students' language and cultural values are denied, they are confined to passive roles within the classroom, and their parents are excluded from participation in educational decisions and activities. The failure of culturally diverse students under these conditions has frequently been attributed, on the basis of "objective" test scores, to deficient cognitive or linguistic abilities.

In short, subordinated group students are disabled educationally in their micro-interactions with educators in very much the same way that their communities have been disempowered (often for centuries) through their macro-interactions with societal institutions. It follows that subordinated group students will succeed educationally and amplify their "voice" or their expression of personal identity to the extent that the patterns of micro-interactions in school reverse the patterns of macro-interactions that prevail in the society at large.

The outcome of this process for both educators and students can be described in terms of *empowerment*. Empowerment can be defined as the collaborative creation of power. Conditions of collaborative empowerment are created when educators attempt to organize their interactions with culturally diverse students in such a way that power is generated and shared through these interactions. This involves becoming aware of, and actively working to change, the ways in which particular educational structures limit the opportunities that culturally diverse students might have for educational and social advancement. It also involves attempting to orchestrate the interactions with culturally diverse students in such a way that students' options for identity formation and critical inquiry are expanded rather than constricted. Teaching for empowerment, by definition, constitutes a challenge to the societal power structure.

REFERENCES

Ada, A. F. (1988). The Pajaro Valley experience: Working with Spanish-speaking parents to develop children's reading and writing skills in the home through the use of children's literature. In T. Skutnabb-Kangas and J. Cummins (Eds.), *Minority education: From shame to struggle.* Clevedon, England: Multilingual Matters.

Au, K. H. & Jordan, C. (1981). Teaching reading to Hawaiian children: Finding a culturally appropriate solution. In H. Trueba, G. P. Guthrie, & K. H. Au (Eds.), *Culture and the bilugual classroom: Studies in classroom ethnography* (pp. 139-152). Rowley, MA: Newbury House.

Berman, P., Chambers, J., Gandara, P., et al. (1992). *Meeting the challenge of linguistic diversity: An evaluation of programs for pupils with limited proficiency in English.* Berkeley: BW Associates.

Bethell, T. (1979, February). Against bilingual education: Why Johnny can't speak English. *Harper's,* pp. 30-33.

Bhatnagar, J. (1980). Linguistic behaviour and adjustment of immigrant children in French and English schools in Montreal. *International Review of Applied Psychology, 29,* 141-149.

Blauner, R. (1969). Internal colonialism and ghetto revolt. *Social Problems, 16,* 393-408.

Bruner, J. S. (1975). Language as an instrument of thought. In A. Davies (Ed.), *Problems of language and learning.* London: Heinemann.

California State Department of Education. (1985). *Case studies in bilingual education: First year report.* Federal Grant #G008303723. Sacramento: California State Department of Education.

Campos, S. J., & Keatinge, H. R. (1988). The Carpinteria language minority student experience: From theory, to practice, to success. In T. Skutnabb-Kangas & J. Cummins (Eds.), *Minority education: From shame to struggle* (pp. 299-307). Clevedon, England: Multilingual Matters.

Collier, V. P. (1987). Age and rate of acquisition of second language for academic purposes. *TESOL Quarterly, 21,* 617-641.

Collier, V. P. (1989). How long? A synthesis of research on academic achievement in a second language. *TESOL Quarterly, 23,* 509-531.

Cummins, J. (1981a). The role of primary language development in promoting educational success for language minority students. In California State Department of Education (Ed.), *Schooling and language minority students: A theoretical framework* (1st ed.) (pp. 3-49). Los Angeles: Evaluation, Dissemination and Assessment Center, California State University, Los Angeles.

Cummins, J. (1981b). Age on arrival and immigrant second language learning in Canada: A reassessment. *Applied Linguistics, 2,* 132-149.

Cummins, J. (1984). *Bilingualism and special education: Issues in assessment and pedagogy.* Clevedon, England: Multilingual Matters.

Cummins, J. (1989). *Empowering minority students.* Sacramento: California Association for Bilingual Education.

Cummins, J. (1991). The development of bilingual proficiency from home to school: A longitudinal study of Portuguese-speaking children. *Journal of Education, 173,* 85-98.

Cummins, J., & Swain, M. (1986). *Bilingualism in education: Aspects of theory, research and practice.* London: Longman.

Cummins, J., Swain, M. Nakajima, K., Handscombe, J., Green, D., and Tran, C. (1984). Linguistic interdependence among Japanese and Vietnamese immigrant students. In C. Rivera (Ed.), *Communicative competence approaches to language proficiency assessment: Research and application.* Clevedon, England: Multilingual Matters.

Delpit, L. (1988). The silenced dialogue: Power and pedagogy in educating other people's children. *Harvard Educational Review, 58,* 280-298.

Diaz, R. M. (1986). Bilingual cognitive development: Addressing three gaps in current research. *Child Development, 56,* 1376-1388.

Dolson, D. (1985). The effects of Spanish home language use on the scholastic performance of Hispanic pupils. *Journal of Multilingual and Multicultural Development, 6,* 135-156.

Donaldson, M. (1978). *Children's minds.* Glasgow: Collins.

Dunn, L. (1987). *Bilingual Hispanic children on the U.S. mainland: A review of research on their cognitive, linguistic, and scholastic development.* Circle Pines, MN: American Guidance Service.

Fordham, S. (1990). Racelessness as a factor in Black students' school success: Pragmatic strategy or pyrrhic victory? In N. M. Hidalgo, C. L. McDowell, & E. V. Siddle (Eds.), *Facing racism in education* (pp. 232-262). Reprint series No. 21, Howard Educational Review.

Freire, P. (1983). Banking education. In H. Giroux & D. Purpel (Eds.), *The hidden curriculum and moral education: Deception or discovery?* Berkeley, CA: McCutcheon Publishing Corporation.

Freire, P., & Macedo, D. (1987). *Literacy: Reading the word and the world.* South Hadley, MA: Bergin & Garvey.

Giroux, H. A. (1991). Series introduction: Rethinking the pedagogy of voice, difference and cultural struggle. In C. E. Walsh (Ed.), *Pedagogy and the struggle for voice: Issues of language, power, and schooling for Puerto Ricans* (pp. xv-xxvii). Toronto: OISE Press.

Gonzalez, L. A. (1986). *The effects of first language education on the second language and academic achievement of Mexican immigrant elementary school children in the United States.* Doctoral dissertation submitted to the University of Illinois at Urbana-Champaign.

Hakuta, K., & Diaz, R. M. (1985). The relationship between degree of bilingualism and cognitive ability: A critical discussion and some new longitudinal data. In K. E. Nelson (Ed.), *Children's language* (Vol. 5). Hillsdale, NJ: Erlbaum.

Hirsch, E. D., Jr. (1987). *Cultural literacy: What every American needs to know.* Boston: Houghton Mifflin Co.

Hodgkinson, H. (1991, September). Reform versus reality. *Phi Delta Kappan*, pp. 9-16.

Kagan, S. (1986). Cooperative learning and sociocultural factors in schooling. In California State Department of Education (Ed.), *Social and cultural factors in schooling language minority students.* Los Angeles: Evaluation, Dissemination and Assessment Center, California State University, Los Angeles.

Kalantzis, M., Cope, B. Noble, G., & Poynting, S. (1990). *Cultures of schooling: Pedagogies for cultural difference and social access.* London: The Falmer Press.

Kemp, J. (1984). *Native language knowledge as a predictor of success in learning a foreign language with special reference to a disadvantage population.* Thesis submitted for the M.A. Degree, Tel-Aviv University.

Kozol, J. (1991). *Savage inequalities: Children in America's schools.* New York: Crown Publishers.

Krashen, S. (1981). *Second language acquisition and second language learning.* London: Pergamon Press.

Krashen, S. (1993). *The power of reading.* Englewood, CO: Libraries Unlimited.

Labov, W. (1970). *The logic of non-standard English.* Champaign, Illinois: National Council of Teachers of English.

Lambert, W. E. (1975). Culture and language as factors in learning and education. In A. Wolfgang (Ed.), *Education of immigrant students.* Toronto: OISE Press.

Macedo, D. (1993). Literacy for stupidification: The pedagogy of big lies. *Harvard Educational Review, 63,* 183-206.

McCaleb, S. P. (1994). *Building communities of learners: A collaboration among teachers, students, families and community.* New York: St. Martin's Press.

McLaughlin, B. (1984). Early bilingualism: Methodological and theoretical issues. In M. Paradis and Y. Lebrun (Eds.), *Early bilingualism and child development*. Lisse: Swets & Zeitlinger B. V.

Oakes, J. (1985). *Keeping track: How schools structure inequality*. New Haven: Yale University Press.

Ogbu, J. (1978). *Minority education and caste*. New York: Academic Press.

Ogbu, J. U. (1992). Understanding cultural diversity and learning. *Educational Researcher, 21*(8), 5-14, 24.

Olson, D. R. (1977). From utterance to text: The bias of language in speech and writing. *Harvard Educational Review, 47*, 257-281.

Ortiz, A. A., & Yates, J. R. (1983). Incidence of exceptionality among Hispanics: Implications for manpower planning. *NABE Journal, 7*, 41-54.

Porter, R. P. (1990). *Forked tongue: The politics of bilingual education*. New York: Basic Books.

Ramirez, C. M. (1985). *Bilingual education and language interdependence: Cummins and beyond*. Doctoral dissertation, Yeshiva University.

Ramirez, J. D., Yuen, S. D., & Ramey, D. R. (1991). *Longitudinal study of structured English immersion strategy, early-exit and late-exit transitional bilingual education programs for language-minority children*. Final Report to the U.S. Department of Education. Executive Summary. San Mateo: Aguirre International.

Ricciardelli, L. (1989). *Childhood bilingualism: Metalinguistic awareness and creativity*. Doctoral dissertation, University of Adelaide, Australia.

Rueda, R. (1989). Defining mild disabilities with language-minority students. *Exceptional Children, 56*, 121-128.

Sayers, D. (1991). Cross-cultural exchanges between students from the same culture: A portrait of an emerging relationship mediated by technology. *Canadian Modern Language Review, 47*, 678-696.

Schlesinger, A., Jr. (1991). *The disuniting of America*. New York: W. W. Norton.

Schweinhart, L. J., Weikart, D. P., & Larney, M. B. (1986). Consequences of three preschool curriculum models through age 15. *Early Childhood Research Quarterly, 1*, 15-45.

Skutnabb-Kangas, T. (1984). *Bilingualism or not: The education of minorities*. Clevedon, England: Multilingual Matters.

Skutnabb-Kangas, T. (1988). Resource power and autonomy through discourse in conflict—A Finnish migrant school strike in Sweden. In T. Skutnabb-Kangas & J. Cummins (Eds.), *Minority education: From shame to struggle* (pp. 251-277). Clevedon, England: Multilingual Matters.

Skutnabb-Kangas, T., & Toukomaa, P. (1976). *Teaching migrant children's mother tongue and learning the language of the host country in the context of the sociocultural situation of the migrant family*. Helsinki: The Finnish National Commission for UNESCO.

Snow, C. E., & Hoefnagel-Hohle, M. (1978). The critical period for language acquisition: Evidence from second language learning. *Child Development, 49*, 1114-1128.

Snow, C. E., Cancino, H., De Temple, J., & Schley, S. (1991). Giving formal definitions: A lingistic or metalinguistic skill. In E. Bialystok (Ed.), *Language processing in bilingual children* (pp. 90-112). Cambridge: Cambridge University Press.

Tizard, J., Schofield, W. N., & Hewison, J. (1982). Collaboration between teachers and parents in assisting children's reading. *British Journal of Educational Psychology, 52,* 1-15.

Verhoeven, L. (1991). Acquisition of biliteracy. *AILA Review, 8,* 61-74.

Wong-Fillmore, L. (1991a). When learning a second language means losing the first. *Early Childhood Research Quarterly, 6,* 323-346.

Wong-Fillmore, L. (1991b). Second-language learning in children: A model of language learning in social context. In E. Bialystok (Ed.), *Language processing in bilingual children* (pp. 49-69). Cambridge: Cambridge University Press.

Zanger, V. V. (1994). "Not joined in": Intergroup relations and access to English literacy for Hispanic youth. In B. M. Ferdman, R-M. Weber, and A. Ramirez (Eds.), *Literacy across languages and cultures.* Albany, New York: SUNY Press.

Bilingual Education and Second Language Acquisition Theory*

Stephen D. Krashen

Introduction

The impression one gets from the popular press is that bilingual education is a mess. We are told that "basic disagreements range across the entire field of bilingual education" (Trombley, 1980a), that the experts disagree on which programs are best, that those who are supposed to benefit from bilingual education often oppose it, that there is little information about how second languages are acquired, and that basic research on all of those issues is either contradictory or lacking.

While we cannot cover the entire field of bilingual education, we will examine some of these disagreements, certain central issues in bilingual education that appear to be unresolved. In the first section, we will briefly describe the issues, the points of contention. Following this, we will review what is known today about the process of second language acquisition. A third section will show how this new information, along with a considerable amount of excellent thinking and research in bilingualism and bilingual education, helps to resolve some of the issues facing parents and educators today. We will see that while bilingual education does have many unresolved problems, the situation is not nearly as bad as it may appear. Basic research and theory already exist that speak to many of the issues in the field today.

The Issues

The aim of this section is merely to present the issues. This is no easy task. There appear to be a bewildering variety of options and programs, each with its supporters and detractors. I will try to present some of these options and some of the points of debate. This will not be a complete survey; it will, however, cover those questions upon which current research and theory can shed some light. The presentation is in the form of definitions, done in the hope that consistent use of terms will alleviate at least some of the confusion that exists in bilingual education today.

*This paper owes a tremendous debt to the research and thinking of James Cummins. I would also like to thank Professors Merrill Swain and John Oller for a very helpful discussion of Professor Cummins' ideas and their relationship to second language acquisition theory, and to Robin Scarcella for her comments.

Bilingual Education Programs

While we could use bilingual education as a cover term for practically all of the programs described below, it will be useful to limit it here. Bilingual education refers to situations in which students are able to study subject matter in their first language (L1) while their weaker language skills catch up. This is Trombley's view of bilingual education: "Bilingual Education is intended to permit students who speak little or no English to learn reading, writing, arithmetic and other basic subjects in their primary language while they are acquiring proficiency in English" (1980b, p. 1). The theory behind bilingual education is that it allows non-English proficient (NEP) children to keep up in subject matter while acquiring English as a second language.

There are, of course, many varieties of bilingual education. Bilingual education programs vary in at least four ways:

1. Language use (manner). It is possible to present subject matter in the first language and leave it up to the English as a Second Language (ESL) component to provide practice in English (bilingual education + ESL). Most programs provide at least some subject matter in both languages, and there are several ways this can be done. Some provide some subjects in English and others in the first language; others use both languages for the same subject. Here again, there are several possibilities. A common method is speaking in first one language and then the other; an explanation is given in both the first language and in English during the same class hour. This is known as *concurrent translation*.

2. Amount of each language used. Not all programs provide exactly 50 percent exposure to each language. Legarreta (1979) informed us, for example, that in one concurrent translation class, Spanish was used 28 percent of the time and English 72 percent, while in a balanced bilingual class (some subjects in Spanish and others in English), the percentage was 50 percent Spanish and 50 percent English.

3. Type of ESL. There are many ways of teaching the second language. Methods include the still popular audiolingual system, which emphasizes repetition and memorization of phrases and sentences, as well as other grammar-oriented approaches, which stress the conscious understanding of rules of grammar, and more conversational methods.

4. Purpose. Bilingual programs vary with respect to whether they are intended to maintain the children's first language indefinitely (maintenance) or are only to help them ultimately adjust to an all-English program (transitional). It is important to note that the announced goals of both transitional and maintenance programs always include acquisition of the second language and subject matter education.

Alternatives to Bilingual Education

1. Submersion or "Sink or Swim"

In submersion programs, NEP children are simply placed in the same classroom as native English speakers and the regular curriculum is followed. There is no organized attempt to provide any special instruction or extra help for these children. Although sympathetic teachers often try to do something, all instruction is in English.

Many people feel that "Sink or Swim" is the best solution. Here are the two most commonly heard arguments for "Sink or Swim," as opposed to bilingual education:

a. Clearly, "Sink or Swim" provides more exposure to English, and the more exposure to English received, the better off children are. In letters to the *Los Angeles Times,* several writers claimed that bilingual education condemns children to second-class status since it fails to provide a full exposure to English, thus denying immigrant students full economic and social opportunity (September 19, 1980).

b. Many people, it is maintained, succeeded via "Sink or Swim." Since they had to learn English, and were surrounded by it, they learned, or so the argument goes.

We will return to these points of view later, after looking at theory and the empirical research.

2. Submersion + ESL

This option is often referred to simply as "ESL," which is a misnomer, since ESL in some form is nearly always a part of bilingual education programs. In submersion plus ESL, NEP children are usually given a separate ESL class for some prescribed period of time, usually an hour per day (termed "pull-out"). The rest of the day is spent in classes with native English speakers, and the NEP students attempt to follow the all-English curriculum.

Those who favor "Sink or Swim" usually support this program as well, on the grounds that it provides more English; more time spent exposed to English; the motivation to learn, since subject matter is taught in English; and the advantages of formal instruction. Lopez, in a letter to the *Los Angeles Times,* speaks for those who hold this view:

> Bilingual classes segregate these [non-English-speaking] students and thus seriously reduce their contact with [the] English speakers and, even more importantly, weaken their drive to communicate with others in English. If you have ever taught a class of immigrants, you know that only the most highly motivated will consistently respond in English if they know you speak their native language....You cannot learn

English well if you do not have the opportunity to interact
with English speakers in thousands of varied situations over a
period of years. This should take place not only in special
classes (English-as-a-second-language classes are the right
idea for immigrant students, but only for a limited time) but
also in regular classes as well as extra-class situations.
(September 19, 1980)

Lopez describes herself as one who had to learn English herself as a
young immigrant and as a bilingual teacher. Her view is shared by some
legislators and some members of the communities who are supposedly
served by bilingual education. According to Trombley:

Many parents think the key to success in the United States is
to learn English, and they do not believe the educators who
tell them their children will learn to speak English better in
bilingual classes. (September 4, 1980b)

Of course, many legislators, immigrants, and members of minority
language communities support bilingual education enthusiastically. We
will evaluate these arguments in a later section of this chapter.

3. Immersion

"Immersion" is often used as a synonym for "Sink or Swim," but this
term has been used in the professional literature to refer to a very different kind of program. Immersion typically refers to programs in which
majority language children (e.g., English-speaking children in the United
States and Canada) are instructed in a second language, that is, programs
in which subject matter is taught in a second language such as Spanish or
French. This need not always be the case, however; and theoretically immersion programs are possible for minority children as well.

Typically, immersion students receive all instruction in the second
language, with the exception of language arts in the first language. Many
programs, however, increase the amount of subject matter instruction in
the first language as children progress. Immersion students are also
"segregated," that is, native speakers of the second language are not
usually included in these programs; and immersion students do not
usually receive formal instruction in the second language.

In early immersion, the second language is used in kindergarten and
for most subjects starting from the first grade. In late immersion,
students may receive one or two years of formal instruction in the second
language before starting subject matter instruction in the L2. Late immersion programs begin around sixth grade, but here again there is variation. There are also partial immersion programs in which some subjects
are taught in the L2 and some in the L1 (Swain, 1978).

Immersion programs in Canada using French as the second language have been carefully followed by researchers. More recently, American immersion programs have been developed using Spanish and other languages.

With this definition of immersion, there really can be no conflict between bilingual education and immersion, since they are aimed at different populations. Nevertheless, immersion is a logical possibility for NEP children (i.e., subject matter instruction in English, segregated from native speakers with L1 language arts), a possibility discussed later.

We also see that immersion research is a rich source of information about second language acquisition for bilingual education specialists.

Table 1 reviews the differences between submersion programs and majority child immersion programs.

Table 1

COMPARISON OF SUBMERSION AND IMMERSION PROGRAMS

Submersion	*(Majority child) Immersion*
Children are mixed with native speakers of the L2	Children are linguistically segregated.
Language of instruction is the majority language.	Language of instruction is a minority language.
Instruction in L1 language arts is not provided.	Instruction in L1 language arts is provided.

Summary of Issues

The issues, then, are these:

1. Does bilingual education retard the development of English as a second language?
2. Are "Sink or Swim" (submersion) and/or ESL methods better than bilingual education?
3. How should ESL be taught?
4. Is there a place for "immersion" for the NEP child?
5. Which bilingual education options are better for language acquisition?

The answers to these questions, contrary to much popular opinion, are not obvious, and not merely a matter of common sense. They should not be resolved by vote but by consideration of empirically based theory and research. In the following section, we will review current second language acquisition theory, an exercise that will be of great use in discussing the issues listed above.

Second Language Acquisition Theory

Current second language acquisition theory will be discussed in terms of five hypotheses about second language acquisition:

1. The Acquisition-Learning Hypothesis

2. The Natural Order Hypothesis

3. The Monitor Hypothesis

4. The Input Hypothesis

5. The Affective Filter Hypothesis

These hypotheses are presented here without extensive supporting evidence, as this evidence has been published elsewhere (Krashen, 1981, 1982b, Dulay *et al.*, 1982).

The Acquisition-Learning Hypothesis

According to this hypothesis, second language acquirers have two distinct ways of developing ability in second languages. Language *acquisition* is similar to the way children develop first language competence. Language acquisition is a subconscious process in two senses: people are often not aware that they are acquiring a language while they are doing so. What they are aware of using the language for some communicative purposes. Also, they are often not aware of what they have acquired; they usually cannot describe or talk about the rules they have acquired but they have a "feel" for the language. Language *learning* is different. It is knowing about language or formal knowledge of a language. Language learning is thought to profit from explicit presentation of rules and from error correction. Error correction, supposedly, helps the learner come to the correct conscious mental representation of a rule. There is good evidence, however, that error correction does not help subconscious acquisition (Brown *et al.*, 1973).

In everyday terms, *acquisition* is picking up a language. Ordinary equivalents for *learning* include grammar and rules.

The Natural Order Hypothesis

The Natural Order Hypothesis states that students acquire (not learn) grammatical structures in a predictable order; that is, certain grammatical structures tend to be acquired early and others, late. For English, a very well-studied language, function words (grammatical morphemes) such as *-ing* (as in: John is going to work now.) and plural/s/ (as in: two boy*s*) are among the earliest acquired. The third person singular ending/s/ (as in: He live*s* in New Jersey.) and the possessive /s/

(as in: John's hat) are acquired much later (in children's first language acquisition, possessive and third person endings may come as much as one year later). It appears that the order of acquisition for first language acquisition is not identical to the order of acquisition for second language acquisition, but there are some similarities. For grammatical morphemes in English, children's second language order is similar to adult second language order. There is thus a "first language order" and a "second language order" (Krashen, 1981).

Two disclaimers about order of acquisition and the Natural Order Hypothesis are necessary. First, linguists do not have information about the order of acquisition of every structure in every language. In fact, we have information only about a few structures in a few languages. As we shall see below, this does not present a practical problem. Also, the order is not rigidly obeyed by every acquirer; there is some individual variation. There is significant agreement among acquirers, however, and we can definitely speak of an average order of acquisition.

As we shall see later, the existence of the natural order does *not* imply that we should teach second languages along this order, focusing on earlier acquired items first and later acquired items later. Indeed, there is good evidence that language teaching aimed at acquisition should not employ a grammatical syllabus.

The Monitor Hypothesis

The Acquisition-Learning Hypothesis merely stated that two separate processes for the development of ability in the second language exist. The Monitor Hypothesis states the relationship between acquisition and learning. It seems that acquisition is far more important. It is responsible for our fluency in a second language, our ability to use it easily and comfortably. Conscious learning is not at all responsible for our fluency but has only one function: it can be used as an editor or monitor. This is illustrated in Figure 1.

Figure 1

**ACQUISITION AND LEARNING IN SECOND
LANGUAGE PRODUCTION**

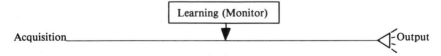

We use conscious learning to make corrections, to change the output of the acquired system before we speak or write, or sometimes after we speak or write (as in self-correction).

Studies (reviewed in Krashen, 1981) suggest that it is not easy to use the Monitor efficiently. In order to use the Monitor Hypothesis, three *necessary* conditions need to be met. These conditions are *necessary* but not sufficient; that is, even if they are met, second language users may not use the monitor very well.

(1) *Time.* In order to use conscious rules, the performer has to have enough time. In normal conversation, there is rarely enough time to consult conscious rules.

(2) *Focus on form.* In order to use conscious rules, just having time is not enough. The second language performer must also be focused on form (Dulay and Burt, 1978) or thinking about correctness. Research has indicated that even when performers have time, as when they are writing, they may not fully use the conscious grammar, since they are more concerned with what they are expressing rather than how they are expressing it.

(3) *Know the rule.* This is a formidable condition, considering our incomplete knowledge of the structure of language. Linguists concede that they have described only fragments of natural languages, and only a few languages have been worked on to any extent. Teachers and students, of course, have access to only a fraction of the linguists' descriptions.

These three conditions place tremendous limits on the use of conscious grammar—and, again, all three must be met to allow effective grammar use—but even this is no guarantee. Research strongly suggests (Krashen, 1981; 1982b) that conscious grammar use is surprisingly light on anything short of a grammar test.

The Input Hypothesis

According to the first three hypotheses, acquisition has the central role in second language performance. If this is so, the crucial question becomes: How do we acquire? Stated in terms of the Natural Order Hypothesis, we can ask how we move from one stage to another, from stage 3, for example, to stage 4 (or more generally from stage i, our current level of competence, i + 1, the next stage that the acquirer is due to acquire, or ready to acquire).

The Input Hypothesis postulates that we acquire by understanding input containing i + 1; that is, by understanding language that contains input containing structures that are a bit beyond the acquirer's current level. We acquire structure by understanding messages and not focusing on the form of the input or analyzing it. We can do this, we can understand language that contains structures we do not "know" by utilizing context, extra-linguistic information, and our knowledge of the world. In second language classrooms, for example, context is often provided via visual aids (pictures) and discussion of familiar topics.

Our usual approach to second language teaching is very different from the Input Hypothesis. As Hatch (1978) has pointed out, we assume the opposite: We first teach students structures and then try to give them practice in "using" them in communication. According to the Input Hypothesis, on the other hand, we acquire structure not by focusing on structure but by understanding messages containing new structure.

The Input Hypothesis also claims that we do not teach speaking directly. Rather, speaking fluency emerges on its own over time. The best way to "teach" speaking, according to this view, is simply to provide "comprehensible input." Speech will come when the acquirer feels ready. This readiness state arrives at different times for different people, however. Also, early speech is typically not accurate; grammatical accuracy develops over time as the acquirer hears and understands more input.

A third part of the Input Hypothesis is the claim that the "best" input should not be "grammatically sequenced," that is, it should not deliberately aim at $i + 1$. We are all familiar with language classes that attempt to do this; there is a "structure of the day" (e.g., the aim of today's lesson is to "learn" the past tense), and both teacher and students feel that the aim of the lesson is to learn and practice this structure. Once the day's structure is mastered, we proceed on to the next. The Input Hypothesis claims that such deliberate sequencing is not necessary and may even be harmful! Specifically, it hypothesizes that if there is successful communication, if the acquirer indeed understands the message contained in the input, $i + 1$ will automatically be provided in just the right quantities. Acquirers will receive comprehensible input containing structures just beyond them if they are in situations involving genuine communication, and these structures will be constantly provided and automatically reviewed.

It may be useful to detail some of the disadvantages of grammatical syllabi, even those that present structures along the natural order. They assume, first of all, that all of our students are at the same level in a given class, that they are all ready for the same $i + 1$. This is hardly ever true. In most classes, a substantial percentage of students will have already acquired the structure of the day, while another large sub-group is nowhere near ready for it. Thus, a teacher's audience for any given structure is usually a small part of the class. Even if the structure of the day is the appropriate one, how do we know when we have provided enough practice? And what about students who miss the structure due to absence? Under current procedures, they often have to wait until the following year. A third problem is perhaps the most serious: It is practically impossible to discuss any topic of real interest in any depth when the hidden agenda is practice of a structure.

Genuinely interesting and comprehensible input solves these problems. According to the Input Hypothesis, if students can follow the general meaning of a discussion, i + 1 will be provided for all of them, different i + 1 for different students.   With natural comprehensible input, students need not worry about missing a class and thereby missing the past tense forever.   It will come up again and again, both in the class discussion and in reading.   Finally, there is no need to worry about contextualizing a different structure every unit.   The focus, at all times, is on helping students understand messages and not rules of grammar.

In other words, input for acquisition need not focus only on i + 1, it only needs to contain it.   Thus, i + 1 will be supplied, and naturally reviewed, when the acquirer obtains enough "comprehensible input."

Evidence supporting the Input Hyupothesis is given in some detail in other publications (Krashen, 1981; 1982b) but it is useful to briefly mention two phenomena in second language acquisition that are consistent with this hypothesis.   The first is the presence of the *silent period,* a period of time before the acquirer actually starts to speak.   The silent period is very noticeable in children's second language acquisition; six- and seven-year-olds, for example, in a new country, may not say anything (except for some memorized sentences and phrases) for several months.   According to the Input Hypothesis, this is a time during which they are building up competence via input, by listening.   When they are ready, they start to talk.

We generally do not allow adults to have a silent period but insist on production right away.   When adults have to talk "too early," before they really have the acquired competence to support production, they have only one choice, and that is to fall back on their first language, an idea first proposed by Newmark (1966).   Here is how this works: performers will "think" in their first language, that is, mentally produce the desired sentence in the first language and then fill in the words with second language vocabulary.   If time permits, performers will note where the syntax or grammar of the sentence in L1 differs from how this sentence should look in the second language and will use the conscious monitor to make changes.   For example, if one wishes to say in French:

(1) The dog ate them.

The learner would mentally produce a sentence similar to (1).   Step ((2) would be to simply plug in French words, giving:

(2) *Le chien a mangé les.*

Some acquirers may consciously know that sentences like (2) are not correct and, given time, can make the necessary correction, giving:

(3) *Les chien les a mangé.*

According to this view, first language "interference" is not something "getting in the way." It is not interference at all but is the result of falling back on old knowledge. Its cure is more acquisition, or more comprehensible input. It is not restricted to adults but will happen in situations where production demands exceed current competence. It is a fairly common occurrence, and we occasionally see it even in acquisition-rich environments, although the number of first language-influenced errors is generally a small minority of the total number of errors children produce. Sentence (2), in fact, was observed in a child second language acquisition situation in an immersion class in Toronto (Selinker *et al.*, 1975).

Table 2 summarizes the Input Hypothesis:

Table 2

THE INPUT HYPOTHESIS

1. We acquire (not learn) language by understanding input that contains structures that are just beyond our current level of competence (i + 1).
2. Speech is not taught directly, but "emerges" on its own. Early speech is typically not grammatically accurate.
3. If input is understood, and there is enough of it, i + 1 is automatically provided. We do not have to deliberately program grammatical structures into the input.

The Affective Filter Hypothesis

The fifth and final hypothesis deals with the role of "affect," that is, the effect of personality, motivation, and other "affective variables" on second language acquisition. Briefly, the research literature in second language acquisition tells us that the following affective variables are related to success in second language acquisition:

1. *Anxiety.* Low anxiety relates to second language acquisition. The more the students are "off the defensive" (Stevick, 1976), the better the acquisition.

2. *Motivation.* Higher motivation predicts more second language acquisition. Certain kinds of motivation are more effective in certain situations, moreover. In situations where acquisition of the second language is a practical necessity, "instrumental" motivation relates to second language acquisition; in many other situations, such as those where acquisition of the second language is more of a luxury, "integrative" motivation predicts success in second language acquisition (Gardner and Lambert, 1972).[1]

---

[1] "Instrumental" motivation is defined as wanting to acquire another language for some practical purpose, e.g., for a profession. "Integrative" motivation occurs when the language is acquired in order to feel a closer sense of identity with another group.

3. *Self-confidence.* The acquirer with more self-esteem and self-confidence tends to do better in second language acquisition (Krashen, 1981).

I have hypothesized that these affective factors relate more directly to subconscious language acquisition than to conscious learning, because we see stronger relationships between these affective variables when communicative-types tests are used (tests that require the use of the acquired system) and when we test students who have had a chance to *acquire* the language and not just learn it in foreign language classes. Dulay and Burt (1977) have made this relationship more explicit and clear by positing the presence of an "affective filter." According to the Affective Filter Hypothesis, acquirers in a less than optimal affective state will have a filter, or mental block, preventing them from utilizing input fully for further language acquisition. If they are anxious, "on the defensive," or not motivated, they may understand the input, but the input will not enter the "language acquisition device." Figure 2 illustrates the operation of the filter.

Figure 2

THE AFFECTIVE FILTER

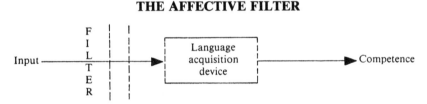

When the filter is "up," input may be understood but will not reach the language acquisition device; it will not strike "deeply" (Stevick, 1976).

The Causative Variable in Second Language Acquisition

We can summarize the five hypotheses with a single claim: People acquire second languages when they obtain comprehensible input and when their affective filters are low enough to allow the input in. In other words, comprehensible input is the only causative variable in second language acquisition. All other factors thought to encourage or cause second language acquisition only work when they are related to comprehensible input.

This hypothesis resolves may problems in the professional literature. For example, some studies seem to show that language teaching is beneficial, while others show that real-world use of the second language is superior (for a review, see Krashen, 1982b). This conflict is resolved by positing that language teaching helps second language acquisition by providing comprehensible input. It seems that language teaching is most efficient for students who have no other source of comprehensible input, that is, foreign language students who have no chance to interact with speakers of the target language and beginners who are not yet advanced enough to understand second language input outside class. Language teaching is of less value when rich sources of comprehensible input are available, e.g., for the intermediate student living in the country where the language is spoken.

The effects of *age* on second language acquisition also reduce down to comprehensible input plus the affective filter. The professional literature consistently supports these generalizations about age and second language acquisition: (1) Older acquirers progress faster in earlier stages (adults are faster than children; older children acquire faster than younger children), but (2) children outperform adults in the long run (Krashen *et al.,* 1979). It usually takes children about six months to one year to catch up to older acquirers (Snow and Hoefnagel-Hohle, 1978).

A possible explanation for these findings is as follows: Older acquirers are faster because they can use production strategies younger acquirers do not usually have. Specifically, older acquirers are able to "beat the system" and perform using a combination of the first language and the conscious grammar, as described earlier. While children also show occasional first language interference, adults appear to be more able to use the first language syntax as a strategy, and with their superior cognitive development, are better able to use the conscious grammar to bring their sentences into conformity with second language patterns. A good "learner" can use a combination of the first language and monitor to begin speaking fairly complex sentences very early, in a matter of hours. While this system has real drawbacks, i.e., it requires constant monitoring and vigilance, it allows the older acquirer to participate in conversation early and obtain more input.

Evidence also suggests (Scarcella and Higa, 1982) that older acquirers are more proficient at conversational management. While younger acquirers get what looks like simpler input, older performers are better able to make the input comprehensible; they ask native speakers for more help, are better at keeping the conversation going, etc.

Older acquirers also have the advantage of greater knowledge of the world—greater cognitive/academic language proficiency (CALP) (Cummins, 1980). This additional extralinguistic information gives older acquirers a greater chance to understand what they hear, both in and out of school.

An explanation for children's superiority in ultimate attainment is simply that the strength of the affective filter is sharply increased at puberty; adults may get sufficient quantities of input, but it does not all get in. The increase in filter strength at this time is due to the biological and cognitive changes the adolescent is going through at puberty (Elkind, 1970; Krashen, 1982a).

Table 3 summarizes explanations for age differences in second language acquisition.

Table 3

AGE DIFFERENCES IN SECOND LANGUAGE ACQUISITION

1. Older acquirers are faster in the early stages of second language acquisition because:
   a. They are better at obtaining comprehensible input (conversational management).
   b. They have superior knowledge of the world, which helps to make input comprehensible.
   c. They can participate in conversation earlier, via use of the first language syntax.
2. Younger acquirers tend to attain higher levels of proficiency in second languages than adults in the long run due to a lower affective filter.

Second Language Teaching

Before proceeding on to the implications of second language theory for bilingual education, it will be useful to examine the implications of theory for language teaching, since language teaching is usually considered one of the goals of bilingual education. While theory should not be the only element considered in language teaching practice (Krashen, 1982b), the five hypotheses given in the previous section have some very clear implications. They predict that any successful second language teaching program will have these characteristics:

1. It will supply input in the second language that is, first of all, comprehensible and, second, interesting and relevant to students. As discussed earlier, the goal of this input will not be to provide practice on specific points of grammar but to transmit messages of interest.

2. It will not force students to speak before they are ready and will be tolerant of errors in early speech. The theory implies that we improve in grammatical accuracy by obtaining more input, not by error correction. [Although error correction will work for some people (monitor users) some of the time (when they have time to think about form) and for some easy-to-learn rules.]

3. It will put grammar in its proper place. Some adults, and very few children, are able to use conscious grammar rules to increase the grammatical accuracy of their output; and even for these people, very strict conditions need to be met before the conscious knowledge of grammar can be applied, given the Monitor Hypothesis presented above. Children have very little capacity for conscious language learning and may also have little need for conscious learning, since they can come close to native speaker performance standards using acquisition alone.

Many different methods come very close to meeting these requirements. Asher's Total Physical Response Approach, Lozanov's Suggestopedia, Terrell's Natural Approach, and materials developed by Winitz are some examples (Krashen, 1982b). In addition, several non-methods also meet these requirements. For example, successful *conversation* with a speaker of the language you are trying to acquire may be the best lesson of all, as long as the speaker succeeds in modifying his or her speech so that you understand. According to the theory, acquirers profit directly not from what they themselves say, but from what native speakers say. Acquirer output makes an *indirect* contribution to acquisition by inviting comprehensible input. Also, pleasure reading or reading for content and intrinsic interest has the potential for supplying the necessary input for acquisition.

Subject Matter Teaching and Second Language Acquisition

Another clear potential source of comprehensible input is the subject matter classroom itself in which subject matter is taught using the second language as a medium of instruction (immersion classes).

Simply, the theory predicts that second language acquisition will occur in subject matter classes taught in the second language if the child can follow and understand the lesson. Language levels necessary for comprehension will differ, of course, for different subjects. It has been suggested, for example, that arithmetic does not require as much control of the second language as science. In the former, there is considerable extralinguistic help in understanding, fewer demands on students in terms of verbal responses, and a more restricted vocabulary (Cazden, 1979).

Applied linguistics research confirms this prediction and helps us see both the advantages and limitations of subject matter teaching as a means of encouraging second language acquisition. English-speaking immersion students, both in the United States and Canada, are in general able to follow the curriculum in a second language, that is, they learn subject matter as well as monolinguals do. Research has shown that they also do far better in acquiring the second language than students who study the second language only in formal classes. Researchers are careful to point out, however, that immersion students do not reach native-like levels in speaking and writing. Also, it takes several years for immersion students to attain these high levels of competence in the second language (see e.g., Lambert and Tucker, 1972; Swain, 1978, 1979). The classroom, thus, has its limits. Immersion students hear the language only from the teacher and not from peers. This may mean both a lack of certain kinds of input (conversational) and the existence of an affective filter.

Subject matter teaching, thus, has both advantages and limitations. It can provide comprehensible input and help second language acquisition; students exposed to the subject matter alone can achieve high levels of proficiency in certain kinds of second language usage. This takes time, however, and such students do not typically reach the native speaker level.

Before proceeding to implications, one major point about the success of immersion programs need to be made. Cohen and Swain (1976) point out that one of the reasons immersion programs succeed, where some kinds of bilingual programs fail, is because the immersion students are "segregated." In early immersion, they note, "all kindergarten pupils are unilingual in the L1. In essence, the successful program starts out as a segregated one linguistically" (p. 47). This linguistic segregation raises the chances of students receiving comprehensible input. The presence of native speakers in a class (submersion) ensures that a good percentage of the language heard by the non-native speaker will be incomprehensible, since teachers naturally will gear much of their speech to the native speakers in a native to native rather than a native to non-native speaker register.

Cohen and Swain (1976) point out several other factors that, in our terms, lead to a lower affective filter in immersion programs. The linguistic segregation "eliminates the kind of ridicule that students exert on less proficient performers" (p. 47), teachers have positive expectations, and the program is voluntary. Also, "in kindergarten, the children are permitted to speak in the L1 until they are ready to speak in the L2" (p. 48). Thus, a silent period in L2 is allowed.

Bilingual Education and Second Language Acquisition

We are now prepared to deal with some of the questions and issues raised in the first section. To do this, we first need to consider what requirements any program must meet in order to promote second language acquisition. From what we have learned from second language acquisition theory, there seem to be two major requirements.

I. Provide Comprehensible Input in the Weaker Language

Clearly, this requirement does not mean merely being exposed to the second language. There is a tremendous difference between receiving comprehensible, meaningful input and simply hearing a language one does not understand. The former will help second language acquisition, while the latter is just noise. It remains noise no matter how much exposure is provided. According to the theory, a small amount of comprehensible input, even one hour per day, will do more for second language acquisition than massive amounts of incomprehensible input.

There are several possible sources of comprehensible input for NEP children. The one that we traditionally turn to is classes in ESL. Simply, the theory predicts that ESL will help to the extent that it supplies comprehensible input. Not all teaching methods do this; some, in fact, supply amazingly little comprehensible input in a second language (e.g., grammar-translation and audiolingual type methods). Both theory and practical experience confirm that repetitive drill does very little for acquisition; and grammar approaches, shown to be ineffective for adults, are even less effective for small children. ESL can make a contribution when it supplies the necessary input to children who have few or no other sources of input (see Terrell, 1977, 1981 for some ideas on how this can be done).

A second source of comprehensible input for NEP children is interaction with other children outside of school, on the playground, and in the neighborhood. This can be an extremely rich source of input, and it may be the case that the availability of this source is responsible for the success of many people who succeeded without ESL or bilingual education.

It should be pointed out that even with informal playground interaction, acquisition of English or of any other language takes time. As mentioned earlier, children in informal environments typically show a silent period and may produce very little for several months. Thus, even under the best conditions, language acquisition is slow.

A third possible source of comprehensible input is subject matter, as discussed in the previous section. It will help second language acquisition if children understand enough of the second language to follow the lesson. Non-English proficient children, however, can make it to this level in "Sink or Swim" programs only if they get the comprehensible input somewhere else or if the linguistic level of the class is somehow lowered.

II. Maintain Subject Matter Education

A bilingual program needs to make sure that NEP children do not fall behind in subject matter. This entails, in many cases, instruction in subject matter using the first language as a medium of instruction. Contrary to the view of critics, this does not necessarily mean less acquisition of English as a second language. In fact, *it may mean more acquisition of English.* To see how this is so, we will describe what observance this requirement can do for NEP children.

First, the school system's basic responsibility is providing subject matter instruction so that NEP children can keep up and obtain the tools they need to live in and contribute to society. Second, subject matter instruction plays an important role in cognitive development. Children who fall behind in subject matter because they do not understand the language of instruction may also be missing the stimulation necessary for normal intellectual development.

The third reason is that subject matter knowledge and the cognitive/academic proficiency it encourages will help second language acquisition. It does this by giving children the context or background needed to understand academic input. In other words, children who are not behind in subject matter and who have normal cognitive development will simply understand more of what they hear, both in English language medium classes and in academic or intellectual discussions outside of class. If children understand more, they will acquire more of the language! Very simply, the more cognitively mature and knowledgeable children are about the *topic* of discussion, the better chance they have to acquire the language.

Anyone who has attempted to acquire a second language has had experiences that illustrate this phenomenon: We find it much easier to understand discussions of topics with which we are familiar and find it difficult to eavesdrop and come into conversations in the middle. (In my own case, I find it easy to read and understand discussions on familiar topics with my intermediate French and German, but I understand very little when I overhear a conversation in these languages.) This illustrates the powerful effect context and background knowledge have on our ability to understand a partially acquired language. The major point here is that understanding is a prerequisite for acquisition. Thus, the more context or background we can provide, the more acquisition will take place.

Children who are behind in subject matter and weak in the second language face double trouble. Their failure to understand will not only cause them to fall further behind but they will also fail to make progress in second language acquisition. Knowledge of subject matter, thus, has an indirect but very powerful effect on second language acquisition despite the fact that it may be provided in the students' first language.

Finally, it can be argued that maintaining subject matter, whether in the first or second language, leads to a better attitude toward school in general and higher self-esteem, factors that contribute to a lower affective filter and better acquisition of English, especially when English is presented in a school situation.

We can also suggest a third requirement for bilingual programs, not one motivated by considerations of second language acquisition but by independent motivations. As we shall see, this requirement may be met by programs that meet the first two requirements, at little or no additional cost.

III. Maintain and Develop Children's First Language

As with nearly all other issues in bilingual education, there is pro and con here as well. Some experts argue that we should make real efforts to maintain the first language. Reasons given include:

1. Speakers of languages other than English make a valuable contribution to our society. Since so few native English speakers successfully acquire a second language, it is foolish to waste this natural resource. Campbell expressed this view in a *Los Angeles Times* (September 5, 1980) interview:

> [The] emphasis on "transition" means we will systematically eradicate foreign languages in elementary school, then spend millions to try to develop these same skills in high school and college....That doesn't make much sense.

2. Maintaining the first language and culture of NEP children may help to build pride and counter negative attitudes members of a linguistic minority may have. There is evidence, in fact, that strongly suggests that those language acquirers who do not reject their own language and culture succeed better in second language acquisition than those who have negative attitudes toward their own group (Gardner and Lambert, 1972).

3. Cummins (1978; 1980) argues that in order to keep up in subject matter and maintain normal cognitive development, students need to develop high levels of first language competence. Specifically, they need to develop not only basic interpersonal and communicative skills in the first language (termed BICS) but also "cognitive competence," the ability to "use language effectively as an instrument of thought and represent cognitive operations by means of language" (Cummins, 1978, p. 397). A lack of development of this aspect of first language competence may explain problems some minority children have in school. When the first language is not used extensively and promoted at home, and is not supported at school, low first language skills, according to Cummins, can exert "a limiting effect" on the development of the second language. Majority language children in immersion programs do not have this problem, since their language is highly developed outside school (Cummins, 1978).

Cummins argues that education in the first language develops CALP (Cognitive/Academic Language Proficiency). CALP developed in one language contributes to CALP in any other, according to Cummins; that is, someone who is able to use Spanish for academic purposes will have developed an ability that will be useful in using any other language for academic purposes.

Arguments against first language maintenance have, in general, attempted to counter any of the above arguments but usually insist that since English is the official language of the United States, taxpayers should not have to support the maintenance or development of minority languages.

Another Look at the Options

We can now ask to what extent different programs meet the conditions described in the previous section. In this section, we will see that both theoretical predictions and empirical evidence show that some programs do satisfy the requirements while others do not and that this success or the lack of it depends not only on the program but also on the characteristics of the students. Most important, it will show that research exists, is not conflicting, and that real generalizations can be made about what works and what does not work in bilingual education. Table 4 presents this analysis.

1. We first consider submersion, or "Sink of Swim" programs. According to Table 4, "Sink or Swim" will satisfy the first requirement by providing comprehensible input in the weaker language only when extra ESL is provided (assuming a form of ESL that indeed provides comprehensible input) and/or when children have sufficient contact with input from the outside. In and of itself, "Sink or Swim" may not meet the first requirement, and children in such situations are in danger of not getting the input needed to acquire English. Such situations clearly exist in submersion programs that include children living in *barrios* where there is little if any social interaction among NEP and native English-speaking children.

The second requirement can only be met by "Sink or Swim" if the children's linguistic competence in English develops quickly enough. Children in "Sink or Swim" are playing a dangerous game of catch-up, hoping their competence in English will be high enough to do school work before they are hopelessly behind in subject matter. "Sink or Swim," even under the best conditions, is a risk.

No "Sink or Swim" program, by definition, attempts to meet the third requirement, development of the first language.

2. Immersion programs for majority children do meet all conditions. As discussed earlier, immersion programs have a better chance of supplying comprehensible input in subject matter classes than do "Sink or Swim" programs. Since all children are at the same linguistic level, there

Table 4
REQUIREMENTS TO BE MET BY PROGRAMS FOR NEP CHILDREN AND CURRENT OPTIONS

Requirements for Programs (predicted by theory)	SUBMERSION ("SINK OR SWIM")			IMMERSION	BILINGUAL EDUCATION		
	Only	+ Informal CI	+ ESL	Majority Child	Minority	Concurrent Translation	Ideal Bilingual
1. Comprehensible input in weaker language.	no	yes	yes [b]	yes	yes [c]	no [d]	yes [e]
2. Maintain subject matter.	no	? [a]	? [a]	yes	yes [c]	? [f]	yes
Additional: 3. Maintain and develop first language.	no	no	no	yes	no	? [f]	yes

a: This program will work if second language ability grows fast enough to reach subject matter threshold before children are too far behind.

b: Yes, if the ESL method supplies comprehensible input.

c: *De facto* immersion programs do not succeed as well as bilingual education, however. May be due to attitudes, teacher expectations, low development of first language, and inappropriate materials.

d: Students tune out weaker language in concurrent translation programs (Legarreta, 1979).

e: Yes, if second language skills are adequate for those classes taught in the second language.

f: Will not succeed unless there is adequate input in the second language.

CI = Comprehensible Input

Ideal Bilingual = Subject matter in primary language, plus comprehensible input in English, either as ESL and/or subject matter instruction in comprehensible English.

is less of a tendency to speak over the comprehension level of the students. This helps to satisfy the first and second requirements. The empirical evidence from the research programs evaluating immersion classes confirms that immersion children develop high levels of competence in the second language and do as well as monolinguals in subject matter.

Immersion programs for majority students also meet the third requirement through the use of language arts classes in the first language. Also, many programs provide for increasing use of the first language as a medium of instruction as children progress in school. Of great importance in meeting this requirement is that in immersion programs for majority students, children's first language is the language of the country, home, and playground; there is little chance that this language will be assigned a lower status.

One could argue that a solution for NEP children is an adaptation of the immersion model. This would entail a completely separate curriculum, all taught in English, to groups consisting only of NEP children. Assuming all children start at the same time and on an equal footing with respect to English competence, it would appear to have the linguistic advantage of having a better chance of supplying comprehensible input as compared to "Sink or Swim." Thus, theoretically, we could expect progress both in language acquisition (first requirement) and subject matter (second requirement) even if little or no contact with English-speaking children outside of school was possible. Judging from reports from majority immersion, we would not expect completely native-like English.

It can be maintained, however, that many "Sink or Swim" programs are already *de facto* immersion programs in that they often involve a majority of NEP children and, in some cases, are composed entirely of NEP children (e.g., in certain inner city areas and on American Indian reservations). These programs do not report overwhelming success. There may be good reasons why, however, reasons that explain why minority-child immersion may look good on paper but may not always work.

First, NEP students who enter immersion programs late will face nearly the same problems they face in "Sink or Swim"; they will not understand and may thus fall behind in subject matter and not improve in English. (Late entering bilingual education students will not have this problem; they can be taught in the first language at least until their English develops sufficiently.)

Also, minority immersion teachers may not have the same kinds of expectations as do majority immersion teachers. They may be less able or willing to make input comprehensible and may set higher standards for second language acquisition than are possible under the circumstances. As Cohen (1976) points out, we have a double standard:

> People applaud a majority group child when he can say a few words in the minority language (e.g., at the beginning of an immersion program) and yet they impatiently demand more English from the minority group child. (p. 85)

Thus, many *de facto* immersion programs look more like "Sink or Swim," with inappropriate materials and input that is too complex and incomprehensible.

3. We turn now to the programs categorized as Bilingual Education in Table 4. Let us first consider the program labeled concurrent translation. In this kind of program, concepts are explained in one language and then repeated in the second. This kind of program may not meet the first requirement for the simple reason that children need not pay attention to the explanation in the second or weaker language, and there is no motivation for teachers to attempt to simplify explanations in the second language. Legarreta (1979) noted that in the concurrent translation program, "Teachers reported that the Hispanic students tune out the English and wait to hear the material explained in Spanish" (p. 533). (This phenomenon also predicts, and correctly I think, the failure of bilingual TV to teach the second language. In many programs, a given character will speak either Spanish or English, but it is quite possible to follow the story line by attending only to one language. Similarly, it predicts that Americans will not acquire centigrade temperature systems from the practice of announcing the temperature in both centigrade and fahrenheit. Most people will simply listen to the version they understand.) Concurrent translation can theoretically meet the second and third requirements, however, since subject matter can be explained in the first language and continued use of the L1 helps to ensure its maintenance. In practice, however, concurrent translation often fails to meet these requirements. This is because, despite its intentions, concurrent translation input in many programs often is incomprehensible, most materials are in English, and primary language input often is provided by under-trained aides or Anglophone teachers who have not fully mastered the children's first language.

The Ideal Bilingual program, shown in Table 4, is one in which subject matter is taught in the primary language and some source of comprehensible input in the second language is supplied. This can be in the form of ESL or comprehensible subject matter instruction using English (as in the balanced bilingual program discussed earlier). Such programs have the potential for satisfying all three requirements, even for children who have little access to English outside of school. Balanced bilingual programs will be successful according to the predictions of the theory, especially if the subject matter classes given in the second language are those where more extra-linguistic context is available to aid comprehensible (e.g., math), while those dealing with more abstract topics—topics that typically employ fewer physical props (e.g., social sicence and language arts)—are taught at first in the primary language (Cazden, 1979).

Empirical Evidence

Our analysis based on the three requirements derived from language acquisition theory bring us to these conclusions:

1. "Sink or Swim" programs will not be effective for children with no extra source of comprehensible input.
2. Adding ESL to "Sink or Swim" will help but will not be as effective as bilingual education in encouraging acquisition of English.
3. Bilingual programs in which subject matter is taught in the first language, and a source of comprehensible input is provided in the second language, whether ESL or not, will succeed best.

Despite years of discussion of bilingual education in the professional literature and many studies of different aspects of bilingualism, little research speaks directly to these three predictions. The research that is available, however, is fully consistent with them.

Legarreta (1979) examined the acquisition of English in kindergarten children in three kinds of bilingual programs (balanced, concurrent translation, and concurrent translation + ESL) and two kinds of "Sink or Swim" programs [with and without ESL where the ESL component consisted of "daily, sequenced lessons in English structure and use, presented orally to small groups" (p. 523)]. The overall exposure time was seven months—relatively short for this kind of study, as Swain (1979) points out—and the number of subjects involved was not large. The results, however, are very interesting.

1. Children in all bilingual education programs outperformed "Sink or Swim" children in listening comprehension and conversational competence[2] tests of English, despite the fact that the "Sink or Swim" children had more exposure to English.

---

[2] The test of conversational competence asked children to use the language in real communication; it thus demands more than knowledge of vocabulary and grammar but also tests abilities such as "the ability to be only as explicit as a situation demands, to elaborate, to make inferences about a situation, to be sensitive to social rules of discourse..." (Legarreta, 1979, p. 525).

2. The balanced bilingual program produced the greatest overall gains in both the second language and the first language (Spanish).
3. "Sink or Swim" with ESL outperformed "Sink or Swim" without ESL on listening comprehension testing but not on the test of conversational competence.

Legarreta (1979) concluded that the use of audiolingual style ESL training is "marginally facilitative" (p. 534), while "an alternate immersion bilingual program, with balanced Spanish and English input, really facilitates both Spanish and English acquisition" (p. 534). This appears to be so, but her data support a deeper generalization: Bilingual programs will work when they supply comprehensible input in the second language and adequate, comprehensible subject matter instruction in either language. The balanced program does this, but so do other versions.

Rosier and Farella (1976) report results from a different context that conform to the same underlying principles. They report of the success of bilingual education for Navajo children at the Rock Point Community School in the heart of the Navajo reservation. In 1960, according to Vorih and Rosier (1978), Rock Point ranked at the bottom of eight Indian schools in student achievement. The introduction of intensive ESL in 1963 helped somewhat, but Rock Point sixth graders were still two years behind national norms. In 1967, bilingual education was introduced, with kindergarten children receiving 70 percent of their instruction in Navajo and first and second graders receiving 50 percent in Navajo. Third through sixth graders had 75 percent of their instruction in English. English is taught in early grades "by TESL methods" (Vorih and Rosier, 1978, p. 264). The program can thus be classified as Bilingual Education + ESL.

Analysis of the Rock Point program confirms the validity of our requirements: Students in the bilingual program, with subject matter in the first language, outperformed non-bilingual education students on a reading test of English. Again, the bilingual students actually had *less* exposure to English but apparently acquired more, confirming that it is comprehensible input and not mere exposure that counts.

Research cited by Cummins (1980) provides even more confirmation. As Cummins (1980) reports it:

> Carey and Cummins (1979) reported that grade 5 children from French-speaking home backgrounds in the Edmonton Catholic School System bilingual program [Canada] (80% French, 20% English from K-12) performed at an equivalent level in English skills to anglophone children of the same IQ in either the bilingual or regular English programs. A similar

finding is reported in a large-scale study carried out by Hébert *et al.* (1976) among grades 3, 6 and 9 francophone students in Manitoba. At all grade levels there was a significant positive relationship between percentage of instruction in French (PIF) and French achievement, but no relationship between PIF and English achievement. In other words, francophone students receiving 80% instruction in French and 20% instruction in English did just as well in English as students receiving 80% instruction in English and 20% in French. (p. 184)

Conclusions

We are now ready to return to the issues raised in the first section of this chapter and attempt to give some answers.

1. Does Bilingual Education Retard the Development of English as a Second Language?

Both theory and empirical research tell us that proper bilingual education need not retard the development of second language competence and should, in fact, promote it. Classes taught in the first language help children grow in subject matter knowledge and stimulate cognitive development, which in turn helps second language acquisition by providing children with the extra-linguistic context necessary for comprehension.

2. Are "Sink or Swim" (Submersion) and/or ESL Methods Better?

Obviously, "Sink or Swim" children have more exposure to English, but they do not necessarily have more comprehensible input; it is comprehensible input, not merely "heard" language, that makes language acquisition happen. Thus, "Sink or Swim" classes, at worst, may be providing children only with noise. The results of this are doubly tragic: Children will fall behind in subject matter and will not acquire the second language.

"Sink of Swim" with ESL will fare somewhat better but will work only if children acquire English fast enough, before they are hopelessly behind in subject matter. It may be that in most cases where "Sink or Swim" worked, children had rich comprehensible input from playmates outside the classroom.

3. How Should ESL Be Taught

Second language acquisition research strongly suggests that methodology *per se* is not the issue: By whatever name, children need comprehensible input to acquire English. This can come in the form of ESL classes taught according to a method that provides such input (e.g., Terrell's Natural Approach) or subject matter taught in comprehensible English.

4. Is There a Place for Immersion for NEP Children?

Theoretically, immersion for NEP children appears to meet the three requirements. Yet, results of *de facto* immersion programs in the United States are not encouraging. This could be due to several factors, including inadequate development of the first language, as suggested by Cummins (1978), differing teacher expectations the failure of late-entering students to obtain comprehensible input, and inappropriate materials.

5. Which Bilingual Education Options Are Better for Language Acquisition?

There are several bililngual education options that will satisfy the requirements given in Table 4 and earlier in the chapter. Balanced bilingual education programs will do this as long as those subjects taught in the second language are comprehensible. There is nothing magic, however, in the 50 percent figure: It need not be the case that exactly one-half of the program be in one language and one half in the other. What counts is that the requirements are met and that NEP students receive enough comprehensible input to improve in their weaker language. This has happened with as little as 20 percent input in the second language in some programs.

Several issues of course remain unsolved, and in a real sense they always will be. As is typical of scientific reasoning, we have discussed hypotheses and some evidence that supports them. We have not provided proof, nor can we. What we have tried to show is that there is substantial information available about how language is acquired, that it is certainly enough to formulate hypotheses, that these hypotheses shed light on some of the basic issues in bilingual education, and that the field is not in a state of helpless confusion. Researchrs are evaluating children's progress, adding to their knowledge of language acquisition, and using this knowledge to better serve the children they study and those who will come after them.

REFERENCES

Brown, R., Cazden, Courtney, & Bellugi, U. (1973). The child's grammar from I to III. In C. Ferguson, & D. Slobin (Eds.), *Studies in child language development* (pp. 295-333). New York: Holt, Rinehart and Winston.

Campbell, Russell (1980, September 5). *Los Angeles Times.*

Cazden, Courtney B. (1979). Curriculum language contexts for bilingual education. In Eugéne J. Briere (Ed.), *Language development in a bilingual setting* (pp. 129-138).

Cohen, Andrew D. (1976). The case for partial or total immersion education. In Antónío Simões (Ed.), *The bilingual child* (pp. 65-89). New York: Academic Press.

Cohen, Andrew D., & Swain, Merrill (1976, March). Bilingual education: The "immersion" model in the North American context. *TESOL Quarterly, 10*(1), 45-53.

Cummins, James (1978). Educational implications of mother tongue maintenance in minority language groups. *The Canadian Modern Language Review, 34,* 395-416.

Cummins, James (1980, June). The cross-lingual dimensions of language proficiency: Implications for bilingual education and optimal age issue. *TESOL Quarterly, 14*(2), 175-187.

Dulay, Heidi C., & Burt, Marina K. (1977). Remarks on creativity in second language acquisition. In Marina K. Burt, Heidi C. Dulay, & M. Finnochiaro (Eds.), *Viewpoints on English as a second language* (pp. 95-126). New York: Regents.

Dulay, Heidi C., & Burt, Marina K. (1978, June). Some guidelines for the assessment of oral language proficiency and dominance. *TESOL Quarterly, 12*(2), 177-192.

Dulay, Heidi C., Burt, Marina K., & Krashen, Stephen (1982). *The language two.* New York: Oxford University Press.

Elkind, David (1970). *Children and adolescents: Interpretive essays on Jean Piaget.* New York: Oxford University Press.

Gardner, Robert C., & Lambert, Wallace E. (1972). *Attitudes and motivation in second language learning.* Rowley, MA: Newbury House.

Hatch, Evelyn M. (1978). Discourse analysis and second language acquisition. In E. Hatch (Ed.), *Second language acquisition: A book of readings.* Rowley, MA: Newbury House.

Krashen, Stephen (1981). *Second language acquisition and second language learning.* London: Pergamon Press.

Krashen, Stephen (1982a). Accounting for child-adult differences in second language rate and attainment. In Stephen Krashen, R. Scarcella, & M. Long (Eds.), *Child-adult differences in second language acquisition.* Rowley, MA: Newbury House.

Krashen, Stephen (1982b). *Principles and practice in second language acquisition.* New York: Pergamon Press.

Krashen, Stephen, Long, Michael A., & Scarcella, Robin C. (1979, December). Age, rate and eventual attainment in second language acquisition. *TESOL Quarterly, 13*(4), 573-582.

Lambert, Wallace E., & Tucker, Richard G. (1972). *Bilingual education of children: The St. Lambert experiment.* Rowley, MA: Newbury House.

Legaretta, Dorothy (1979, December). The effects of program models on language acquisition by Spanish-speaking children. *TESOL Quarterly, 13*(4), 521-534.

Lopez, Rosa Maria (1980, September 19). *Los Angeles Times.*

Los Angeles Times. (1980, September 19).

Newmark, L. (1966). How not to interfere with language learning. *International Review of American Linguistics, 40,* 77-83.

Rosier, Paul, & Farella, Merilyn. (1976, December). Bilingual education at Rock Point—Some early results. *TESOL Quarterly, 10*(4), 379-388.

Scarcella, Robin, & Higa, C. (1982). Input and age differences in second language acquisition. In Stephen Krashen, Robin Scarcella, & Michael A. Long (Eds.), *Child-adult differences in second language acquisition.* Rowley, MA: Newbury House.

Selinker, Larry, Swain, Merrill, & Dumas, Guy (1975, June). The interlanguage hypthesis extended to children. *Language Learning, 25*(1), 139-152.

Snow, Catherine E., & Hoefnagel-Hohle, Marian (1978, December). The critical period for language acquisition: Evidence from second language learning. *Child Development, 49*(4), 1114-1128.

Stevick, Earl W. (1976). *Memory, meaning, and method.* Rowley, MA: Newbury House.

Swain, Merrill (1979). Bilingual education: Research and its implications. In C. Yorio, K. Perkins, & J. Schachter (Eds.), *On TESOL '79.* Washington, DC: TESOL.

Swain, Merrill (1978, May). French immersion: Early late or partial? *Canadian Modern Language Review, 34,* 577-585.

Terrell, Tracy D. (1977, November). A natural approach to second language acquisition and learning. *Modern Language Journal, 41*(7), 325-337.

Terrell, Tracy D. (1981). The natural approach in bilingual education. In *Schooling and language minority students: A theoretical framework* (1st ed.), Los Angeles, CA: Evaluation, Dissemination and Assessment Center, California State University, Los Angeles.

Trombley, William (1980a, September 7). Bilingual education: Even the experts are confused, *Los Angeles Times.*

Trombley, William (1980b, September 4). Is bilingual education able to do its job? *Los Angeles Times.*

Vorih, Lillian, & Rosier, Paul. Rock Point community school: An example of a Navajo-English bilingual elementary school program. *TESOL Quarterly, 12*(3), 263-269.

Part Two
Strategies for Implementation

Communicative Approaches to Second Language Acquisition: From Oral Language Development into the Core Curriculum and L2 Literacy

Alan N. Crawford

Introduction

Instruction in English as a second-language is the keystone of programs aimed at the academic needs of language minority students. It is especially important where only small numbers of students speak the same mother tongue or where a lack of trained personnel and appropriate instructional materials prevents the implementation of programs of bilingual education. It is also the major element of those full bilingual education programs where we use the native language for academic instruction while students develop sufficient English to benefit from academic instruction in their new second language.

The foundation for communicative approaches to second language acquisition is based on concepts, theories, and hypotheses that have converged around the interaction of constructivist notions about making meaning. Vygotsky (1978) defined the zone of proximal development as "the distance between the actual developmental level as determined by independent problem solving and the level of potential development as determined through problem solving under adult guidance in collaboration with more capable peers." This key concept emphasizes the social dimension of learning that results from the support of mothers, teachers, older siblings, and other caregivers. The collective wisdom of the cooperative learning group has an obvious role here as well.

The author gratefully acknowledges the contribution of the late Tracy D. Terrell, who wrote the original chapter on "The natural approach in bilingual education" in the first edition to *Schooling and Language Minority Students: A Theoretical Framework* (1981).

The concept of *scaffolding* involves the temporary support provided by teachers when students are engaged in a task within the zone of proximal development. Bruner (1978) described scaffolding as a temporary launching platform designed to support and encourage children's language development to higher levels of complexity. Pearson (1985) explained the temporary nature of scaffolding as the gradual release of responsibility. Good teachers intuitively use such scaffolding strategies as questioning, prompts, illustrations and other visual resources, demonstrations, dramatization, gestures, comprehension monitoring, graphic organizers, and rephrasing. These strategies enable students to sustain participation in learning activities.

Approximation is a related process in which students imitate language and test hypotheses about it. The process of approximation underlies oral and written language in that students are acquiring new skills and understandings within the context of authentic wholes. Students exhibit behaviors in which they approximate the language behavior of their models, growing closer and closer to their levels of proficiency. In his view of successive approximation, Holdaway (1979) describes the process as one in which Vygotsky's adults and more capable peers use the output from learner responses to construct, adjust, and finally eliminate the scaffolding that permits learning to progress.

At this point, we should also examine the dichotomy between skills-based and constructivist models of instruction. Skills-based models focus on the disassembly or fragmentation of curricular elements so that isolated skills and concepts can be mastered within a linear paradigm. A constructivist view of instruction conversely focuses on the construction of meaning, using what the learner already knows and combining it with new ideas to be integrated. The latter model is learner-based, an important factor in working with the students from diverse backgrounds who are often at-risk in any case. Within the constructivist view, language acquisition is embedded in function. When we teach skills, we teach them as needed in a meaningful context, not in a systematic, artificial, and fragmented way.

The purpose of this chapter is to link the constructivist paradigm to communicative approaches to second language acquisition and to related instructional strategies for English learners. In addition, we will extend the third stage of Terrell's natural approach, the emergence of speech, into more advanced levels of language development. This will include access to the core curriculum through specially designed academic instruction in English (SDAIE), which was formerly called *sheltered English instruction*.

Finally, we will examine the development of literacy in English. The approach and strategies presented will reflect many aspects of whole language instruction. They will be consistent with communicative approaches to second language acquisition and with Krashen's underlying hypotheses about that process. We will see that the paradigm shifts that occur within second language acquisition, content/language integration in the core curriculum, and whole language approaches in literacy and the language arts encompass a broad convergence and overlapping among these processes.

A Historical Perspective

Until recent years, most students in the public schools have tried to learn a second language using such grammar-based approaches as the grammar-translation and audiolingual methods. The grammar-translation approach is most familiar to us as the one used in the foreign language courses we took in high school and college in the 1950s and even later (Chastain, 1975). We learned vocabulary from lists which paired words in the foreign language with their English counterparts. We studied the grammar of the new language again in terms of our own. Our first language was always the window through which we viewed, and contrasted, our new second language. We rarely became functional in that language because of the classes we took. At best, we scored well on tests of grammar, translated with difficulty, and read with halting comprehension.

The audiolingual approach is rooted in structural linguistics and behavioral psychology. This combination results in a methodology based on a grammatical sequence, with mimicry and the memorization of pattern drills, but without the heavy grammatical analysis of the grammar-translation approach (Chastain, 1975). The audiolingual approach is characterized by the following: (a) it is based on the unconscious mastery of sequenced grammatical forms; (b) learning is the result of teaching patterned oral drills; (c) the emphasis is on correct oral production of grammatical forms in response to oral stimuli; (d) language skills are acquired in the natural sequence of listening, speaking, reading, and writing; and (e) there is no reference to the primary language during instruction (Finocchiaro, 1974).

The typical audiolingual lesson consists of a dialogue followed by a series of related pattern drills. The purpose of the dialogue is to present the meaning of the vocabulary or grammatical element being taught within the context of a real situation. For example, a dialogue to introduce the grammatical concept of prepositions of position might appear as follows:

Rosa: *Where is the ball, Diego?*

Diego: *It's on the table, Rosa.*

Rosa: *No, it fell under the table.*

Diego: *Pick it up and put it in the box, Rosa.*

We would teach this dialogue using a repetition drill, illustrating it with pictures or dramatizing with actual objects and students. We would then practice the new elements using pattern drills that develop a habitual response through repetition. Based upon a stimulus or cue from the teacher, the students respond, making one incremental change in the pattern at a time. They usually begin by responding as a total group. As they gain confidence, smaller groups respond separately, until individual students are confident enough to respond alone. The result is usually an artificial and boring program based on a grammatical continuum that does not reflect the sequence in which elements are naturally acquired.

The results of recent research have brought about major changes in educators' conceptions of how a second language is acquired and how this acquisition is best promoted in the elementary and secondary classroom. There has been a major paradigm shift away from the grammar-based approaches to language acquisition and toward those we call *communicative*. This change has been particularly apparent in the second language acquisition of English learners.

Underlying Principles of Communicative Approaches

Krashen's Hypotheses

Krashen (1982a and 1982b) has offered five important hypotheses that underlie current practice in most communicative approaches to second language acquisition.

The Acquisition-Learning Hypothesis. In his acquisition-learning hypothesis, Krashen illustrates the difference between the infant's subconscious acquisition of the primary language and the high school French student's conscious learning of a second language. We *acquire* language subconsciously, with a *feel* for correctness. *Learning* a language, on the other hand, is a conscious process that involves knowing grammatical rules. Of course, the infant is almost always successful in acquiring language, while the high school foreign language learner is usually not.

The Natural Order Hypothesis. According to Krashen's natural order hypothesis, grammatical structures are acquired in a predictable sequence, with certain elements usually acquired before others. He has concluded that the orders for first and second language acquisition are similar, but not identical. It is important to note, however, that Krashen does not conclude that sequencing the teaching of language according to this natural order is either necessary or desirable. The content of grammatical approaches to second language acquisition is organized around sequences of grammatical structures. The content learned when the primary language is acquired in infancy is whatever the infant needs and is interested in at that time.

The Monitor Hypothesis. Krashen's related monitor hypothesis describes how the learner's conscious monitor or editor functions to make corrections as language is produced in speaking or writing. Several conditions are necessary for the application of the monitor: (a) time to apply it, a situation not present in most ordinary oral discourse, especially in classroom settings; (b) a focus on the form or correctness of what is said, rather than on the content of the message; and (c) knowledge of the grammatical rule to be applied. These conditions serve to illustrate why so few students learn to understand and speak a foreign language in a grammar-translation or audiolingual high school or university foreign language course.

The Input Hypothesis. Among Krashen's most important contributions is his input hypothesis. He concludes that growth in language occurs when we receive comprehensible input, or input that contains structure at a slightly higher level than what we already understand. The input hypothesis corresponds to Vygotsky's zone of proximal development. The context of the input provides clues to maintain the integrity of the message. According to the input hypothesis, a grammatical sequence is not needed. The structures are provided and practiced as a natural part of the comprehensible input that the learner receives, much as it occurs with infants acquiring their primary language. Krashen characterizes this comprehensible input as caretaker speech about the *here and now*.

The Affective Filter Hypothesis. In his affective filter hypothesis, Krashen concludes that several affective variables are associated with success in second language acquisition. These include high motivation, self-confidence and a positive self-image, and low anxiety in the learning environment. Krashen (1981) relates the input hypothesis to the silent period, the interval before speech in either the primary or second language in which the learner listens to and develops an understanding of the language before beginning to produce language.

Other Underlying Principles

Results from recent research have led to other major changes in educators' conceptions of how a second language is acquired and how this acquisition is best facilitated in the elementary and secondary classroom.

Similarities Between Primary and Second Language Acquisition. An important similarity between primary and second language acquisition is the formation of an incomplete and incorrect interlanguage by both primary and second language learners (Selinker, Swain, and Dumas, 1975). Most children move through similar stages of development in this incomplete language. It is often called *telegraphic speech* because it resembles the incomplete patterns we use to carry meaning in telegrams (Terrell, 1982). Selinker, Swain, and Dumas point out the danger that this interlanguage may become fossilized, stopping short of its continued development into fluency in the absence of native language speakers.

In a related study, Ervin-Tripp (1974) conducted a meta-analysis of research comparing first and second language acquisition. She found that the development of syntax by second language learners parallels the order of development of primary language learners. Dulay and Burt (1974b) similarly found that learners from diverse language backgrounds tend to acquire English grammatical structures in approximately the same order. Chinese and Spanish-speaking children, for example, acquired the copula at approximately the same stage of language development, even though the copula is present in Spanish, but not in Chinese. Their conclusions lead to questions about the actual effects of interference from the primary language. In a related study, they found that fewer than 5% of children's errors in the second language could be attributed to interference from the primary language (Dulay and Burt, 1974a). This leads us to additional reservations about the use of an ESL curriculum based on grammatical sequences.

Chamot (1981) pointed out another similarity, the lack of student interest in abstract language concepts. Instead, students should use language for functional purposes based upon immediate needs and interests, just as infants do.

The role of correction is also similar in both primary and second language acquisition. According to Terrell (1982) and Krashen and Terrell (1983), we should view correction as a negative reinforcer that will, at best, raise the affective filter and the level of anxiety in a language classroom, whether with children or adults. When there is no interference with comprehension, we should recognize that the correction of errors has no more place in the second language acquisition program than it does when infants acquire their primary language. Caregivers may expand incorrect or incomplete forms, such as *Kitty gots four feets,* and say *Yes, Kitty has four feet.* There is little evidence, however, that this expansion has any positive effect.

These similarities between primary and second language acquisition are not consistent with either grammar-translation or the audiolingual approach. Children learning their first language don't rely on grammatical rules or on systematic acquisition of vocabulary. With its emphasis on early production instead of a silent period, on correct production instead of an acceptable, though immature and incomplete, interlanguage, and on grammatical sequence instead of function and communicative competence, the audiolingual approach bears little resemblance to the way primary or second languages are successfully acquired.

Other Factors Associated with Second Language Acquisition. Many investigators have found strong associations between the successful acquisition of second languages and student attitudes. Oller, Hudson, and Liu (1977) reported that positive self-esteem was associated with performance in second language instruction. Oller (1981) further indicated that improved performance in second language acquisition is conversely associated with improved self-esteem.

Gardner and Lambert (1972) found a strong relationship between students' motivation to learn a second language and their attitude toward the group that the language represents. In a related vein, Saville-Troike (1976) found that negative stereotyping of English learners' cultural group can have a negative effect on their efforts to learn a second language spoken by those who hold that negative stereotype.

The age of English learners is another factor associated with second language acquisition. Because immigrants typically enter school when they first arrive, they enter second language acquisition programs at many different ages. Although the age of entry into programs is therefore determined by age at arrival instead of the optimum age for second language acquisition, it will be useful to examine the effects of age on acquisition.

According to Lenneberg's (1967) critical period hypothesis, primary language acquisition must occur before the onset of puberty. Snow and Hoefnagel-Höhle (1978) investigated the implications of the critical period hypothesis for second language acquisition and found that subjects from 12 to 15 years of age and adults made the fastest progress in acquiring Dutch during the first months of learning. At the end of the first year, those from 8 to 10 years of age and from 12 to 15 years of age demonstrated the best proficiency in Dutch, while those from 3 to 5 years of age were lowest, indicating that Lenneberg's hypothesis was not supported for second language acquisition.

In an analysis of similar studies, Krashen, Long, and Scarcella (1979) found that adults developed second language proficiency faster than children, that older children developed faster than younger children, and that those who had natural exposure to second languages during childhood tended to be more proficient than those who began as adults. Cummins (1980) also concluded that older students acquired second language cognitive/academic language proficiency (CALP) more rapidly than younger students because of the greater development of CALP in the primary language and its interdependence with CALP in the developing second language.

Collier (1987) examined the relationship between the age of LEP students and their acquisition of English. She found that students who entered the ESL program at ages 8 to 11 were the fastest achievers and that they reached the 50th percentile in all subject areas within two to five years. The lowest achievers entered the program at ages 5 to 7, and they were one to three years behind students from 8 to 11 years of age. Students from 12 to 15 years of age had the most difficulty acquiring English. It was projected that they would need from six to eight years of instruction to reach grade-level norms in academic achievement.

When Collier (1989) later analyzed other research on age and academic achievement in English, she found that students who had primary language academic instruction, whether in English or another native language, generally required from four to seven years to reach national norms on standardized tests in reading, social studies, and science, and as little as two years in mathematics and language arts, including spelling, punctuation, and grammar. She also found that those students from ages 8 to 12 who brought at least two years of schooling from their home country in their primary language needed from five to seven years to reach the same levels of achievement in English reading, social studies, and science, and two years in mathematics and language arts. Young students with no schooling in the primary language from either the home country or the new host country needed seven to ten years of instruction in reading, social studies, and science. Adolescent students with no second language instruction and no opportunity for continued academic work in the primary language were projected, in the main, to drop out of school before reaching national norms, both those with a good academic background and those with interrupted schooling.

Ervin-Tripp (1974) concluded that older language learners are more effective because they take advantage of the generic similarities of languages in learning the second one. They learn new symbolic representations for concepts and ideas they already have in their primary language. They have better skills in managing memory heuristics, and they have greater capacity to solve problems and form generalizations.

Communicative Approaches to Second Language Acquisition

The implications of Krashen's hypotheses and of related similarities between first and second language acquisition are that approaches to second language acquisition should provide comprehensible input, focus on relevant and interesting topics instead of grammatical sequences, and provide for a silent period without forcing early production. There are approaches to second language acquisition that meet these criteria. They are categorized as *communicative* approaches, and those most appropriate for elementary and secondary classrooms include the total physical response method, the natural approach, and the confluent education approach.

The Total Physical Response Method

Asher's (1969, 1979, 1982) total physical response or TPR method is an important communicative approach in the initial stages of second language acquisition. The TPR method provides for comprehensible input, a silent period, and a focus on relevant content, rather than on grammar or form. The focus of TPR is on physical response to verbal commands, such as *Stand up* and *Put your book on the desk*. Because little emphasis is given to production, the level of anxiety is low.

Lessons can be given to small groups or to an entire class. In the beginning, the teacher models one-word commands. This is done first with a few students, then with the entire group, then with a few students again, and finally with individual students. The teacher would say, for example, *Sit,* and then model by sitting down. Later, the teacher would issue the command without modeling. As the students' levels of language increase, the teacher begins to use two- and three-word commands, such as *Stand up* and *Bring the book.* The students demonstrate their understanding by physically carrying out the commands. The order of commands is varied so that the students cannot anticipate which is next. Old commands are combined with new ones in order to provide for review. Whenever the students do not appear to comprehend, the teacher returns to modeling. After a silent period of approximately ten hours of listening to commands and physically responding to them, a student then typically reverses roles with the teacher and begins to give those same commands to other students. It is important for the teacher to maintain a playful mood during classroom activities.

The total physical response approach can be extended to higher levels of proficiency by using the technique of nesting commands. The teacher might say the following:

> *Manuel, take the pencil to Enrique, or open the door. Esperanza, if Manuel took the pencil to Enrique, stand up. If he opened the door, close your eyes.*

A high level of understanding is necessary to carry out such commands, but no oral production is needed. Parents of young children will recognize that their infants can understand and carry out such commands long before they begin to speak themselves.

The Natural Approach

Terrell's (1977) original concept of the natural approach provided for three major characteristics: (a) classroom activities were focused on acquisition, that is, communication with a content focus leading to an unconscious absorption of language with a feel for correctness, but not an explicit knowledge of grammar; (b) oral errors were not directly corrected; and (c) learners could respond in the target language, the native language, or a mixture of the two.

Krashen and Terrell (1983) later presented four principles that underlie the natural approach to language acquisition. The first is that comprehension precedes production, which leads to several teacher behaviors: the teacher always uses the target language, focuses on a topic of interest to the students, and helps the students maintain comprehension.

The second principle is that production emerges in stages ranging from non-verbal responses to complex discourse. Students can begin to speak when they are ready, and speech errors are not corrected unless they interfere with communication.

The third principle is that the curriculum consists of communicative goals. Topics of interest, not a grammatical sequence, make up the syllabus. Finally, activities must lead to low anxiety, a lowering of students' affective filter. The teacher accomplishes this by establishing and maintaining a good rapport and friendly relations with and among students.

Terrell's (1981) natural approach is based on three stages of language development: (a) preproduction (comprehension); (b) early production; and (c) emergence of speech.

The Preproduction Stage. Topical, interesting and relevant, comprehensible input is provided by the teacher in the first stage, which closely parallels Asher's TPR approach. The teacher speaks slowly, using gestures to maintain comprehension. Students may respond with physical behaviors, shaking or nodding their heads, pointing at pictures or objects, or saying *yes* and *no*. It is important that input is dynamic, lively, fun, and comprehensible. Using a pet turtle, the teacher might say:

> *This is a turtle. His name is Herman. Is he red? Who wants to hold him?* [Hand to student.] *Who has the turtle? Does Tran have the turtle? Yes, he does. Does Rosa have the turtle? No, she doesn't.*

This basic input can be repeated with other objects in the classroom. We can also use large-format illustrations and posters. For example:

> *Here is a picture of a circus. Are there animals in the picture? Yes. How many animals are there? Yes, four. Point to the lion. Where is the elephant?*

If each student in the group is given a different illustration, the teacher might provide such input as:

> *Who has a picture of a boat? Yes, Eloy, you do. Is the boat large? Eloy, give your picture to Zipour. Who has a picture of an airplane? Yes, Araceli has a picture of an airplane.*

These examples include three primary preproduction techniques: using TPR, using TPR and naming objects, and pictures. The required responses include movement, pointing, nodding or shaking the head, and using the names of other students in the group. We should remember that nodding the head for an affirmative response and shaking it for a negative one are not appropriate in all cultures. Students may also have to acquire these nonverbal behaviors.

Since the emphasis at this stage is on listening comprehension, verbal responses in the primary language are also acceptable. This may be a problem if the teacher is unable to understand the students' mother tongue, but they usually find a way to help the teacher understand.

Classroom props allow for relevant expansion of this and subsequent stages of the natural approach. Any manipulative or concrete object is helpful, including flannel boards and puppets. Large colorful illustrations, such as those in travel posters and big books, are also very helpful. Sources of free color illustrations include calendars, outdated or otherwise, large posters available from textbook and trade book publishers, food group posters available from the National Dairy Council, and colorful illustrations in the annual reports of many large corporations, usually available on request through announcements in major business magazines.

The Early Production Stage. In the stage of early production, the student begins to produce one-word utterances, lists, and finally two-word answers, such as *little dog* and *in house.* Some of the latter, such as *me like* and *no want,* are grammatically incorrect or incomplete. Krashen and Terrell (1983) indicate that error correction has a negative effect that raises anxiety level and is not helpful. According to Crawford (1986), we should view these errors as immature language, not incorrect language. In the presence of good models, most of these errors will disappear in time, just as they do among infants developing their primary language.

Several types of questions can be used to elicit the one- and two-word responses within the reach of students as they transition into the early production stage:

Question Type	Question
Yes/no	*Are you thirsty?* *Do you like hamburgers?*
Here/there	*Where is the picture of the car?*
Either/or	*Is this a pencil or a book?*
One-word	*How many oranges are there?*
Two-word	*What animals are in the picture?*

As in the preproduction stage, these strategies should be integrated into activities that permit a variety of responses, ranging from physical responses from those not ready for production, to brief oral responses from those who are.

Does Jaime have a picture of a tree? [Yes.] Is the tree red? [No.] Who has a picture of an airplane? [Rigoberto.] Does it go fast or slow? [Fast.] Where is the picture of the tree? [There.] Look at Bo-Gay's picture. How many children are there? [Three.] What are they doing? [Playing ball.]

As the students begin production, conversations should increasingly require one-word responses. Within the same conversation, the teacher can address questions calling for longer responses to those children who are ready.

Sven, show us your picture. What is in Sven's picture? [Hamburger.] Yes, it is a hamburger. What is on the hamburger? [Catsup.] Is there apple on the hamburger? [No. Laughter.] What else is on the hamburger? [Lettuce, mayonnaise.] How does it taste? [Good.] What do you like with a hamburger? [French fries. Soda.] I like a milk-shake with mine.

Terrell suggests several other formats to elicit language from the students:

Activity	Example
Add-on sentence	*I like ice cream.* *I like ice cream and cake.* *I like ice cream, cake, and....*
Open-end sentence	*Playing basketball is....*

He also recommends the use of oral lists, interviews, and the discussion of charts, tables, graphs, newspaper advertisements, and pictures.

The Emergence of Speech Stage.   During the stage of emergence of speech, students begin to produce structures that are longer, more complex, more rich in vocabulary, and more correct. This production proceeds from three-word phrases to sentences, dialogue, extended discourse, and narrative. At this stage, Terrell recommends such activities as preference ranking, games, group discussions, skits, art and music, radio, TV, filmstrips, pictures, readings, and filling out forms.

Terrell (1981) suggested three general techniques to focus students in this stage on using language instead of on form: games; affective-humanistic activities; and problem-solving tasks. Games are helpful for providing comprehensible input in low anxiety situations. He recommended some of the affective-humanistic activities suggested by Galyean (see section below), including dialogues about personal topics, such as weekend activities, interviews, preference ranking, and the preparation of personal charts, tables, and graphs. An example of a chart that incorporates preference ranking follows below:

Favorite Pizzas

Name	Cheese	Sausage	Pepperoni	Tomato	Anchovy	Mushroom
Rita		X		X		X
Nguyen		X				
Abdul						
Sofik	X		X	X		
Petra		X		X		X

Does Nguyen like pizza? [Yes.] What kind of meat does Nguyen like? [Sausage.] How many like tomato on their pizza? [Three, Rita, Sofik, and Petra.] How does Abdul like pizza? [He doesn't like it.] Which students like the same kind of pizza? [Rita and Petra.] Is there a topping that no one likes? What is it? [Anchovy.] How do we know? [Nobody wants anchovy.]

Not only is the chart a valuable source of comprehensible input, but the process of gathering the data for the chart is fun as well.

Krashen and Terrell (1983) describe several other problem-solving activities. One is a task analysis of a daily activity, such as washing a car or getting ready for school. Teachers and students can organize other information into charts and tables for problem-solving activities, including student class schedules, physical characteristics and clothing, airline, bus, and train schedules, and department sale information. Maps of the community are particularly effective and very useful for preparing students to live in a new environment. In addition, students can work on developing speech for particular situations, such as ordering food in a restaurant, purchasing clothing, and making appointments. Analyzing advertisements is another worthwhile problem-solving activity.

Terrell (1981) also suggested that we can provide comprehensible input in such a way that students can acquire extensive English proficiency through studying science, social studies, music, art, and mathematics. Process skill science programs, such as McGraw Hill's Elementary Science Study (ESS) program, for example, offer a powerful means for promoting English acquisition and science learning at the same time. In *Mystery Powders* (1974), for example, students are given five white powders: salt, sugar, laundry or cooking starch, plaster of Paris, and baking soda. They must perform various experiments in which they taste, touch, smell, heat, and mix the powders with water or vinegar in order to identify them or mixtures of them. The teaching strategies can involve all of the stages of the natural approach, as shown in the commands and questions in Table 1. The teacher should anticipate participation through physical responses, in incomplete utterances in the new and immature second language, and in the mother tongue.

Table 1

AN APPLICATION OF THE NATURAL APPROACH TO
MYSTERY POWDERS, ELEMENTARY SCIENCE STUDY

Preproduction - Terrell (corresponds to Asher's Total Physical Response [TPR])

Point to the spoon.
Taste the first white powder.
Pick up the vinegar.
Put some of the first powder on the aluminum foil.
Raise your hand if you think Powder #2 is salt.
If your mixture has salt and starch, stand up; but if it has salt and sugar,
*   put your head on the table*

Early Production - Terrell

Yes/No:	*Is the first powder red?*
Either/Or:	*Does the sugar taste good or bad?*
	Is the vinegar here or over there?
One word:	*How many powders are there?*
	Who found baking soda in Mixture #4?
Fill blank (oral):	*When you look at salt through the magnifying glass, it looks _____.*
Lists:	*What powders do you think we have?*
Two words:	*How does the starch taste?*
	What did we do with the plaster?
	Tell me how you test for starch.

Emergence of Speech - Terrell

Preference ranking:	*Put the powders in order from best taste to worst.*
Three-or-more word responses:	*Why did we use heat with the powders?*
	Which test do you think you should use first with the Mystery Liquids?
	Tell me two ways to identify salt.

The Confluent Education Method

The confluent education method of language teaching (Galyean, 1977) places emphasis on four components of humanistic teaching: (a) a focus on the actual ongoing interests of the class; (b) practicing language structures with student-generated language; (c) student-to-student sharing with interpersonal, self-disclosing communication; and (d) self-awareness and self-realization leading to personal growth. Students experience activities that help them grow physically, emotionally, intellectually, and spiritually.

Instructional strategies include "centering" activities to prepare students for learning. These involve breathing activities, imagining, visualization, and body movement designed to lower anxiety. Focus activities provide opportunities for children to learn and share within groups. Conversational activities consist of using English sentence patterns in lively discussions. They include movement, art, pantomime, role play, and creative expression. The source of content is the students themselves, their needs, interests, and values. Galyean described several processes inherent in the method: (a) language practice takes place as a part of class interaction; (b) close interpersonal relationships among class members are fostered; and (c) self-reflection and self-disclosure are encouraged. Elements of the confluent method are often found in the natural approach.

Other Communicative Approaches

Two other approaches are included within the communicative category, although neither seems to have immediate utility in elementary and secondary classrooms. They are the Lozanov method, which is also referred to as Suggestopedia and Super Learning, and community language learning.

The Lozanov Method. The Lozanov method (Bancroft, 1978; Schaefer, 1980) has its origins in Europe and the former Soviet Union. Major elements of the method include a comfortable learning environment, with soft lighting and cheerful room decorations, and teachers trained as actors and psychologists who can suggest the meanings of words through action and gesture. Classes are intensive, lasting for four hours each day and meeting six days a week. Ideally, six men and six women are enrolled in each class. The suggestopedic cycle consists of a review of previous material, the use of dialogues, and a session in which new material is memorized by students reclining on special chairs and breathing according to a prescribed yoga rhythm. Music is often provided in the background.

Adaptations of the method in the United States include these essential elements: (a) an attractive, softly lit classroom; (b) a dynamic teacher; and (c) a state of relaxation combined with mental alertness on the part of the students. The latter is produced through Zen breathing, yoga and mind-calming exercises, and music. The focus of the approach corresponds to the lowering of Krashen's affective filter by reducing anxiety. A recent iteration of Suggestopedia is Dhority's Acquisition through Creative Teaching (ACT) approach (1991). It should be noted that in a study carefully crafted to compare superlearning with traditional strategies, Wagner and Tilney (1983) found no significant differences between the two groups in either learning vocabulary or in alpha brain wave rhythms.

Community Language Learning. Community language learning (La Forge, 1971) has its origins in an application of the group counseling process to language learning. The community is a small group of language learners guided by a counselor expert in the target language. The community or group dynamic is the key to diminishing anxiety in the language learning situation. The role of the counselor is to provide rote translation of ideas expressed in their own language for members of the group to use. A silent period is an accepted part of the approach. The clients proceed from complete dependence on the language counselor in the beginning stages to a point where they can function in the language with intervention from the counselor, when needed.

The Curriculum of a Communicative Program

Teachers who would advocate teaching the first person present indicative tense to a child in a second grade classroom would be incredulous at the suggestion that a parent teach the same concept to a three-year-old at home. Of course, both children can use the tense correctly, and neither as the result of instruction. This leads us to conclude, as do Krashen, Terrell, Galyean, and others, that the content of second language acquisition programs should be based primarily on content, not on grammatical sequence.

Topical Curricula. Under the assumption that needed language structures will emerge and be acquired naturally within the context of topical lessons, a communicative ESL curriculum is usually organized around a set of topics in order to ensure the introduction of new vocabulary and concepts of interest and utility to the students. Grammatical sequences also appear as a subcategory of some communicative curricula, as we shall see below.

Terrell (1981) suggested that, at the elementary and secondary levels, a grammatical continuum is not appropriate in the language acquisition process. He recommended the use of a topical curriculum that de-emphasizes the form or correctness of the message and that emphasizes instead its content. He suggested that the content should be limited to the following until students demonstrate production of more than one-word responses: following commands for classroom management; names of articles in the classroom; colors and description words for articles in the classroom; words for people and family relationships; descriptions of students; names of clothing, school areas, school activities; names of objects in the school that are not in the classroom; and foods, especially those eaten at school.

Later in the acquisition process, topics of interest to students would include the students' families, their homes and neighborhoods, their favorite activities, and pleasant experiences they have had. They also enjoy discussing their preferences about food, colors, television programs and films, and other aspects of their lives.

Like Terrell, Asher (1982) advocates the use of a topical curriculum. He suggests, however, that it should be organized into behaviors, objects that these behaviors are acted upon, and qualifiers or modifiers, such as adverbials and adjectivals, as outlined below:

Behaviors	Objects	Qualifiers
action verbs	nouns	adverbials prepositions adjectivals possessives

For example, the teacher might use the behavior *put,* the object *book,* and the qualifier *on the table* to produce the command, *Put the book on the table.* According to Asher, these elements can be combined and presented in a variety of creative and interesting ways.

Galyean (1980) organized a very comprehensive curriculum for her confluent approach to second language acquisition. It is entitled *My Language Is Me,* which reflects the focus of confluent education on the self. The curriculum is organized into eight topical units: School, Home, Me and My World, Amusements, Transportation, The City, Nature, and It's a Small World. Each topic is then subdivided into a sequence of grammatical objectives and structures.

Chamot (1983) offers several recommendations that very effectively tie the ESL program to the core curriculum. She suggests that vocabulary and concepts from content areas of the curriculum be used in ESL activities and that reading and writing instruction in English be increased for older students, especially those with literacy skills in the native language. Instead of focusing on the correct pronunciation of words in oral reading, teachers should emphasize silent reading comprehension, including extensive experiences with expository text in the content areas of the core curriculum.

Grammar in the Communicative Approach Curriculum. In spite of the advocacy of topical curricula by most authorities in the communicative approaches, some do find a place for grammatical structures. Terrell (1991) reexamined the place of grammar in communicative approaches with respect to adults. He postulated that, instead of relying on input to produce language following the silent period, many adults rely on output, indicating that grammar may have more importance than previously thought in their language development. Indeed, most of us who work in fields related to language acquisition recognize our own need for references to the grammar of any language we attempt to acquire.
we attempt to acquire.

Terrell concluded that, for some adults, we should consider using grammar instruction as an advance organizer to help language learners make sense of input. He also recommended using meaning-form focus in activities that contain many examples of a single grammatical relationship, that is, activities in which one grammatical concept is intentionally exemplified repeatedly, as described by Rutherford and Sharwood-Smith (1981). Terrell further suggested that, by using the monitor, learners might acquire their own output, instead of acquiring only comprehensible input from others. Although he addressed this discussion to adults, it has obvious implications for more capable secondary school English learners. Teachers should give serious consideration to the expressed wishes of those of their students who request some type of referencing to grammar.

Access to the Core Curriculum Through Specially Designed Academic Instruction in English

A major issue in the acquisition of English as a second language is the extent of access to the core curriculum during that process. In a study of programs for limited-English-proficient students in California, Berman et al. (1992) concluded that most English learners, especially those at the intermediate and senior high school levels, did not have access to aspects of the core curriculum that would permit them to receive a diploma. Instead, they were clustered in what was characterized as "a steady diet of ESL classes."

Many communicative strategies can be adapted to provide access to this core curriculum through a scaffolding process we now call *specially designed academic instruction in English* (SDAIE), which was formerly called *sheltered English instruction*. The topics treated in this highly contextualized instruction are the important content areas of the core curriculum.

Strategies for Providing Access to the Core Curriculum

Specially designed academic instruction in the content areas of the curriculum in the second language adds substantially to the knowledge and vocabulary that students need as a base for comprehension as they read and think in any language (Krashen, 1985). These strategies are consistent with the philosophy of communicative approaches to second language acquisition, and they additionally provide access to academic areas of the curriculum in such a way that communication is maintained.

Cummins (1981) provides a set of intersecting continua that are very useful for conceptualizing the issue of balancing the complexity of curriculum content with demands on language proficiency (see Figure 1 in the Cummins' chapter). The vertical continuum extends from cognitively undemanding to cognitively demanding, ranging, for example, from a conversation about what students ate for lunch on the cognitively undemanding side to a third grade mathematics lesson about the distributive principle of multiplication on the cognitively demanding side.

Cummins's intersecting horizontal continuum extends from context-embedded to context-reduced, ranging, for example, from a science lesson on classification taught with concrete manipulatives on the context-embedded side to an abstract lecture/discussion about the principles of democracy on the context-reduced side. Specially designed academic instruction in English will be most effective in subject areas of the curriculum that can be presented concretely, such as mathematics, science, art, music, and physical education. Although there are aspects of social studies that can be taught concretely, such as geography and map skills, there are so many abstract concepts taught that instruction in this area might well be delayed until students acquire additional English proficiency.

The purpose of a specially designed academic instruction approach to the core curriculum in English is to provide a focus on context-embedded activities, ensuring that comprehensible input is provided while treating increasingly cognitively demanding aspects of the core curriculum. The Los Angeles Unified School District (1985) prepared a set of English-language teaching strategies that provides the necessary scaffolding in content areas for intermediate English learners. They recommend that teachers simplify input by speaking slowly and enunciating clearly, using a controlled vocabulary within simple language structures. Where possible, they should use cognates and avoid the extensive use of idiomatic expressions. They suggest that teachers make frequent use of nonverbal language, including gestures, facial expressions, and dramatization. They also recommend the use of manipulatives and concrete materials, such as props, graphs, visuals, overhead transparencies, bulletin boards, maps, and realia. Comprehension should be maintained through extensive use of gestures, dramatization, illustrations, and manipulatives. Teachers should check frequently for understanding by asking for confirmation of comprehension, by asking students to clarify, repeat, and expand, and by using a variety of questioning formats. Schifini (1985) recommends a focus on student-centered activities, especially at the secondary level where lecturing and textbook use predominate.

Richard-Amato and Snow (1992) provide valuable strategies for content-area teachers of English learners. For mainstream teachers, they recommend providing a warm learning environment, recording lectures and talks on tape for later review, rewriting some key parts of text material at lower levels, asking native-English-speaking students to share notes with English learners, and avoiding competitive grading until students have achieved sufficient English proficiency to compete successfully with native speakers. In addition to strategies suggested by LAUSD and Schifini above, they recommend that teachers reinforce key concepts frequently, that they establish consistent routines in the classroom, that they provide sufficient wait time for students to respond to questions, that corrections be in the form of expansion and mirroring in correct form, and that they avoid forcing students to speak until they are ready. They also suggest that teachers frequently summarize and review, demonstrate that they acknowledge and value the language and culture that students bring to the classroom, and make effective use of teaching assistants or aides who speak their students' native language.

There are several other strategies that provide scaffolding for English learners in specially designed academic instruction activities in English. The highly contextualized interactions that take place in cooperative learning can make the difference between what Krashen (1985, 1991) describes as submersion, or *sink or swim,* and immersion, the type of scaffolded subject-matter instruction described above. Cooperative learning is most effective when, in the words of Vygotsky, more capable peers, that is, stronger speakers of English, are included in groups with English learners at various levels.

It benefits all students when no one has all of the information or skills needed to complete a task, but rather when all have opportunity and a need to contribute. According to Hamayan and Perlman (1991), assigning a function to each student, such as materials director, timekeeper, supervisor to keep the group on task, or recorder, helps ensure that each has a role and is actively involved.

Johnson (1988) suggests creating cross-language pairs in which a group of English learners is taught in English to do something, such as an art activity. Each of them must then teach the activity to an English-speaking student. This creates a need to communicate, making English functional and goal-oriented. In addition, the English learner has the status of the person who knows how to accomplish the task, while the English speaker does not. Doughty and Pica (1986) also reported that interaction in small groups could be greatly increased by ensuring that group members needed to know each other's information in order to complete a task.

Cathcart-Strong (1986) has found that a sufficient amount of time is needed in group activities so that English learners can elicit needed comprehensible input from English-speaking peers. They also need abundant opportunities to initiate interaction with adults. These are most likely to occur in problem-solving situations within small groups.

Krashen and Terrell (1983) describe several useful grouping techniques for acquisition activities. Teachers can form restructured groups according to some arbitrary criterion, such as the amount of money students have in their pockets, the color of their shirts, or the time they went to bed the night before. In a one-centered group, a single student becomes the focus of the activity. For example, one student might think of something, and the other students ask questions in order to guess what it is. A unified group activity is one in which everyone in the group has a piece of the information needed to solve a problem. Therefore, everyone must participate. Dyads or buddy groups are those in which two students work together. Finally, some activities can be conducted with an entire class or with a large group of students in the class. In all of these activities, the focus is on the message transmitted, not on its form.

Structures for Integrating English Learners

English learners are often organized into classrooms for the purpose of providing native language instruction, a practice that tends to segregate them from English-speaking students unless other arrangements are made. The isolation of English learners from English-speaking students can lead to fossilization, a stopping-in-place of language development caused by a lack of comprehensible input from expert English speakers. Krashen and Terrell (1983) indicate that exposure to the interlanguage, that is, the incorrect or incomplete structures of English learners, in the classroom should not be a problem if it is not the only input to which they are exposed.

The Eastman model (Krashen and Biber, 1988) of the Los Angeles Unified School District effectively alleviates this problem at the elementary level. Spanish-speaking students are organized for native language instruction in reading and the language arts during the morning, along with a natural approach program of ESL. In the afternoon, Spanish-speaking students are mainstreamed with English-speaking students in art, music, and physical education. As Spanish-speaking students gain English proficiency, they begin to receive specially designed academic instruction in English in the more concrete areas of the curriculum, such as mathematics and science. Social studies in English is introduced later.

Friedlander (1991) described three different newcomer program models for addressing the same problem at the secondary level. She identified general goals that newcomer programs share in common, including providing students with a strong academic foundation, developing English language proficiency, providing for orientation and basic survival skills, developing multicultural understanding and intercultural communication, promoting persistence, and enhancing self-esteem. Additional key features of identified programs were access to counseling, tutoring, health, interpretation services and specialized teacher training.

The English Language Center in Hayward, California, provides a half-day program at a separate site that gradually prepares students to learn successfully in their neighborhood schools. This permits them to have regular school experiences with English-speaking students during the other part of the day. All of its teachers have had personal immigrant experiences.

The Newcomer Center within Crenshaw High School in Los Angeles provides four options to serve Cantonese, Korean, and Spanish-speaking students. They include a full bilingual strand for preliterate students, a modified bilingual strand for students reading between fourth and eighth grade level in the primary language, and an accelerated bilingual strand for students achieving at grade level in the primary language. There is an English language development strand for students who could not be served in their primary language because of a lack of teachers. Teachers use cooperative and group learning techniques in a thematic approach to the content curriculum.

The International High School at LaGuardia Community College in New York provides a separate-site, full-time program. Rather than serving as a transition to a regular secondary school, the International High School is the final destination. In addition, students are able to continue their studies in the community college curriculum. Instead of providing primary language instruction, the program offers all instruction in English, with language learned in a meaningful context and embedded in content areas. Students are not separated into homogeneous language groups.

Other Supportive Strategies

There are many other strategies that provide the scaffolding needed in specially designed academic instruction in English. The development of thematic teaching units serves to provide a broader context for students' understandings in the content/language integration fostered by such instruction in English. Elementary teachers will find that they can organize units around literature themes, such as *change*. They might begin with literature study in *The Very Hungry Caterpillar,* examining *change* in the metamorphosis of a butterfly. Through the integration of mathematics and science, they can study change by graphing the amount of rust on a piece of metal over time. In the area of social studies, they can analyze *change* in behavior as one grows older. The concept of *change* is revisited throughout the curriculum in all content areas, providing reinforcement of vocabulary and language structures that will tend to be used often.

At the secondary level, Short (1991) recommends close collaboration between ESL and content teachers so that a theme such as deforestation might be the focus of a unit of study in both the language and science classes in which English learners are enrolled. Chan and Chips (1989) suggest previewing lessons in the native language, providing audiotapes for students to use following lessons, providing extra wait time for English learners to think about their responses to questions, providing study guides, and conducting read-alouds of textbook materials before they are read by the students themselves.

Finally, we should reinforce once again the idea that students should learn academic content from the core curriculum in the native language until they are ready for specially designed academic instruction in English when they reach a level of intermediate fluency in English. Schifini (1985) describes these intermediate learners as those who can engage in extended discussion in English. This instruction follows that provided in the primary language when students have enough background in the new second language to benefit from content instruction in it with the support inherent in what Krashen (1985) at that time termed a sheltered approach.

Teachers will find that students who have mastered a numeracy concept in the native language, for example, will find the same concept much more comprehensible in the second language than will the student who is learning the concept for the first time. It is for the latter student, in fact, that primary language instruction in that subject area is vital. Students who have developed language proficiency at an academic level in the primary language will gain more both in the further development of the numeracy concept and in the second language development that will surely accompany it in specially designed academic instruction in English.

There is, however, a situation in which specially designed academic instruction in English may be the preferred mode, or even the only mode, for teaching. It is the case of students who speak a primary language in which instruction cannot be provided. This may result from a lack of personnel proficient in the language, of materials, or of sufficient numbers of students to support such a program.

Extending Communicative Approaches into L2 Literacy

Only a few years ago, it was commonly held that English learners should not begin learning to read and write in English until they had reached an intermediate level of English fluency. We now recognize that the processes of reading and writing in English can begin early in the acquisition process, especially for those students who have developed literacy skills in the primary language. In addition, literacy can play a major role in support of the acquisition of English as a second language. Krashen and Terrell (1983) describe reading in the second language as an important source of comprehensible input. In the same way that we find parallels between communicative approaches to second language acquisition and specially designed academic instruction in English, we can identify many aspects of communicative approaches that parallel access to literacy in students' new second language—English.

Communicative Approaches and Whole Language

The convergence between communicative approaches to second language acquisition and literacy is particularly prominent in *whole language.* Coote and Stevens (1990) define whole language as "the interplay of all aspects of language needed to communicate with others, or when others, present or past, communicate with us," a definition that encompasses second language acquisition, including literacy.

Goodman (1986) views learning as proceeding from whole to part, without any basis in a sequence of skills. He places the major focus on authentic language use in the real world. Both of these ideas about whole language are consistent with communicative approaches to second language acquisition. Smith (1989) reinforces the importance of authenticity in stating that "literacy is a social phenomenon. Individuals become literate not from the formal instruction they receive, but from what they read and write about and who they read and write with." We can readily interchange listening and speaking for reading and writing in the Smith citation.

Rigg (1991) has identified major purposes of language within whole language, including the construction of knowledge and the creation and communication of purposeful and authentic meaning. Freeman and Freeman (1988) describe whole language as whole to part; as learning-centered; as having meaning and purpose; as including the four modes of listening, speaking, reading, and writing; and as reflecting high teacher expectations for students. Finally, Altwerger, Edelsky, and Flores (1987) describe whole language as a set of beliefs or a perspective about language, not as a method.

These mutually supporting concepts about whole language are entirely consistent with the underlying principles of communicative approaches to second language acquisition. Let us now examine some approaches and strategies to reading and writing that promote second language acquisition within a whole language perspective.

Early Literacy Experiences

Most English learners have had some emergent literacy experiences at home and in the community—recognizing cereal and soft drink labels; knowing brands of automobiles; being read to; and watching a parent read, refer to a calendar, or write a check. They have begun to understand the underlying concept of print representing spoken ideas, often even for the second language they are only beginning to understand.

A print-rich environment in the classroom is an important step toward providing meaningful material to read. Students don't need to know letter names or sound/symbol correspondences to begin recognizing and discussing labels, their own names, and other forms of print to which they are exposed. Surrounding them with sources of print in the classroom will serve to supplant missing or inadequate experiences.

The Key-Vocabulary and Language Experience
Approaches to Reading

The language experience approach (LEA) advocates a major source of written language for providing authentic, meaningful, early literacy experiences in English for English learners. If students have an extremely limited background in the language of initial instruction, especially if it must be English as a second language, then the key-vocabulary approach of Veatch *et al.* (1979) may serve well to bridge to literacy from a strong, communicatively based second language acquisition program.

As a part of the natural approach, Terrell (1981) recommended that key words be written on the chalkboard in the second language for older students who are literate in their native language. In the early production stage of Terrell's natural approach, students may express themselves quite appropriately in one- or two-word utterances as they begin to acquire a second language. It is altogether proper that they also begin to read key vocabulary that they have asked their teacher to write for them. They may later produce lists of related ideas, such as foods to eat at a carnival or fair, words that describe a favorite friend, or things to do after school. These topics and this output reflect the oral language common in the early production phase of Terrell's natural approach to language acquisition.

During an individual meeting with the teacher, each student in the key-vocabulary approach selects a word of personal importance. The teacher writes it on a card. After the student traces the word with a finger, the teacher records it in a key-word book and records a sentence or phrase that is dictated by the student about the word. The student then reads the dictation back to the teacher and illustrates it. Finally, the student copies the word and the sentence.

Most bilingual teachers who teach reading in the mother tongue recognize that student motivation to begin reading and writing in English early is strong. Although it is most beneficial for students to learn to read and write in the native language (Cummins, 1986, 1989; Krashen and Biber, 1988), where possible, teachers can begin an early introduction to literacy in English in order to take advantage of that motivation. The key-vocabulary and language experience approaches should be used with caution to ensure that the second language acquisition program does not evolve into an English literacy program presented before the student is ready. Being able to read and write in the mother tongue is always the most desirable base from which to establish literacy in English later because of the positive transfer of literacy skills to English.

Moving from the dictation of key vocabulary to predictable language patterns in the language experience approach is a natural step, and one that quickly leads to more traditional LEA strategies (Heald-Taylor, 1986). A dictation about foods to eat at the fair might result in each of several students dictating an idea conforming to this predictable pattern:

I eat hot dogs at the fair.

I eat popcorn at the fair.

I eat cotton candy at the fair.

Using the language experience approach in the second language is an excellent way to initiate students into print of interest and relevance to them (Moustafa and Penrose, 1985; Nessel and Jones, 1981; Dixon and Nessel, 1983). According to Crawford (1993), LEA also provides a means through which students can experience literature in their second language that is above their ability to read and comprehend. A teacher or aide can tell or read a story aloud. The students can then dictate the story back, that is, retell it for the teacher or aide to record, although probably in a less complicated version than the original. Peck (1989) found that listening to stories in this way helps students develop a sense of story structure, which should be reflected in the dictated version and in enhanced abilities to predict in this and other stories. The dictated text allows students to think, talk, read, and write about the piece of literature and to be exposed to its valuable cultural content. At the same time, they are actively interacting with it at a level of comprehension and of English language proficiency appropriate for their stage of development. They will be able to activate background knowledge from this experience that will transfer positively into the second language when they later read the literature for themselves in their new second language.

Beginning a LEA activity with a piece of literature or a story will often result in a better structured dictation than the random list of sentences that sometimes results from LEA dictations stimulated by an illustration, a manipulative, or other prompts. Heller (1988) describes a process for eliciting dictations that incorporates aspects of story grammar and supports the composing process. She recommends adding several components to traditional LEA procedures, including the activation of background knowledge, the setting of a purpose and identification of a target audience for the dictation, the discussion of a model LEA dictation, the modeling of metacognitive strategies by teachers who describe their thoughts about creating an interesting story, and asking the students to make notes about the story they will dictate. They can then discuss, edit, and rewrite the dictated story in much the same way that the writing process would be applied in independent writing.

Shared Reading

Another valuable form of written text for English learners early in the reading process is the big book, particularly those big books with predictable or repetitive language patterns. Teachers read to students, who then read with them and finally back to them, although this *reading* may consist of telling the story while looking at the illustrations (Trachtenburg & Ferruggia, 1989). Using big books provides an opportunity for the teacher to model so that students can clearly see what they will later do in their own independent reading. In addition, students begin to notice correspondences between letters in familiar texts and the sounds they represent (Holdaway, 1979).

According to Lynch (1986), the shared reading process begins with consideration of the book language that has probably already been acquired by students whose parents or siblings read to them. For those who lack this experience, shared reading takes on increasing importance. English learners will tend more than other students to come from homes where printed material is scarce or where parents' own literacy skills may be limited. We cannot make assumptions about the conceptual knowledge about print that they bring to the classroom (Crawford, 1993).

By looking at the cover and at illustrations inside a book together, students begin to understand that they can make predictions based on what they already know, their background knowledge, and what they think the author wants to say to them. As the teacher begins to read the story to them, they will note and discuss connections between their predictions and the story line.

Many teachers are concerned about how students can begin to read a big book or a predictable book before they have learned to read, that is, to decode or call the words. Smith (1989) describes the process as one of demonstration in which the teacher or parent reads the big book to the student, who in turn *reads* it back to the teacher or parent. As students gain confidence through this early successful experience with reading and through a process of approximation, they begin to read with increasing accuracy and faithfulness to the actual text. When students read to the teacher as a group, a process that Peetoom (1986) calls echoic reading, there is even a greater sense of success because individual errors are not noted. Students can either correct themselves or go right on, with a correspondingly low level of anxiety about reading. This process is very much parallel with the need for a low level of anxiety in the acquisition of a second language and with the role of correction in that process.

Students soon begin to identify which parts of the text tell about corresponding parts of the story, and they begin to recognize certain words of interest to them. In terms of the frequency of their appearance in primary texts or in the number of syllables they contain, these words are not necessarily easy words from an adult's point of view. They are instead easy from a student's point of view in terms of interest and utility. Such easy words as *elephant* and *yellow* are more likely to be readily remembered and identified on second or third reading than more difficult words, such as *come* and *me*.

As Lynch (1986) points out, repetition of familiar stories leads to increased success, not to boredom on the part of the students. Their abilities to predict will grow, and they will increase the kind and variety of cues they use to predict, moving from illustrations and background knowledge of a story to familiar words and other visual cues. The later use of graphophonic cues, the phonics and structural analysis skills of so much concern to some educational decision makers, emerges then as a result of this process, not as its cause (Smith, 1988).

Strategies to Promote Reading Comprehension

In recent years, we have moved away from the controlled environment of the traditional basal reader into authentic children's literature, including fiction and non-fiction trade books. According to Crawford (1993), students are exposed to oral and written ideas that demand higher levels of background knowledge, vocabulary, and language proficiency. In their work with English learners, teachers face great challenges in providing for the equitable access of all students to quality literature while helping them make progress in reading and writing.

We have tended to place these at-risk students in perpetual compensatory or remedial programs where we expect them to learn to read and write by acquiring isolated skills through interaction with incomplete fragments of language. These students rarely move successfully into the mainstream curriculum, more frequently leaving these programs when they leave school, all too often as dropouts.

Whether or not English learners read literature from the primary or from the second language, we can organize a set of strategies to support their reading comprehension into three categories: prereading strategies, guided reading strategies, and postreading strategies. The contrast among these recommended strategies and those ordinarily used for English learners is significant. The recommended strategies resemble most closely the enrichment or additional activities that teachers of English learners never have time for because they are busy installing the isolated skills that the students seem to lack. We need to develop those skills directly and, within the context of language, in an authentic mode.

The recommended strategies are those that will provide the underlying support or scaffolding needed for reading comprehension. It is the isolated skills that teachers should set aside. We should view skill development as an outcome of learning to read, not as its cause (Samuels, 1971; Smith, 1985). Only on those rare occasions when a student's needs suggest that a directed skill lesson is needed should teachers seek out an appropriate one in the teachers' editions and workbooks of traditional reading and language arts programs.

Prereading Strategies

Background knowledge. There is increasing recognition of the importance of bringing background knowledge to bear on making sense of new information (Smith, 1988). The activation of this background knowledge, and often its development, constitutes a vitally important prereading activity. The background knowledge that we have acquired about the world forms the structure through which we assess new information and incorporate it. We use this knowledge to make and verify predictions about the new information to which we are exposed. According to Krashen (1991), background knowledge also makes second language input more comprehensible and therefore facilitates second language acquisition.

All students have acquired background knowledge, but there is often a discontinuity between the background knowledge a student has and the assumptions that teachers, authors, and textbook publishers make about that knowledge. This discontinuity must be assumed to be deeper when the student comes from a language or culture different from that of the student for whom the materials were designed or intended. A story about a birthday leads most American children to activate background knowledge about a party, a cake with candles, and gifts. The same story might lead a Mexican child to think about a piñata, yet children from Senegal and Morocco don't think about birthdays at all because they are not celebrated in their cultures. If children who lack a schema for a birthday cake are to read a literature selection in which the American celebration plays a significant role, then background knowledge must be activated or developed as a prereading activity.

Group discussion. The activation or development of background knowledge in students without previous exposure can often be accomplished through a sharing of the group's knowledge. Although no individual student may know a great deal about a topic, many children in a group will have some knowledge (María, 1989). A skillful teacher can lead a group discussion to elicit the information to be shared.

Semantic mapping. A useful strategy for providing structure to the development of background knowledge is semantic mapping (Heimlich and Pittelman, 1986). Knowledge is activated from long-term memory, shared with other students, and discussed in terms of needed vocabulary. It is then recorded in a graphic format that promotes organizing schemata so that relationships become more clear. The resulting semantic map may also serve as an advance organizer that will promote reading comprehension when the students later read the selection.

A teacher might write a word on a chart, chalkboard, or transparency and ask students to tell what they know about that concept. Although most students won't know much about the concept, many will know something. The process of discussing and systematically recording their background knowledge on a semantic map permits them to share what they know while the teacher organizes it into logical categories. Semantic maps are widely used to develop vocabulary in the same way.

According to Crawford (1993), semantic mapping is not a strategy to use with English learners every day. The nature of the literature selection, the desirability of formally structuring the background knowledge into a semantic map, and the existing background knowledge of the students should all be factors in deciding when and if the gains from devoting a considerable amount of instructional time to the activity are warranted.

Ordinarily, a semantic map for activating background knowledge or vocabulary is developed and completed during one or two related lessons and is not referred to subsequently. Teachers often find, however, that they must deal with such concepts as *feelings* on repeated occasions. It can be useful to return to a semantic map on such a topic, to add to it, and to consider new additions in contrast with earlier ones. We can identify this elaborated strategy as the cumulative semantic map.

In Figure 1, for example, a teacher might introduce the new word *furious* from a piece of literature and ask students where it should be

Figure 1

CUMULATIVE SEMANTIC MAP OF FEELINGS

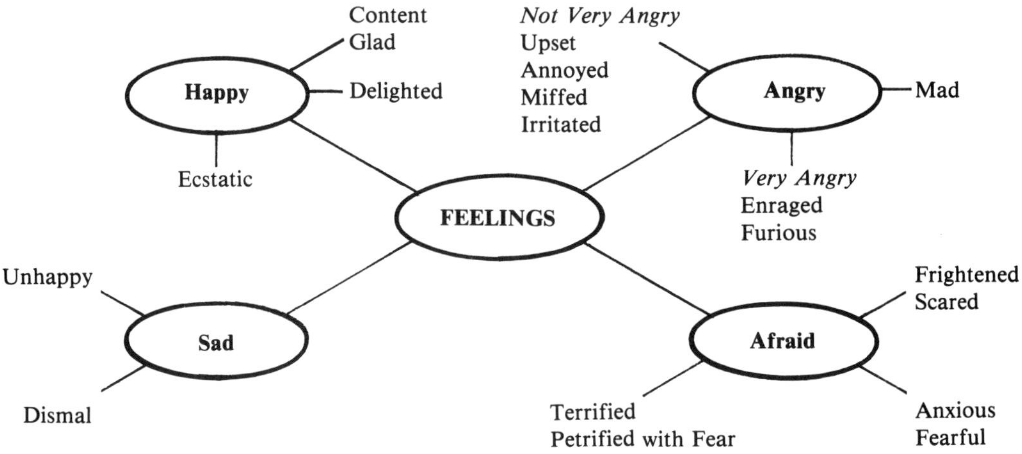

added to an existing cumulative semantic map for words about feelings. At that point, the students can discuss how angry *furious* is as compared with *miffed, enraged,* and *upset,* which were added to the semantic map on earlier occasions. When written on removable self-stick notes, the various words can be arranged and rearranged in ascending order of increasing anger as students negotiate their meanings with one another.

In a later writing assignment, students can again refer to the cumulative semantic map when they want to select just the right word to convey the degree of anger they have in mind. Discussing the choice of word with the teacher or other students will be particularly helpful. When students are ready to add yet another synonym for *angry* a week or a month later, they will have the opportunity to review other words or expressions for the same feeling, but within a context of known or somewhat familiar vocabulary. We can view a well-developed cumulative semantic map as a graphic thesaurus. Other suitable topics for cumulative semantic maps might include *seeing (stare, peek, glare,* etc.), *motion (crawl, creep, dawdle, dash, poke along, lope,* etc.), and *touching (poke, tap, jab, stroke,* etc.).

Advance organizer. The advance organizer is another useful tool for activating background knowledge. It is perhaps most common to find advance organizers provided in content area textbooks, but they can also be a useful addition to literature readings, whether prepared by authors and publishers or by teachers. Some stories or literature selections provide a brief summary, often on a book jacket or on the back cover of a softcover book. Occasionally, this includes a question or comment designed to entice the reader into reading the selection. Teachers can use these to interest their students in stories, to activate background knowledge, and to help them make predictions about the story. Even an adult will rarely purchase a paperback novel without examining the advance organizer or publisher's teaser on the back cover, not to mention the illustration on the front cover.

Vocabulary development. When English learners read in their second language, the lack of vocabulary knowledge is often an obstacle to comprehension. This can be a problem in the primary language as well, because they may have insufficient academically related background knowledge and the primary language vocabulary development that would accompany it. We can consider vocabulary as an aspect of background knowledge, but we will treat it separately here in order to examine several concepts that relate more specifically to vocabulary.

Let us consider two different aspects of the question of vocabulary development for English learners. One is the richness of language that surrounds them. It is well recognized that students become familiar with the meanings of words when those meanings are highly contextualized, not when they are studied in isolation as new vocabulary words. It follows, then, that a richer language environment should result in increased exposure to contextualized vocabulary and, therefore, to understanding of their meanings.

We often postpone or even eliminate instruction for English learners, however, in the very areas of the curriculum where new vocabulary words will be offered in the most highly contextualized ways—in science, social studies, art, music, health, and other areas of the curriculum. According to Crawford (1993), we must ensure that these areas of the curriculum are provided for English learners and that they are presented so that contextualized exposure to a rich vocabulary is promoted. Instruction in these areas should include the use of cooperative learning, problem solving, and other vocabulary-rich strategies.

In a study by Nagy, Anderson, and Herman (1987), they found that, although the proportion of words learned was low, a major factor in vocabulary development by third, fifth, and seventh grade students was the sheer volume of reading that students did and the amount of vocabulary to which they were exposed. Stanovich (1986) elaborated this idea further in his treatment of individualized differences and the *Matthew effect,* the idea that those who read more (the rich) read better (get richer). In a related vein, Smith (1986) observed that good readers read, and poor readers take tests and do drill sheets.

Another aspect of vocabulary is the issue of direct instruction. Although many vocabulary words will be acquired incidentally, some literature or content selections will contain a few vocabulary words that must be clearly grasped if the text is to be understood. There will be other words not known to the students that need not be addressed through direct instruction because they are not critical to understanding the selection or because they can be quickly analyzed through the context in which they appear.

Many of the strategies recommended for the activation or development of background knowledge constitute direct approaches to vocabulary instruction. Semantic mapping is one of these strategies, but its application should be limited to those key and conceptually difficult vocabulary terms that are more in the realm of background knowledge. Otherwise, there will be little time left for reading after prereading activities are completed.

Some words may be analyzed through brief discussion following read-aloud activities by the teacher. They will have been presented in context, and someone in the group will likely have some knowledge of most vocabulary words. Others may be analyzed by reviewing the illustrations in a story or an appropriate illustration, manipulative, or visual aid provided by the teacher. Because illustrations provide important visual information, paging through a selection and discussing them provides an opportunity for presenting new vocabulary and for making predictions about the text. A partial or complete read-aloud of a literature selection as a prereading activity is equally productive.

Guided Reading Strategies. According to Smith (1985), we learn to read by reading. This fundamental and obvious idea should underlie our thinking as we consider how English learners' time is spent during reading instruction. Rather than having students study about reading by mastering skills, we must instead maximize the amount of reading they do. Some obvious counterproductive strategies are pencil-and-paper exercises and the still-common round-robin oral reading, which usually results in one student laboriously reading aloud a passage never before read, even silently, while the rest of the students in the group pretend to listen or read along.

From our own experiences with second language acquisition, we should also recall the importance of reading for comprehension, as opposed to word calling. Most of us had the experience of being asked to read aloud in a high school or university foreign language class. We read with great intensity, attempting to correctly soften the intervocali *d* in Spanish or accurately pronounce the difficult initial *r* of French. When we finished, the teacher asked us to tell about the content of what we read in our own words. Of course, we had little idea, because we had been focusing on pronunciation. We must remember that communication and comprehension are the focus of reading and writing, just as they are in a communicative approach to oral language development. There are many guided reading strategies that will help us ensure that students focus on comprehension rather than on correct pronunciation.

When students begin to read themselves, they may benefit from having their teacher read to them from the selection first. Occasionally, the teacher may find that presenting the entire selection as a read-aloud is helpful. When a parallel version of a text is available in the students' primary language, a teacher or aide may read it aloud before the students read later in English. Students in school are not bored or disturbed by several exposures to the same literature selection, any more than a three-year-old objects to hearing the same story before bed every night. The familiarity of a story that is an old friend becomes a real comfort. Familiarity with the background knowledge and structure of a story permits a student to read with good comprehension and with fewer time-consuming visual cues, especially for students' early literacy experiences in English. The teacher's read-aloud also provides the teacher with the opportunity to model predicting, thinking about context, and other strategies by talking through some of the metacognitive processes used during the teacher's oral reading.

With beginning readers, their first reading may take the form of group echoic reading with a teacher or lead reader, usually following a read-aloud by the teacher (Peetoom, 1986). As the lead reader reads very expressively, the time gap between that person and the group of students will diminish. When an individual or a part of the group stumbles, the lead reader should take charge and read until the group is together again. This activity lowers anxiety about oral reading because students' approximations, a very natural aspect of early reading, are not noticeable and comprehension is maintained. Most important, everyone is reading.

Peetoom (1986) also describes timed and repeated readings in which students read aloud passages of about 150 words from carefully selected literature. With practice, students read them more accurately and in less time. Dowhower (1987) has reported that such repeated and rehearsed readings can result in gains in the reading rate, accuracy, and comprehension of second grade students, with some evidence of transfer to unpracticed passages as well. As part of Dowhower's study, students read along with an audiotape until they read easily, or they practiced reading a passage until they could read at a pre-established set rate. This may be an especially useful independent activity for student dyads working together. Again, they will be reading instead of completing written drill and practice activities on skill development. Samuels (1979) associated repeated readings with the development of automaticity, the stage at which students read and recognized words unconsciously, permitting their full attention to focus instead on meaning. Automaticity in reading seems to parallel the process of oral production without employing the monitor in language acquisition. It also has much in common with Terrell's (1986) concept of *binding,* where a linguistic form evokes meaning without any delay.

Middle and upper grade elementary students and secondary students should read silently on an extensive basis. It is through more rapid silent reading that students can read for the most practice and be exposed to the most background knowledge and contextualized vocabulary. It is more difficult for teachers to provide extra support to English learners, however, because their need for it may be less obvious during the largely independent activity of silent reading.

One strategy for providing this support during the silent reading of literature selections is to direct or structure students' reading with questions. Some whole language advocates would decry this as an annoying and unnecessary strategy that is destined to destroy any enjoyment of the selection by the student. That may indeed be the case for some students. The reality is, however, that many English learners struggle to read, and their many failure experiences can result in a lack of motivation and interest in reading. Their teachers often have difficulty reading themselves during silent sustained reading (SSR) because of their need to supervise closely the reading of their sometimes reluctant students.

According to Crawford (1993), guiding students' reading with questions provides valuable support in maintaining comprehension. It brings key story concepts to their attention as they read, and, perhaps more important, it provides moral support, interest, and motivation from someone who cares about them. Students who cannot, or will not, read a lengthy selection alone may do so a page or two at a time within the security of a supportive teacher-directed group. Their reading can be structured by questions that elicit predictions, with timely resolution of those predictions through discussion and any needed mediation.

Beck and McKeown (1981) reported that having students develop a story map of the major events or ideas of a selection was even more effective if questions were developed to guide them toward identifying unifying events and ideas. Peetoom (1986) suggests chunking stories by having students read them in manageable and comprehensible sections. Questions can be used very effectively and naturally to accomplish this chunking.

Although there is considerable debate about the value of teaching reading comprehension skills through direct instruction, there are sufficient other reasons to guide silent reading with questions. A teacher will take no longer to formulate and ask a higher-order comprehension question than a low-level recall question before asking students to read to find the answer. It is often said that teachers have low expectations for English learners. Guided silent reading provides an opportunity for students to make inferences and predictions, identify cause and effect relationships, and apply other higher-order critical thinking skills when their comprehension is supported (Crawford, 1993).

Postreading Strategies. After students read, there are other opportunities to provide scaffolding. We have already considered the retelling
of stories told or read to students as a means of producing text through
LEA for them to read themselves. Retelling is also an excellent
postreading activity. An oral retelling provides students with the opportunity to negotiate with one another about the meaning of the selection.
It is often through this process that students can incorporate new information gained through reading into existing background knowledge.
Koskinen *et al.* (1988) found that the verbal rehearsal that occurs in the
retelling process also serves to improve the reading comprehension of less
proficient readers. Some students may elect to retell in their primary
language what they read or heard in their second language. Brown and
Cambourne (1990) observe that retelling also promotes multiple readings
of text as a part of the negotiation process.

Retelling also provides a means for integrating writing into the
program. Students can prepare a written retelling either through a
cooperative learning process or through individual or paired writing
(Strickland and Feeley, 1985). As a result of their earlier discussion, of
the knowledge they gained through reading and of such prereading activities as semantic mapping and the examination of story grammar,
students are better prepared to write a well-structured retelling. Like the
modeling that teachers provide during reading, teachers should also
model retelling with an actual example.

The most obvious postreading activity should not be overlooked—
more reading. If we are to be successful in providing quality literature
that students will choose to read and in supporting their comprehension,
then we should expect gains in all areas of the English language arts.
Krashen (1985, 1993) has concluded that reading is more powerful than
direct instruction in developing vocabulary, grammar, spelling, and
reading comprehension. He advocates extensive free voluntary reading
with messages that are understood in low-anxiety situations. Finally, he
feels that good writing is promoted more by extensive reading than by
writing.

The Writing Process

A major principle of whole language is the interdependence of listening, speaking, reading, and writing. Hudelson (1984) observed that
second language learners address the four language processes as a totali-
ty, not as separate entities. According to Fitzgerald (1993), writing

begins when children can draw, and there is no need to wait for reading. We can certainly extend these ideas to English learners, who should be encouraged to write in English early, especially if they have writing skills in their native language. The errors they make should be viewed in the same way that we view errors in oral production, as part of the natural process of acquisition.

In keeping with the constructivist orientation of this chapter, Ferreiro (1991) described the process of writing as one of making meaning through construction and reconstruction. Samway (1993) reinforced this idea in her study of how a sample of non-native-English-speaking elementary students in grades two through six evaluated their own writing and that of others. Although these high-risk students were experiencing difficulties in school, they tended to focus on meaning in their evaluative comments. Most of their comments were categorized as *crafting,* how well a story had been developed, or *understanding,* making sense of the text.

For English learners, we have already seen that writing flows out of a variety of language acquisition activities, including the key-vocabulary and language experience approaches to reading and the postreading strategy of written retellings. The structuring of their writing or their selection of vocabulary may be supported through the use of semantic maps and cumulative semantic maps.

Writing Workshop. Samway (1992) describes the writing workshop as an important strategy for providing a writing program for ESL learners. She describes writing as both a solitary and a social act in which students write for real audiences in a collaborative mode. She advocates the establishment of classroom work stations for editing, illustrating, and publishing. Among the activities one might see during that part of the day set aside for writing workshop are: whole class meetings for mini-lessons; children writing, with some beginning a first draft, while others are revising or editing; conferences among students or with the teacher; children searching for writing topics; research, such as reading, watching a film, or interviewing another student; illustrating; word-processing on a computer; publishing final, clean copies; making book covers; and sharing their writing, often from a place of honor called the author's chair.

In a typical writing workshop cycle (Samway, 1992), students begin on the first day with a mini-lesson to generate topics. Supporting prewriting activities might include listening to literature, brainstorming, clustering and mapping activities, storytelling, interviewing and opinion surveys, and field trips. After modeling by the teacher, individual students list topics, select one of interest, and then write for ten to twenty minutes. On the second day, students read their pieces aloud to each other in dyads, describing their purpose, what they liked best about it, and any problems they had. They confer with each other, maintaining a mutually supportive role. At the end of the session, some of the students share their progress with the entire class.

On the third day, students consider the comments of their dyad partner and revise accordingly. On the fourth day, the teacher might model editing with a piece of personal writing in a mini-lesson. Students then edit their own work for clarity, mechanics, word use, and spelling. At the end of the session, some students share their progress with the class. On the fifth day, students publish their completed work. As a result of the five-day cycle, students have written for a real audience, conferred about their writing, and published their work.

In a six-month observational study of six upper elementary grade Southeast Asian students, Urzúa (1987) found that feedback among children in the writing process caused them to develop a sense of audience. Their peers asked them questions and made suggestions about their writing. The students also developed a sense of voice, preferring to select their own writing topics. Finally, she observed that they developed a sense of power in language as they learned to add to their writing, to discuss vocabulary with one another, and to take risks as they manipulated language.

Teachers should employ a variety of other writing activities to maintain interest in the process. Bromley (1989) suggests that at-risk students keep a buddy journal, a diary in which two students write back and forth to each other. Similarly, Arthur (1991) recommends the use of dialogue journals to promote authentic communication for ESL learners at the middle school level.

Invented Spelling. Consistent with the communicative approach principle of minimizing error correction and with the developmental nature of second language acquisition and literacy, teachers should accept the invented spellings of their students as a very natural aspect of their growth in writing. Gentry (1981, 1982) describes five developmental stages of spelling. In the precommunicative stage, students demonstrate some knowledge of letter forms, but no knowledge of letter-sound correspondences. Teachers will be unable to decipher their efforts, but children can usually "read" them to the teacher, at least at the time they are written.

In the semiphonetic stage, students begin to approximate an alphabetic orthography and to conceptualize the alphabetic principle. They begin to demonstrate the relationship between sound and letter, and they sometimes use letter names as words. They begin to understand the left-to-right convention of English, and they may begin to segment words. Consonants tend to predominate over vowels.

In the phonetic stage, students begin to map letter-sound correspondences in reference to sounds, but not to conventions. They generally segment words appropriately. At this point, teachers can decipher their writing with only occasional difficulty. During the transitional stage, students follow basic spelling conventions, with vowels in most syllables. They use morphological features and a larger number of learned (and correctly spelled) words.

In the correct stage, students have learned most basic rules of the English orthographic system. They are aware of such word structures as prefixes, suffixes, contractions, compound words, and homonyms, and they continue to learn some less common spelling patterns and rules. It is at this stage that they begin to recognize when a word *looks* correct, a phenomenon that corresponds to the natural approach characteristic in which English learners begin to recognize when something *sounds* right or *feels* right. They are able to spell a large number of words automatically.

Nathenson-Mejia (1989) found that, in their English writing, Spanish-speaking students in the beginning stages of English spelling made extensive use of their Spanish pronunciation in their invented spellings in English. Edelsky (1982) made the same observation in a more generic sense. She took the positive point of view that students are applying some primary language writing skills to writing in the second language, rather than the negative point of view that it reflects interference from the first language on the second.

The Role of Evaluation in the Communicative Program

Current views of the scope of second language acquisition include not only listening and oral communicative competency, but they now also extend into specially designed academic instruction in English through content/language integration in the core curriculum and into literacy in English. Assessment must be considered in a similarly broad scope. The issue of assessment is further complicated by conflicts between the need for data to meet legal and fiscal requirements and those needed to make instructional decisions.

An Assessment Model

The Council of Chief State School Officers (1992) has proposed an assessment model for limited English proficient students that addresses the following purposes for evaluation: (1) screening for language background other than English; (2) classification into a category restricting participation in English-only classrooms; (3) placement into appropriate language programs; (4) monitoring student progress; and (5) monitoring student academic success and program effectiveness. They recommended that initial screening consist of a home language survey conducted in the language of the home within ten days of school registration. They further recommended that the data gathered incorporate place of birth, first language acquired, and educational background, including location of schools previously attended, language of instruction, and level completed.

In the area of classification, they cited the most commonly used instruments as the Language Assessment Scales (LAS), the IDEA Proficiency Test, the Bilingual Syntax Measure, and the Basic Inventory of Natural Language (BINL). They raised many concerns about the use of a single instrument or tool for classification.

In the area of placement, they suggested that states should work together to develop assessment processes, implying accordingly that none of those currently available were satisfactory. Their expressed concerns about the use of a single assessment tool for classification purposes should be even greater for placement of children in educational programs. They recommended that educators should develop means of assessing content knowledge, whether in English or the native language, and that they use achievement test scores within a context of their relationship to other sources of data. They also recommended that tests of both achievement and language proficiency be based on sound psychometric practice and empirical research.

Within the area of monitoring, the Council of Chief State School Officers considered the issue of reclassification, the decision about when English learners become eligible to participate in the mainstream English curriculum. They recommended that rather than indicating that the student *leave* the language-assistance program, reclassification should instead indicate a change in the *nature* of language-assistance services provided. They suggested the use of measures of English and non-English language proficiency and of achievement to ensure that students have skills comparable to native English speakers in knowledge of subject matter and of English. Finally, they recommended that programs following reclassification should be seamless, not dichotomous, providing needed support on a continuing basis.

In summary, the dilemma for educators is the discrepancy between the need for one kind of assessment to meet legitimate legalistic and fiscal needs and for another kind of assessment to meet instructional needs. The focus of this treatment of assessment will be on instructionally related assessment.

Implications for Assessment in Communicative Approaches

If a second language curriculum were designed to teach grammar, then the assessment tool to evaluate outcomes would logically consist of discrete point measures of the mastery of grammatical elements. Within the topical curriculum advocated by most proponents of communicative approaches, and in keeping with their advocacy of language being functional and authentic, we would expect wide variation in the acquisition of competence with respect to these topics and in related measures of assessment.

According to Terrell (1977), evaluation in the communicative second language acquisition program must focus on oral competence. He states that instruction should focus first on the transmittal of the message, second on the use of appropriate vocabulary, third on form or correctness, and last on pronunciation. Accordingly, we would expect evaluation to be a very dynamic and individualized process, depending on the topics of interest to individual students and on their stages of development in communicative competence.

Krashen and Terrell (1983) focus on global communicative competence in contrast to discrete point linguistic competence. In the area of listening comprehension, they suggest such strategies as answering questions after listening to a recorded dialogue, a narrated story, a radio or TV program, a song, or a film. They suggest that teachers can evaluate speaking proficiency by holistically scoring performance in conversational interchanges, recounting events, giving directions, reports in class, and, at the higher levels, in debate and argumentation.

McGroarty (1984) concluded that communicative competence may refer to many different aspects of language for students with different needs and reasons for enrollment in programs. She found that English learners in elementary and secondary schools need a diverse set of language skills, including literacy, in order to make normal school progress. One of the greatest needs she saw was for students to master and use context-reduced language.

Saville-Troike (1991) recognized the need for language assessment that provided information about the English learner's readiness for success in a regular English-medium classroom. She recommended using standardized reading tests already in use with English learners to assess academic language proficiency. Because of its strong generic relationship to academic progress, she emphasized the use of the vocabulary subtest score for children beyond the third grade.

Crawford (1982) suggested that the informal reading inventory (IRI) shows promise as a measure of English proficiency when used as a test of listening comprehension or reading capacity. The teacher can use the IRI to determine readiness for reading instruction in given materials by reading a selected passage aloud to the student. Crawford reported that students who respond correctly to 75% of comprehension-level questions about the material usually have sufficient English language proficiency to read it with support from the teacher. According to Antonacci (1993), story retelling is an important tool for assessing students' formation of story concept in the reading process.

Pierce and O'Malley (1992) proposed a series of what they characterize as alternative assessments. They defined alternative assessment as any method of determining what a student knows or can do, as criterion-referenced, as authentic in reflecting typical classroom and real-life tasks, as integrative of language skills, and as including the incorporation of teacher observation, performance assessment, and student self-assessment. They referred to performance assessment as an exercise in which students demonstrate specific skills and competencies in relation to a continuum, as judged by a professional rater. Finally, they recommended the use of portfolios as a record of student work over time and in various modes to show depth, breadth, and development, with possibilities for adding student reflection and self-monitoring.

Pierce and O'Malley's concept of assessment might be difficult to accommodate to the need for the formal classification and reclassification of students. It is, however, ideal for monitoring student placement and progress in programs. It is also appropriate for providing data for informed instructional decisions, particularly within the philosophies underlying communicative approaches to second language acquisition, to content/language integration in specially designed academic instruction in English in the core curriculum, and to related whole language approaches to literacy.

Portfolio Assessment

The assessment strategy that is perhaps most consistent with the constructivist paradigm underlying both communicative approaches to second language acquisition and the whole language approach to literacy is the portfolio. It is authentic and holistic, and it represents a developmental view of students' progress. Pierce and O'Malley (1992) suggest that portfolio assessment be used for making instructional decisions about moving students into mainstream programs. The materials included in the portfolio should therefore reflect the criteria used for making such decisions. They indicate that portfolio assessment can also be used for diagnosis and placement, monitoring student progress, feedback on the effectiveness of instruction, communication with other teachers, feedback to students, and communication with parents.

The contents of the portfolio may vary widely, depending on its purpose. Teachers should consider including a log of personal reading, perhaps in the form of a response journal. A personal writing log, accompanied by periodic samples of students' published writing, is a useful component. Videotapes or audiotapes of students' reading, storytelling, and other language development activities provide a valuable record of students' progress in English as well as in the primary language.

Summary and Conclusions

Communicative approaches to second language acquisiton reflect Vygotsky's zone of proximal development, Bruner's concept of scaffolding, and Holdaway's concept of approximation in that teachers or others provide just enough support to maintain comprehension while students acquire language subconsciously. The natural approach is the most widely applied communicative approach. It is consistent with Krashen's hypothesis in that it involves providing comprehensible and meaningful input from a topical curriculum with a low anxiety level. Early production, correction, and the use of grammatical sequences are minimized. This is the language learning environment of the infant, who is almost always successful in effortlessly learning the mother tongue.

When English learners have intermediate English proficiency, they should have access to the full core curriculum through the careful application of communicative approach strategies in specially designed academic instruction in English. The focus of this instruction should be on maintaining comprehension through the pacing of teacher input and through the extensive use of nonverbal language and of props and illustrations.

At an appropriate time, English learners should receive instruction in English reading and writing through strategies that ensure continued comprehension and communication. Whole language strategies are very consistent with communicative approaches to second language acquisition. They focus on constructing meaning, they proceed from whole to part, they treat authentic, relevant, and functional language, and they center on the learner.

In the early stages of literacy, teachers will find that the key-vocabulary and language experience approaches can provide English learners with access to print that is consistent with their stage of production. When they are able to begin reading simple text, we should provide scaffolding through prereading activities that develop background knowledge and vocabulary. We should support reading comprehension through guided silent reading and postreading activities, such as oral and written retelling. Extensive silent sustained reading is potentially the most valuable activity for continued growth in English language development in the areas of vocabulary, reading comprehension, grammar, spelling, and writing.

Student progress in English language acquisition, in the core academic curriculum, and in literacy is enhanced for students who have developed a high level of proficiency in the primary language, including listening, oral language, reading, and writing skills at cognitive/academic levels. In addition, background knowledge they develop from the core curriculum in the primary language provides a strong base for learning in English.

REFERENCES

Altwerger, B., Edelsky, C., & Flores, B. M. (1987). Whole language: What's new? *The Reading Teacher, 41,* 144-154.

Antonacci, P. A. (1993). Natural assessment in whole language classrooms. In A. Carrasquillo & C. Hedley (Eds.), *Whole language and the bilingual learners* (pp. 116-131). Norwood, NJ: Ablex.

Arthur, B. M. (1991). Working with new ESL students in a junior high school reading class. *The Journal of Reading, 34,* 628-631.

Asher, J. J. (1969). The total physical response approach to second language learning. *Modern Language Journal, 53,* 3-17.

Asher, J. J. (1979). Motivating children and adults to acquire a second language. *SPEAQ Journal, 3,* 87-99.

Asher, J. J. (1982). The total physical response approach. In R. W. Blair (Ed.), *Innovative approaches to language teaching* (pp. 54-66). Rowley, MA: Newbury House.

Bancroft, W. J. (1978). The Lozanov method and its American adaptations. *Modern Language Journal, 62,* 167-175.

Beck, I. L., & McKeown, M. G. (1981). Developing questions that promote comprehension: The story map. *Language Arts, 58,* 913-917.

Berman, P., Chambers, J., Gandara, P., McLaughlin, B., Minicucci, C., Nelson, B., Olsen, L., & Parrish, T. (1992). *Meeting the challenge of language diversity.* Berkeley, CA: BW Associates.

Bromley, K. D'Angelo (1989). Buddy journals make the reading-writing connection. *The Reading Teacher, 43,* 122-129.

Brown, H., & Cambourne, B. (1990). *Read and retell: A strategy for the whole-language/natural learning classroom.* Portsmouth, NH: Heinemann.

Bruner, J. (1978). The role of dialogue in language acquisition. In A. Sinclair, R. J. Jarvella, & W. M. Levelt (Eds.). *The child's conception of language* (pp. 241-256). New York: Springer-Verlag.

Cathcart-Strong, R. L. (1986). Input generation by young second language learners. *TESOL Quarterly, 20,* 515-530.

Chamot, A. U. (1981). Applications of second language acquisition research to the bilingual classroom. *Focus: National Clearinghouse for Bilingual Education,* pp. 1-8.

Chamot, A. U. (1983). Toward a functional ESL curriculum in the elementary school. *TESOL Quarterly, 17,* 459-471.

Chan, J., & Chips, B. (1989, April). Helping LEP students survive in the content-area classroom. *Thrust,* pp. 49-51.

Chastain, K. (1975). *Developing second-language skills: From theory to practice.* Chicago: Rand McNally College Publishing Company.

Collier, V. P. (1987). Age and rate of acquisition of second language for academic purposes. *TESOL Quarterly, 21,* 617-641.

Collier, V. P. (1989). How long? A synthesis of research on academic achievement in a second language. *TESOL Quarterly, 23,* 509-539.

Coote, P., & Stevens, R. (1990). *Whole language: A New Zealand approach.* Christchurch, NZ: Christchurch College of Education.

Council of Chief State School Officers (1992). *Recommendations for improving the assessment and monitoring of students with limited English proficiency.* Washington, DC: Author.

Crawford, A. N. (1982). From Spanish reading to English reading: The transition process. In M. P. Douglas (Ed.), *Claremont Reading Conference Yearbook* (pp. 159-165). Claremont, CA: Claremont Reading Conference.

Crawford, A. N. (1986). Communicative approaches to ESL: A bridge to reading comprehension. In M. P. Douglass (Ed.), *Claremont Reading Conference Yearbook* (pp. 292-305). Claremont, CA: Claremont Reading Conference.

Crawford, A. N. (1993). Literature, integrated language arts, and the language minority child: A focus on meaning. In A. Carrasquillo & C. Hedley (Eds.), *Whole language and the bilingual learner* (pp. 61-75). Norwood, NJ: Ablex.

Cummins, J. (1980). The cross-lingual dimensions of language proficiency: Implications for bilingual education and the optimal age issue. *TESOL Quarterly, 14,* 175-187.

Cummins, J. (1981). The role of primary language development in promoting educational success for language minority students. In California State Department of Education (Ed.), *Schooling and language minority students: A theoretical framework* (1st ed.) (pp. 3-49). Los Angeles: Evaluation, Dissemination and Assessment Center, California State University, Los Angeles.

Cummins, J. (1986). Empowering minority students: A framework for intervention. *Harvard Education Review, 56,* 18-36.

Cummins, J. (1989). *Empowering minority students.* Sacramento: California Association for Bilingual Education.

Dhority, L. (1991). *The ACT approach: The use of suggestion for integrative learning.* Philadelphia: Gordon and Breach Science Publishers.

Dixon, C. N., & Nessel, D. (1983). *Language experience approach to reading and writing: LEA for ESL.* Hayward, CA: Alemany Press.

Doughty, C., & Pica, T. (1986). "Information gap" tasks: Do they facilitate second language acquisition? *TESOL Quarterly, 20,* 305-325.

Dowhower, S. L. (1987). Effects of repeated reading on second-grade transitional readers' fluency and comprehension. *Reading Research Quarterly, 22,* 389-406.

Dulay, H. C., & Burt, M. K. (1974a). Errors and strategies in child second language acquisition. *TESOL Quarterly, 8,* 129-143.

Dulay, H. C., & Burt, M. K. (1974b). Natural sequences in child second language acquisition. *Language Learning, 24,* 37-53.

Edelsky, C. (1982). Writing in a bilingual program: The relation of L_1 and L_2 texts. *TESOL Quarterly, 16,* 211-228.

Ervin-Tripp, S. M. (1974). Is second language learning like the first? *TESOL Quarterly, 8,* 111-127.

Ferreiro, E. (1991). La construcción de la escritura en el niño. *Lectura y Vida, 12,* 5-14.

Finocchiaro, M. (1974). *English as a second language: From theory to practice.* New York: Regents.

Fitzgerald, J. (1993). Literacy and students who are learning English as a second language. *The Reading Teacher, 46,* 638-647.

Freeman, D., & Freeman, Y. (1988). Whole language content lessons. *Elementary ESOL Education News, 11,* 1-2.

Friedlander, M. (1991). *The newcomer program: Helping immigrant students succeed in U.S. schools.* Washington, DC: National Clearinghouse for Bilingual Education.

Galyean, B. (1977). A confluent design for language teaching. *TESOL Quarterly, 11,* 143-156.

Galyean, B. (1980). *My language is me: A confluent program in English for K-3 NES/LES students* (Publication No. 3725). Los Angeles: Los Angeles Unified School District, Instructional Planning Division.

Gardner, R., & Lambert, W. (1972). *Attitudes and motivation in second-language learning.* Rowley, MA: Newbury House.

Gentry, J. R. (1981). Learning to spell developmentally. *The Reading Teacher, 34,* 378-381.

Gentry, J. R. (1982). An analysis of developmental spelling in GNYS AT WRK. *The Reading Teacher, 36,* 192-200.

Goodman, K. (1986). *What's whole in whole language?* Portsmouth, NH: Heinemann.

Hamayan, E. V., & Perlman, R. (1991). *Helping language minority students after they exit from bilingual/ESL programs.* Washington, DC: National Clearinghouse for Bilingual Education.

Heald-Taylor, G. (1986). *Whole language strategies for ESL students.* San Diego: Dormac.

Heimlich, J. E., & Pittelman, S. D. (1986). *Semantic mapping: Classroom applications.* Newark, DE: International Reading Association.

Heller, M. F. (1988). Comprehending and composing through language experience. *The Reading Teacher, 42,* 130-135.

Holdaway, D. (1979). *The foundations of literacy.* Sydney: Ashton Scholastic.

Hudelson, S. (1984). Kan yu ret an rayt en Ingles: Children become literate in English as a second language. *TESOL Quarterly, 18,* 221-238.

Johnson, D. M. (1988). ESL children as teachers: A social view of second language use. *Language Arts, 65,* 154-163.

Koskinen, P. S., Gambrell, L. B., Kapinus, B. A., & Heathington, B. S. (1988). Retelling: A strategy for enhancing students' reading comprehension. *The Reading Teacher, 41,* 892-896.

Krashen, S. D. (1981). Bilingual education and second language acquisition theory. In California State Department of Education (Ed.), *Schooling and language minority students: A theoretical framework* (1st ed.) (pp. 51-79). Los Angeles: Evaluation, Dissemination and Assessment Center, California State University, Los Angeles.

Krashen, S. D. (1982a). *Principles and practice in second language acquisition.* New York: Pergamon Press.

Krashen, S. D. (1982b). Theory versus practice in language training. In R. W. Blair (Ed.)., *Innovative approaches to language teaching* (pp. 15-30). Rowley, MA: Newbury House.

Krashen, S. D. (1985). *Inquiries and insight: Second language teaching, immersion & bilingual education, literacy.* Hayward, CA: Alemany Press.

Krashen, S. D. (1991). *Bilingual education: A focus on current research.* Washington, DC: National Clearinghouse for Bilingual Education.

Krashen, S. (1993). *The power of reading.* Englewood, CO: Libraries Unlimited Inc.

Krashen, S., & Biber, D. (1988). *On course: Bilingual education's success in California.* Sacramento, CA: California Association for Bilingual Education.

Krashen, S. D., & Terrell, T. D. (1983). *The natural approach: Language acquisition in the classroom.* New York: Pergamon/Alemany.

Krashen, S. D., Long, M. A., & Scarcella, R. C. (1979). Age, rate and eventual attainment in second language acquisition. *TESOL Quarterly, 13,* 573-582.

La Forge, P. G. (1971). Community language learning: A pilot study. *Language Learning, 21,* 45-61.

Lenneberg, E. (1967). *Biological foundations of language.* New York: Wiley.

Los Angeles Unified School District (1985). *Strategies for sheltered English instruction.* Los Angeles: Author.

Lynch, P. (1986). *Using big books and predictable books.* New York: Scholastic.

María, K. (1989). Developing disadvantaged children's background knowledge interactively. *The Reading Teacher, 42,* 296-300.

McGroarty, M. (1984). Some meanings of communicative competence for second language students. *TESOL Quarterly, 18,* 257-272.

Moustafa, M., & Penrose, J. (1985). Comprehensible input PLUS the language experience approach: Reading instruction for limited English speaking students. *The Reading Teacher, 38,* 640-647.

Mystery powders (1974). New York: McGraw-Hill.

Nagy, W., Anderson, R. C., & Herman, P. (1987). Learning word meanings from context during normal reading. *American Educational Research Journal, 24,* 237-270.

Nathenson-Mejia, S. (1989). Writing in a second language: Negotiating meaning through invented spelling. *Language Arts, 66,* 516-526.

Nessel, D. D., & Jones, M. B. (1981). *The language-experience approach to reading.* New York: Teachers College, Columbia University.

Oller, J., Jr. (1981). Research on the measurements of affective variables: Some remaining questions. In R. Anderson (Ed.), *New dimensions in second language acquisition research* (pp. 14-27). Rowley, MA: Newbury House.

Oller, J., Jr., Hudson, A., & Liu, P. (1977). Attitudes and attained proficiency in ESL: A sociolinguistic study of native speakers of Chinese in the United States. *Language Learning, 27,* 1-27.

Pearson, P. D. (1985). Changing the face of reading comprehension instruction. *The Reading Teacher, 38,* 724-738.

Peck, J. (1989). Using storytelling to promote language and literacy development. *The Reading Teacher, 43,* 138-141.

Peetoom, A. (1986). *Shared reading: Safe risks with whole books.* Richmond Hill, Ontario, Canada: Scholastic.

Pierce, L. V., & O'Malley, J. M. (1992). *Performance and portfolio assessment for language minority students.* Washington, DC: National Clearinghouse for Bilingual Education.

Richard-Amato, P. A., & Snow, M. A. (1992). Strategies for content-area teachers. In P. A. Richard-Amato & M. A. Snow (Eds.), *The multicultural classroom: Readings for content-area teachers* (pp. 145-163). White Plains, NY: Longman.

Rigg, P. (1991). Whole language in TESOL. *TESOL Quarterly, 25,* 521-542.

Rutherford, W., & Sharwood-Smith, M. (1985). Consciousness raising and universal grammar. *Applied Linguistics, 6,* 274-282.

Samuels, S. J. (1971). Letter-name versus letter-sound knowledge in learning to read. *The Reading Teacher, 24,* 604-608.

Samuels, S. J. (1979). The method of repeated readings. *The Reading Teacher, 32,* 403-408.

Samway, K. D. (1992). *Writers' workshop and children acquiring English as a non-native language.* Washington, DC: National Clearinghouse for Bilingual Education.

Samway, K. D. (1993). "This is hard, isn't it?": Children evaluating writing. *TESOL Quarterly, 27,* 233-257.

Saville-Troike, M. (1976). *Foundations for teaching ESL.* Englewood Cliffs, NJ: Prentice-Hall.

Saville-Troike, M. (1991). *Teaching and testing for academic achievement: The role of language development.* Washington, DC: National Clearinghouse for Bilingual Education.

Schaefer, D. A. (1980). My experiences with the Lozanov method. *Foreign Language Annals, 15,* 273-278.

Schifini, A. (1985). *Sheltered English: Content area instruction for limited English proficient students.* Los Angeles: Los Angeles County Office of Education.

Selinker, L., Swain, M., & Dumas, G. (1975). The interlanguage hypothesis extended to children. *Language Learning, 25,* 139-152.

Short, D. J. (1991). *Integrating language and content instruction: Strategies and techniques.* Washington, DC: National Clearinghouse for Bilingual Education.

Smith, F. (1985). *Reading without nonsense.* New York: Teachers College Press.

Smith, F. (1986). Keynote address, California Reading Association, Fresno, California.

Smith, F. (1988). *Understanding reading.* Hillsdale, NJ: Erlbaum.

Smith, F. (1989). Overselling literacy. *Phi Delta Kappan, 70,* 352-359.

Snow, C. E., & Hoefnagel-Höhle, M. (1978). The critical period for language acquisition: Evidence from second language learning. *Child Development, 49,* 1114-1128.

Stanovich, K. E. (1986). Matthew effects in reading: Some consequences of individual differences in the acquisition of literacy. *Reading Research Quarterly, 21,* 360-406.

Strickland, D. S., & Feeley, J. T. (1985). Using children's concept of story to improve reading and writing. In T. L. Harris & E. J. Cooper (Eds.), *Reading, thinking and concept development* (pp. 163-173). New York: College Entrance Examination Board.

Terrell, T. D. (1977). A natural approach to second language acquisition and learning. *Modern Language Journal, 6,* 325-337.

Terrell, T. D. (1981). The natural approach in bilingual education. In California State Department of Education (Ed.), *Schooling and language minority students: A theoretical framework* (1st ed.) (pp. 117-146). Los Angeles: Evaluation, Dissemination and Assessment Center, California State University, Los Angeles.

Terrell, T. D. (1982). The natural approach to language teaching: An update. *Modern Language Journal, 66,* 121-132.

Terrell, T. D. (1986). Acquisition in the natural approach: The binding/access framework. *Modern Language Journal, 70,* 213-227.

Terrell, T. D. (1991). The role of grammar instruction in a communicative approach. *Modern Language Journal, 75,* 52-63.

Trachtenburg, P., & Ferruggia, A. (1989). Big books from little voices: Reaching high risk beginning readers. *The Reading Teacher, 42,* 284-289.

Urzúa, C. (1987). "You stopped too soon": Second language children composing and revising. *TESOL Quarterly, 21,* 279-304.

Veatch, J., Sawicki, F., Elliott, G., Flake, E., & Blakey, J. (1979). *Key words to reading: The language experience approach begins.* Columbus, OH: Merrill.

Vygotsky, L. S. (1978). *Mind in society.* Cambridge, MA: Harvard University Press.

Wagner, M. J., & Tilney, G. (1983). The effect of "superlearning techniques" on the vocabulary acquisition and alpha brainwave production of language learners. *TESOL Quarterly, 17,* 5-17.

Primary Language Instruction: A Bridge to Literacy

Marguerite Ann Snow

Introduction

One of the greatest challenges currently facing American schools is educating the burgeoning population of students who do not speak English. How best to teach these elementary and secondary students is the subject of much debate. This chapter makes a case for the use of the primary language in the schooling of language minority students by exploring relevant research in the language acquisition and language education literature and suggesting ways in which teachers can support the use of the primary language while their students are developing their English language skills.

Any discussion of the use of the primary language in the schooling of language minority students must first begin with an understanding of who these students are. The language minority population in American schools represents a very complex mosaic of languages, native countries and cultures, familial circumstances, and educational experiences. Given this complexity, it is difficult indeed to characterize this diverse school-age audience. Yet an understanding of this profile provides a critical backdrop for our discussion in this chapter of the role of the primary language in the school of language minority students.

Limited English proficient (LEP) students fall into three broad categories: (1) recent immigrants; (2) early immigrants; and (3) U.S.-born learners. These three categories of students differ along a number of key dimensions, perhaps the most critical of which is the degree to which they have been exposed to literate practices or have developed literacy skills in their native language either in the home or at school. In fact, Williams and Snipper (1990) classify language minority

The author gratefully acknowledges the efforts of the late Dorothy Legarreta-Marcaida whose chapter, "Effective Use of the Primary Language in the Classroom," in the first edition of this volume was a valuable source of inspiration for this chapter.

students according to the degree to which they can read and write in their native language. In their scheme, language minority students are labeled as preliterate, literate, or postliterate.

Age of arrival has been shown to be a critical variable. Early immigrants may have left their home countries in the early primary grades and hence schooling in the first language may have been interrupted. Collier (1987) found that children who arrive in the U.S. at ages 4 to 7 and are schooled exclusively in English may need up to five years to reach the same levels of academic achievement as older LEP students who have had some instruction in their primary language. Recent immigrants, on the other hand, have typically developed academic language proficiency in their native language and, in some cases, initial proficiency in English in their home countries, but need assistance in transferring concepts and skills learned in their first language to English.

The U.S.-born LEP child, of course, comes into school with no prior schooling and, particularly for those who live in ethnic communities, often little exposure to English in their daily lives. Depending upon literacy practices in the home, these children may or may not read and write in their native language. For these language minority students, schooling in the U.S. represents the only opportunity for native language literacy development.

The profile is, in fact, even more complex than the categories reflect. Many other factors may be present. Language minority students coming from rural, poor, or war-torn countries may have experienced gaps in their education. Especially for secondary school immigrants, these gaps often mean little or poor literacy in the native language. Because their schooling has been disrupted, they may lack basic study skills and knowledge of school culture to fall back on as they learn English in the American schooling setting. Their difficulties are compounded by the fact that the level of cognitive complexity and sequential content knowledge of high school subject matter is very dependent on prior knowledge. Once in the U.S., other factors, such as the high transiency of students from migrant worker families, the tension of being in undocumented status, work pressures on students helping to support their families financially, family responsibilities such as caring for younger siblings, and trips back to the native country create gaps in schooling which are difficult for these students to overcome. For these students, the amount of time remaining in school is a critical factor. Collier (1989) found that, for the late immigrant, if academic work in the primary language is not continued at home or at school while these students are learning English, there may not be enough time left in secondary school to make up for the lost periods of academic instruction.

Even for those students who have had the benefit of consistent, high quality instruction in their home countries, these learners, once in the U.S., may find the adjustment process difficult. They often encounter very different kinds of teaching styles (possibly more student-centered than teacher-centered) and learning styles (less need for rote memorization and more emphasis on analytical thinking), and emphasis on different skills (e.g., focus on writing rather on than grammar instruction). Moreover, these older students must deal with the adjustment to a new language, culture, and school setting while undergoing the inevitable growth pains experienced by teenagers. All this takes place in the typically impersonal setting of the American high school where, for the newly arrived immigrant, the school day must seem like a whirlwind of ever changing classrooms, subjects, and teachers. Thus, although these learners may have been successful students in their home countries, the transition may, nevertheless, not be as smooth as expected.

In short, we know that all students do not bring the same kinds of knowledge, language habits, and strategies for learning to school. We as educators must recognize the tremendous heterogeneity to be found among our language minority students and take responsibility for presenting all students with a range of options for organizing knowledge and using language. Perhaps the perception of diversity as an educational "problem" should be reexamined. Heath and Mangiola (1991) offer us a strategy for dealing with the tremendous linguistic and cultural variety in our classrooms: "Let us then not think of students of diverse backgrounds as bringing 'differences' to school, but instead as offering classrooms 'expansions' of background knowledge and ways of using language" (p. 17). Furthermore, Garcia (1991) helps us find a common ground, noting that these students "display a portrait of unrealized academic success" (p. 1). The perspective taken in this chapter is that primary language instruction is a bridge to literacy, a key link in assisting language minority students to realize success.

Primary Language Instruction: Can It Be Justified?

This section will provide a rationale for instruction in the primary language. Justification comes from a variety of different perspectives, including the calls for a language competent society, the positive consequences of bilingualism on cognitive development, and the development of social-cultural identity.

A Language Competent Society

Clearly, the goal of our educational system is to produce students who are proficient in English in all realms of use—for social and academic needs, for use in the home, and in the job force. Consider the paradox, however, when it comes to efforts to preserve these students' native language skills. Why do we offer foreign language instruction to monolingual English-speaking students while our school system, in general, is set up to eradicate the home language of the language minority students who come into American schools? In fact, this paradox is put in bold perspective. It is calculated that the Defense Language Institute in Monterey, California, each year provides instruction in more than 40 languages to 6,000 full-time students who are members of the U.S. military. A 47-week course in Korean, for example, costs [based on 1989 estimates] about $12,000 per student. Despite the effort on the parts of the students and instructors and the considerable costs involved, its graduates achieve lower levels of oral proficiency in Korean than a five-year-old native speaker of Korean brings to school (Crawford, 1989, p. 164). In the 1992-93 school year in the Los Angeles Unified School District alone, 4,513 limited English proficient Korean speakers were enrolled whose native language is at risk of, at best, weakening or, at worst, extinction.

Senator Paul Simon of Illinois was one of the first at the national level to recognize this potential crisis. In his 1980 book *The Tongue-Tied American,* Simon notes that:

> Because of our rich ethnic mix, the United States is home to millions whose first language is not English. One of every fifty Americans is foreign-born. We are the fourth largest Spanish-speaking country in the world. Yet almost nothing is being done to preserve the language skills we now have or to use this rich linguistic resource to train people in the use of a language other than English. (p. 4)

Bilingualism in most countries around the world is considered a fact of life—a symbol of educational attainment in the academic setting, a necessity in the global marketplace. In countries as diverse as Sweden, China, and Canada, societal bilingualism is commonplace, and education in more than one language is supported by the government. Even in the U.S., during the nineteenth century, more than a dozen states offered instruction in languages such as German, Swedish, Norwegian, Danish,

Dutch, Polish, Italian, Czech, French, and Spanish (Lessow-Hurley, 1990). But then World War I brought about attitudes of nationalism which contributed to the decline in language instruction and the value placed on bilingualism. The War's aftermath of isolationism exacerbated this decline. World War II, in contrast, brought a renewed interest in language study for defense needs. With the launching of Sputnik in 1957, this effort was followed by an even greater emphasis on language study and the commitment to narrow the perceived educational gap with the Soviet Union (Thompson *et al.,* 1990). More recently, bilingualism has become a highly politicized issue. The English-only movement and ballot initiatives in many states to make English the official language have brought the issue of bilingualism and native language use into the national spotlight.[1] Despite this movement, however, calls for a language competent American society continue to be reiterated by educators who value multiculturalism (Tucker, 1984, 1990; Padilla, 1990). The use of the primary language in the schooling of language minority students is justified on the grounds of sustaining the rich natural resource these students bring to the American classroom.

Cognitive Consequences

A glance at the history of research in this country on the relationship between intelligence and bilingualism offers two contrasting pictures. Early studies of the cognitive consequences of bilingualism were quite consistent in their results. [see Legarreta-Marcaida (1981) and Hakuta (1986) for reviews of these studies.] For instance, Thompson (1952) writes:

> There can be no doubt that the child reared in a bilingual environment is handicapped in his language growth. One can debate the issue as to whether speech facility in two languages is worth the consequent retardation in the common language of the realm. (p. 367)

Darcy (1953) reviewed 110 studies in the literature and found either no effect or adverse effects on intelligence associated with bilingualism.

The tide began to shift when a widely cited UNESCO document entitled *The Use of Vernacular Languages in Education* (1953) reported on

---

[1] See, for example, James Crawford's coverage of the English-only versus English-plus debate in the U.S. in *Language Loyalties: A Source Book on the Official English Controversy.* (Crawford, 1992).

successful programs around the world that used the native language as the medium of instruction. Perhaps the major turning point in the debate occurred with the publication of a study by Canadian researchers Peal and Lambert (1962) whose findings stood in stark contrast to the earlier conclusions. Based on their research, they describe a bilingual as:

> a youngster whose wider experiences in two cultures have given him advantages which a monolingual does not enjoy. Intellectually his experience with two language systems seems to have left him with a mental flexibility, a superiority in concept formation, a more diversified set of mental abilities....In contrast, the monolingual appears to have a more unitary structure of intelligence which he must use for all types of intellectual tasks. (p. 20)

Macnamara (1966) underscored this change in perspective in a critical review of the early studies. He found them so fraught with methodological irregularities, such as failure to control for socio-economic status, sampling techniques that were questionable, and use of instruments that were not valid, that these early findings could no longer be considered credible.

More recent work confirms that children who grow up bilingual or become bilingual at an early age demonstrate advantages in several areas of cognitive functioning over monolingual children (Snow, 1990). One type of advantage is in the area of metalinguistic awareness, the ability to analyze the form as well as the content of language and the knowledge of how to talk about language. Certain kinds of metalinguistic skills, such as the realization that words have no intrinsic connection to the objects to which they refer, develop much earlier in bilingual children than in their monolingual counterparts. Interestingly, the metalinguistic skills so critical in learning to read, which are typically developed by monolingual children who come from highly verbal homes, can also be seen in bilingual children from families of low income and low educational backgrounds. These advantages do not appear for low income monolingual peers and seem to take place only when language minority students use their bilingual skills over an extended period of time or in what Lambert (1980) first called "additive" language learning environments. In contrast, the "subtractive" bilingual model where the home language is replaced by the school language does not provide for any period of stable bilingualism during which the positive consequences of being bilingual can emerge (Snow, 1990, p. 65).

Social-cultural Identity

Krashen and Biber (1988) conclude that "possibly the most important advantage of full bilingualism is that it can help lead to a healthy sense of biculturalism" (p. 27). In contrast, many language minority students perceive the negative messages about their language and culture which emanate from school and society at large and develop what Cummins has called "cultural ambivalence." A strong primary language component in school can mitigate against these negative images, validating language minority students' home language and culture and helping to develop a strong sense of self-identity as these students adjust to life in a new country, a new language, or a new school culture. As Snow (1990) points out: "Schools should be operated in ways that maximize the self-esteem of their students—because that is a worthy goal in itself, but also because students with high self-esteem work harder, learn better, and achieve more" (p. 64).

Research in Bilingual Education: What Are the Findings?

Another justification for use of the primary language in the schooling of language minority students can be found in the extensive research carried out in bilingual education. Since the passage of the Bilingual Education Act in 1968, controversy regarding the effectiveness of bilingual education has raged in both academic circles and the popular press.[2] This section will begin with a brief discussion of early research regarding the effectiveness of bilingual education and then move on to a description of more recent studies which elucidate the key features of successful instructional programs for language minority students.

The highly publicized Baker and de Kanter (1983) review of the results of 28 bilingual education programs concluded that there was no consistent evidence to support the effectiveness of transitional bilingual education (TBE). It interesting to note that they had initially reviewed more than 300 studies, but rejected all but 28 as methodologically unsound (e.g., the studies failed to randomly assign subjects or reported grade-equivalent scores instead of raw scores on standarized tests) (Crawford, 1989). In their conclusions, Baker and de Kanter noted, "An occasional, inexplicable success is not reason enough to make TBE the law of the land....The time spent in using the home language in the classroom may

---

[2] For interesting discussions of the politics of bilingual education, see the articles by Secada and Mulhauser in Cazden, and Snow (1990).

be harmful because it reduces [the time for] English practice'' (in Crawford, 1989, p. 92).

A counterpunch to the Baker and de Kanter report was provided by Willig (1985) who used a sophisticated statistical procedure called "meta-analysis" to reanalyze the Baker and de Kanter results. The results of Willig's analysis, in contrast, revealed small to moderate differences favoring bilingual education.

More recently, a number of studies have shown the effectiveness of programs with a primary language component for language minority students. In a longitudinal evaluation of an Australian bilingual program, Gale *et al.* (1981) found that aboriginal students taught in their primary language and in English performed significantly better on 10 different oral and written measures of English after seven years of schooling than aboriginal students who had only received instruction in English. Saville-Troike (1984) investigated the acquisition of oral and written English and academic performance in the subject areas of 19 children, ages 7 to 12. She found that the two major factors that correlated significantly with the students' academic achievement in English were development of English vocabulary and opportunity for on-going cognitive development in their primary language.

Six California programs with successful bilingual programs are presented in Krashen and Biber (1988). Results of standardized testing demonstrated that language minority students who received primary language instruction did as well or better than comparison children in both English and academic achievement, supporting the authors' claim that time spent developing background knowledge and literacy in the primary language enhances the abilities and competencies ultimately underlying school success.

Collier's (1987) comprehensive research makes an important contribution to our understanding of the age factor in schooling language minority students. Findings from her work support the claim that older LEP students who arrive in this country at ages 12 to 15 experience the greatest difficulty with acquisition of English for academic purposes when these students are schooled only in English. Such students in grades 7 to 12, Collier believes, cannot afford even one or two years' loss of cognitive and academic development in the subject areas while they are attempting to master English. Thus, her results suggest content subjects taught in the primary language must be available to secondary LEP students while they are learning English. Once students are sufficiently proficient in English, content area courses taught in English can be introduced.

A study commissioned by the U.S. Department of Education to SRA Technologies sought to avoid the major methodological weaknesses which had been exposed in the Baker and de Kanter and Willig reviews. In this comprehensive eight-year study, comparison groups were carefully matched and the instructional treatments of the three programs were carefully considered (Ramirez, Yuen, and Ramey, 1991). The objective was to compare three alternative programs at the elementary school level:

1. *Early exit TBE:* In this type of program, initial instruction was provided in the children's primary language, typically to introduce initial reading skills, for approximately 30 to 60 minutes per day. All other instruction was in English. Instruction in the primary language was phased out over the next two years so that by grade two, virtually all instruction was in English and students were expected to be exited from the program and mainstreamed into English-only classrooms by the end of first or second grade.

2. *Late exit bilingual education programs:* Students in this program received a minimum of 40 percent of their total instruction in Spanish (Spanish language arts, reading, and content areas such as mathematics and social studies). Students remained in the program through the sixth grade.

3. *Structured immersion:* All instruction in the program was in English. Teachers had specialized training in working with LEP students and strong receptive skills in the students' primary language, Spanish, although the use of Spanish was restricted to clarification. Students were mainstreamed within two or three years.

In their final report, the authors concluded that the complexity of the study precluded a direct comparison of the effectiveness of the three programs; however, comparisons of early-exit and structured immersion were possible and a thorough analysis of the three late-exit programs was reported. Results are as follows:

- After four years in the respective programs, LEP students in early exit and structured immersion programs demonstrated comparable skills in mathematics, language, and reading when tested in English.

- Differences were found among the three late-exit sites in achievement levels for mathematics, English language, and English reading at the end of the sixth grade. Students in the two sites with the most consistent level of primary language use (in the other site students were exited earlier than the sixth grade) exhibited the highest scores in English language and English reading. Interestingly, these two sites differed in the relative amount of instruction provided in English and Spanish from first through six grade. Yet students from the program with the greatest use of Spanish achieved the same results in English language and reading by the end of sixth grade as the students from the program with the most use of English.

- When compared with the norming population, students who were provided with a substantial and consistent primary language program learned mathematics, English language, and English reading skills as fast or faster than the monolingual comparisons.

In sum, Ramirez, Yuen, and Ramey (1991) concluded that providing LEP students with substantial amounts of instruction in their primary language does not impede their acquisition of English language skills. In other words, it is as effective as being provided with large amounts of English. Moreover, students are able to master content area subjects and, consequently, make normal progress through the standard school curriculum when instructed in their primary language.

Cazden (1992), in her review of the "Ramirez Report," highlights several important implications of this research. First, she noted, "The most obvious implication is that the amount of time spent using a second language in school can no longer be considered the most important influence on learning it. Such correlation has been an important assumption in all arguments against bilingual education" (p. 6). The results of this study, she notes, provide strong support for the threshold level posited by Cummins.

Cazden also points out two other factors identified in the study which are of critical importance in the school success of language minority students. First, it was found that the parents of the late-exit students were the most involved of the three programs (and, interestingly, had the lowest income levels). "More late-exit parents tend[ed] to monitor their child's homework and slightly more tend[ed] to help the child complete homework" (Ramirez, Yuen, and Ramey, 1991, Vol. 1, p. 361). Clearly, the extensive use of the primary language in the late-exit program had the concomitant effect of creating access to the school for the parents and encouraging increased attention at home to their children's schoolwork. Second, the late-exit teachers and principals had more graduate education and more specialized training for working with language minority students than the teachers in the other two program types. Furthermore, the late-exit teachers were more proficient in Spanish than the other teachers and were as proficient as the others in English. The current state of the art in bilingual program evaluation is perhaps best summed up by Wong Fillmore (1992), "a self-avowed" advocate of bilingual education, who concludes, "Bilingual education done well gives excellent results; bilingual education done badly gives poor results, just as one would expect" (p. 367).   Hence, the question remains, What are the characteristics of bilingual education done well?   Or phrased another way, What constitutes effective instruction for language minority students?

Recent Research: What Does It Reveal about Effective Instruction?

More recently, the trend in research in bilingual education has moved away from program comparisons of the type just described toward attempts to document instructional practices that are effective with linguistically and culturally diverse students. Some of the findings dealing with effective features will be highlighted in this section.

In one of the first attempts to describe the characteristics of effective instruction, Tickunoff and Vasquez-Faria (1982) identified five instructional features which, in their research, were significantly related to effective instruction for LEP students: (1) active teaching, (2) using both the native language and the second language for instruction, (3) integrating English language development with academic skills, (4) using cultural referents, and (5) communicating a sense of self-efficacy and high student expectations.

In a comprehensive study of *special alternative instructional projects* (SAIPs) in which instruction was provided primarily in English as an alternative to bilingual instruction, Tickunoff *et al.* (1991) found that the exemplary programs, in spite of their emphasis on English instruction, still offered students opportunities to use their native languages. Specifically, Lucas and Katz (1991) described a variety of ways in which students and teachers used the primary language and the school context provided support for the use of the primary language. Specific uses across the nine exemplary SAIP sites (labeled A-I) are summarized in

Table 1 below. From these findings, it is clear that even in programs in which English is the main language of instruction, exemplary programs find many ways to facilitate the use and development of the students' primary languages both at school and at home.

Table 1

USE OF THE PRIMARY LANGUAGE BY STUDENTS AND TEACHERS ACROSS THE NINE EXEMPLARY SPECIAL ALTERNATIVE INSTRUCTIONAL PROGRAMS

Sites*	A	B	C	D	E	F	G	H	I
Students' use of L_1:									
To assist one another	x	x	x	x		x	x	x	x
To tutor other students							x		
To ask/answer questions	x	x	x	x		x		x	
To use bilingual dictionaries		x	x	x		x		x	
To write in L_1	x	x		x	x	x		x	
To interact socially	x	x	x	x	x	x	x	x	x
Teachers' use of L_1:									
To check comprehension	x	x				x		x	
To translate a lesson		x				x		x	
To provide instruction	x	x							
To interact socially	x	x	x		x	x	x	x	
L_1 support in the larger school context:									
Content instruction in L_1	x	x		x			x		x
Instruction in L_1 culture, history, and/or language arts	x	x		x		x	x		x
Library books in L_1	x	x			x			x	x
Communication to parents in L_1	x	x	x		x	x			
Parents encouraged to read to students in L_1	x	x			x				

NOTE: x denotes the use of L_1 for the specified purpose.
*Sites B and E include students at the secondary level.

Another recent study, a two-year study commissioned by the California State Legislature, examined 15 exemplary elementary schools from more than 100 nominated by county offices of education, universities, and professional organizations. In *Meeting the Challenge of Cultural Diversity* (Berman *et al.,* 1992) (commonly referred to as the Berman, Weiler Report) the researchers concluded, among other findings, that students in classes using native language instruction tended to operate at higher skill levels than those using English instruction. They also found that preschool programs in the students' primary languages were found to be highly advantageous.

Historically, research and policy in bilingual education have tended to focus on elementary school programs where enrollments of LEP students have been greater. The secondary LEP population is burgeoning, however, and can no longer be ignored. In California, for example, in the period from 1989-1992 there has been a 42 percent increase in the number of LEP students enrolling in secondary schools (Minicucci and Olsen, 1992). Two recent studies provide much-needed research in the post-elementary setting.

Lucas, Henze, and Donato (1990) extended the research on effective schooling which had focused on urban elementary schools in low income neighborhoods to the secondary level in schools with large populations of Latino language minority students. Data were collected at five school sites in California and one in Arizona. Criteria for site selection included both qualitative and quantitative factors. Nominations for successful secondary schools were solicited from a variety of people familiar with schools with large numbers of language minority students, including educators at state, county, and district levels. Once the recommendations were received, the principals of the schools were contacted to determine whether their schools had received any formal recognition from local, state, or federal agencies for their programs for language minority students and whether they could provide quantitative evidence of their success (e.g., drop-out rates, standardized tests scores that compared favorably to other minority schools).

From the data collected, which included audiotapes and notes from interviews with school site personnel and students, student questionnaires, classroom observations, records and documents from each school which included such items as policy statements and program descriptions, eight key features emerged which Lucas, Henze, and Donato concluded were the most important in promoting the success of language minority students at the six school sites:

1. Value is placed on the students' languages and cultures.
2. High expectations of language minority students are made concrete.
3. School leaders make the education of language minority students a priority.
4. Staff development is explicitly designed to help teachers and staff serve language minority students more effectively.
5. A variety of courses and programs for language minority students is offered.
6. A counseling program gives special attention to language minority students.
7. Parents of language minority students are encouraged to become involved in their children's education.
8. School staff members share a strong commitment to empower language minority students. (pp. 324-325)

Given the focus in this chapter on the use of the primary language, the first key feature identified by Lucas, Henze, and Donato seems worthy of elaboration. In the exemplary school sites, it was found that value was placed on the students' languages and cultures in a number of important ways. First, the ability to speak another language in addition to English was treated as an advantage rather than a liability. A number of teachers and counselors at the schools had learned Spanish in order to function more effectively in their jobs—an effort well-noted by a student who commented "when teachers are bilingual, it makes our learning easier. They treat us equally" (p. 323). A second way in which the schools exemplified how they valued students' languages and cultures could be found in the school curricula. Although these high schools made English literacy a primary goal, they also encouraged students to continue to develop their Spanish skills by offering Spanish courses for native speakers. Advanced placement classes in which students could earn college credit and content courses taught in Spanish were offered so that students could advance through the curriculum while developing their English skills. Moreover, students were allowed to speak their native language when English language development was not the focus of instruction. Thus, throughout the campuses visited by the team of researchers, students were heard to speak Spanish freely with each other and with Spanish-speaking staff members.

In addition to showing respect for the students' native languages, it was clear that the students' cultures were valued as well. This respect was apparent in obvious ways such as the celebration of customs and holidays, but also in more meaningful ways throughout the year. Teachers made a point of learning about the students' past experiences; some, for instance, had visited Mexican schools to better understand the students' previous educational experiences. At the same time, faculty and staff did not treat students "simply as members of an undifferentiated ethnic group" (p. 325). They recognized students' individual interests and problems and avoided stereotypes and generalization by acknowledging that students from Mexico, Nicaragua, El Salvador, Cuba, and other Spanish-speaking countries have different histories and customs and speak different varieties of Spanish. Mexican immigrants, Mexican-Americans, and Chicanos were also viewed as having their own distinct characteristics, socioeconomic backgrounds, and histories of educational attainment. Effort was made in hiring practices not only to employ high quality instructional staff, but also to find teachers and counselors reflecting the student composition to serve as role models and advocates for the students. As one student remarked, "Mr. A encourages students to break stereotypes by being good in chemistry, physical science, and physics" (p. 327).

In a study seeking to investigate the attitudes of language minority junior high students about what constitutes effective instruction, Snow *et al.* (in press) interviewed 66 students from six junior high schools in a large urban school district. The findings from the oral interviews revealed that the students rated highly such activities as journal writing, cooperative learning, peer editing, group work, and study skills. When asked to provide their own "ingredients" for the ideal classroom, they called for increased student participation, more hands-on projects, and opportunities for discussion of issues that concern them. They also emphasized the importance of parental support in the success of the language minority student. One student commented, in Spanish:

> Los padres lo deben ayudar mucho, que le aconsejen mucho, que le aconsejen que debe hacer, asi gana buenos grados.

> [The student's] parents should help him a lot; they should advise him; they should advise him what to do, so that he gets good grades.

Finally, Garcia (1991) summarizes recent research on effective instruction for linguistically and culturally diverse students, citing five implications for instruction:

- Any curriculum, including one for diverse children, must address all categories of learning goals (cognitive and academic, advanced as well as basic). We should not lower our expectations for these students; they, too, need to be intellectually challenged.

- The more linguistically and culturally diverse the children we teach, the more closely we must relate academic content to the child's own environment and experience.

- The more diverse the children, the more integrated the curriculum should be. That is, multiple content areas (e.g., math, science, social studies) and language learning activities should be centered around a theme. Children should have opportunities to study a topic in depth, and to apply a variety of skills acquired in home, community, and school contexts.

- The more diverse the children, the greater the need for active rather than passive endeavors, particularly informal social activities such as group projects, in which students are allowed flexibility in their participation with the teacher and other students.

- The more diverse the children, the more important it is to offer them opportunities to apply what they are learning in a meaningful context. (p. 7)

Classroom-Based Research: What Are the Implications?

A Rationale for Interaction

The emerging picture of effective instruction for language minority students is an interactive, student-centered classroom. Yet, the Ramirez et al. (1991) study discussed earlier found that teachers in all three types of programs they examined offered language minority students a passive language learning environment with limited opportunities to produce language (either the primary language or English) or to develop complex language and thinking skills.

Research in both first and second language acquisition provides a rationale for the interactive classroom. The interactionist perspective is reflected in the view of human development that draws predominantly from the work of the Russian psychologist Vygotsky and others such as Jerome Bruner who belong to a school of social science referred to as *Neo-Vygotskianism*. A key feature of this school of human development is that higher-order functions develop out of social interaction. Vygotsky (1978) talked about the *Zone of Proximal Development* (ZPD) which he defined as "the distance between the actual developmental level as determined by individual problem solving and the level of potential development as determined through problem solving under adult guidance or in collaboration with more capable peers" (p. 86).

Tharp and Gallimore (1988) apply the notion of ZPD to the classroom: "Teaching consists in assisting performance through the ZPD. Teaching can be said to occur when assistance is offered at points in the ZPD at which performance requires assistance" (p. 31). Wood, Bruner, and Ross (1976) coined the metaphor *scaffolding* to describe the ideal role of the teacher in assisting the learner through the ZPD. The teacher's responsibility in the interactionist view is to structure and model appropriate solutions to problems by building a scaffold from the learner's current state of competence which extends his/her skills or knowledge to a higher level of competence.

The major implication of interactionist theory for language learning is that language is learned by taking part in social interaction. According to Wells (1981), children learn their first language through interaction with caregivers "which gives due weight to the contribution of both parties, and emphasizes mutuality and reciprocity in the meanings that are constructed and negotiated through talk" (p. 115). *Negotiation of meaning* is a very descriptive term. It is a complex, collaborative process which occurs regularly in the strategies used by parents in talking to their young children. The term connotes the reciprocity entailed in the process of human communication. Negotiation of any kind involves a give and take, a back and forth until the parties reach agreement. These processes have been applied to teaching in the form of "instructional conversations" in which teachers encourage the expression of students' own ideas, build upon information students provide and experiences they have had, and guide them to increasingly sophisticated levels of understanding (Goldenberg, 1991).

Wong-Fillmore (1985) was interested in how teachers' language use affects language learning. Specifically, she asked the question, When does teacher talk work as input? In a large-scale study of over 40 elementary classrooms which had sizable numbers of LEP students, Wong-Fillmore examined the characteristics of the language used in lessons that seemed to work well for language learners. Several of her findings are relevant for our purposes here. First, she found that clear separation of languages was essential. In other words, translation or concurrent instruction in both languages did not promote success in language learning. Separation of languages forces students to utilize all the cues available in instruction to negotiate the message; they cannot wait for the message to be delivered in their first language. Thus, instruction for language minority students should be delivered in the primary language or the second language, not used interchangeably in concurrent translation.[3]

Another finding of the study was that the emphasis in successful classrooms was on communication. Wong-Fillmore noted that the language used in the classroom was "in the service" of communicating subject matter to students. Successful teachers negotiated meaning with their students. Teachers talk that works as input was rich in its variety; it builds in redundancy through the use of routines and patterns and provides students with multiple cues to meaning. It helps learners expand and refine their linguistic repertoire by gaining greater command over the forms, functions, and uses of language.

Hawkins (1988) looked for instances of scaffolding or assisted performance in the classroom setting. After extensive observation, she found that scaffolding occurred only in classroom situations that were highly interactive *and* cognitively demanding. Thus, true teaching in the Tharp and Gallimore sense can occur only when students are given the opportunity to negotiate meaning in interactive, cognitively demanding situations.

Thus far in our discussion of the interactive classroom, we have been concerned with the importance of interaction between the teacher and the learner. It is also important to consider the potential benefits of

---

[3] Perez and Torres-Guzman (1992) note, however, that while bilingual educators are, in general, in agreement about the separation of languages for instruction, the value of switching back and forth for some teaching purposes has been demonstrated. They cite examples from the literature in which the use of the two languages or "code switching" has been effective in the teaching of poetry and in peer teaching situations; they also discuss the New Concurrent Approach in which planned code-switching was found to be as effective as, and in some subjects, more effective than, the language separation approach which is generally advocated.

interaction between learners in the negotiation of meaning process. Studies have shown that in a typical class, teachers talk for at least half, and often for as much as two-thirds of any class period. In fact, Long and Porter (1985) estimate that in an average language class of 30 students in a public secondary school, students have a chance to talk about 30 seconds per lesson, or just one hour per student per year. They see group work as an "attractive alternative to the teacher-led, 'lockstep' mode" (p. 207). It improves the quantity and quality of student talk and helps individualize instruction. Careful selection of groups and assignments can take into consideration the great variety of personalities, attitudes, motivations, interests, cognitive and learning styles, and linguistic and cultural backgrounds in a typical classroom. Group work also promotes a positive affective climate. For many students, being called upon in front of the whole class is very stressful. Small groups provide a much less threatening environment, often freeing students up to take more risks. It may also motivate learners because it is more tailored to individual differences and provides a change of pace from the typical teacher-controlled format.

Work in cooperative learning grew out of concern that competitive classrooms do not promote access to learning for all students equally. To counteract the traditional classroom organizational structure, Kagan (1986) reconfigures the classroom, dividing the class "into small teams whose members are all positively interdependent" (p. 241). In order to accomplish any assigned task, all members of the team have a designated role or responsibility. Groups are assigned a group grade, creating the interdependence on members which makes cooperative learning different from the more general group work activities described above. Research on the value of cooperative learning shows positive results on academic achievement, race relations, and the development of mutual concerns among students in a wide variety of settings, subject areas, and grade levels. The approach also appears to be particularly effective with low achieving students.

The Language of School

A number of scholars have attempted to describe the types of language used in school. Snow (1987) characterizes the language of the home as "contextualized." It tends to deal with shared background knowledge about the family, the house, pets, or common experiences such as holidays, vacations, or important events. In addition, the language used in the home often has a "here and now" focus. Talk centers around concrete objects within the present time frame. In contrast, the language of school is "decontextualized"—it does not assume shared background knowledge among participants. Furthermore, the language of school becomes more decontextualized as students progress through school. By the upper elementary school grades, information is mainly disseminated through reading texts and lectures rather than through experiential activities more typical of the early school years. To be successful in school, language minority students must learn the kinds of language skills required to perform academic tasks which rely on written messages.

Heath (1986) has examined the kinds of language used in both home and school settings. From her observations, she concludes that implicit in the American school curriculum are six very specific kinds of language demands. First, students need to use language to label and describe the objects, events, and information that "non-intimates" present them. This language function in school typically takes place in the form of "display" or "factual" questions where the teacher already knows the answer. A second common language function is the use of language to recount past events or information in predictable order and format. Heath refers to this function as "event casts" and gives the following example to illustrate: "Teachers to class: What happened the other day when someone didn't follow the rules for putting books away?" A third type of language used is that needed to follow directions from oral and written sources. This function includes many of the management routines found in school: lining up for recess, changing groups, preparing to go home. A fourth demand is the use of language to sustain and maintain the social interactions of the group. In school, this often means subordinating individual or personal goals to maintain group relations. Thus, students are taught to share, to wait their turn, and so on. The use of language to obtain information from non-intimates is the fifth demand. Children need to know how to request and clarify information. Once they are given information, they are expected to generalize from one situation to other similar situations. For instance, the procedures for cleaning up might be the same regardless of the kind of project that students are working on at any given time. Finally, the sixth demand is the ability to use language to account for one's unique experiences, to link these experiences to generally known ideas or events, and to create new information or integrate ideas in innovative ways.

Heath and Mangiola (1991) define literate behavior as learning to:

- Interpret texts

- Say what they "mean"

- Tie them into personal experience

- Explain and argue with passages of text

- Make predictions based on the text

- Hypothesize outcomes of related situations

- Compare and evaluate

- Talk about doing all of the above (p. 41)

In their study of a cross-age tutoring project involving at-risk fifth graders at a California school with a large language minority student population, Heath and Mangiola (1991) investigated the development of literate behavior. Twice a week the fifth graders read to their first grade tutees. The tutors took field notes about the tutoring sessions, reported to the first grade teachers on their tutees' progress, and viewed and analyzed videotapes of the tutoring sessions. They also met with the researchers to talk about the tutoring sessions and to discuss what they themselves did as readers and writers. The goal of the discussions was to help the tutors see themselves as becoming experts about the processes of reading, writing, and talking about what can be learned from personal experience, books, and the oral retelling of others.

Importantly, the tutors and tutees were allowed to read and interact in either English or Spanish. It was felt that whether the students read in one language or the other, they would ask the same kinds of questions and make the same progress in their reading and writing, since literate behaviors are fundamental skills that are transferable to all areas of academic performance. Results of the analysis revealed that the students who began the program speaking and reading exclusively in Spanish began to read and discuss books with their tutees in English. Another impressive result of the project was that students had numerous authentic occasions for extensive, highly motivated, and varied student writing (e.g., field notes, letters to tutees and teachers, book synopses) of the kind that engaged students in real communication with an audience—a stark comparison to the more typical "dead-end" writing assignment directed at the teacher.

Rosebery, Warren, and Conant (1992) report on a study of the effects of a collaborative inquiry approach to science with language minority students. Two groups of students, most of whom had never studied science before and some who had had very little schooling, were exposed to "doing science" in ways practicing scientists do. The goal was to teach the students to use language, to think, and to act as members of the scientific community. One of the groups was seventh and eighth grade Haitian Creole speakers who were taught science in their primary language. The second group comprised high school students from a variety of language and cultural backgrounds who attended a basic skills program for academically weak students. Results were reported for the Haitian Creole students from both the seventh and eighth grades and from the high school group.

Before the onset of the inquiry science program, interviews with the students showed no evidence that they understood what it meant to reason scientifically. The researchers concluded that the students did not differentiate the discourse context for science. In other words, the students' responses demonstrated their belief that in the teaching of science: (1) literal comprehension was valued over inferential reasoning, and (2) questions were asked by "knowing" adults to ascertain whether students knew the right answer. By June, after exposure to the inquiry approach, however, the students began to show signs of reasoning in terms of a larger explanatory framework. They used the content knowledge about water pollution and aquatic ecosystems which they had learned to generate explanations and hypotheses. More importantly, from the students' use of language—they presented multiple hypotheses and used conditional statements—they demonstrated awareness of the tentative character of hypothesis formation. This use of language was in contrast to their initial concern with finding the right answer. The June interviews suggested that hypothesis making now functioned as part of a larger inquiry process linking conjecture and experimentation. The students had begun to learn how to appropriate scientific discourse for their own uses in the science classroom.

Program Models: What Works for Language Minority Students?

Two program models will be highlighted in this section which place a significant value on the use of the primary language in the schooling of language minority students. The first model is known as the "Case Studies Project." It was developed by consultants at the California State Department of Education in 1980 and has been implemented, in some form or another, in schools around the state since the early 1980s. In fact, the Los Angeles Unified School District adopted the philosophy and curriculum of the Case Studies Project based on its positive experience with its implementation at Eastman School in East Los Angeles. The "Eastman Model" is in place in 15 schools in the Los Angeles Unified School (where it is now called Project MORE) and 4 sites in the San Diego City Schools.

The second model to be described is a relatively new innovation both in California and around the country. "Bilingual" or "Two-way" immersion education combines the most significant features of bilingual education for language minority students and of immersion education for language majority students. In this model, English-speaking and LEP students are grouped for purposes of instruction. For example, in a two-way Spanish immersion program, native English speakers and native Spanish speakers would share the same classroom. The English speakers learn in Spanish as they would in a regular Spanish immersion program; the Spanish speakers receive initial instruction in their primary language. The goal is for the two groups of students to interact in their respective first and second languages, thereby receiving and giving peer input to one another. In a bilingual immersion program, the teacher must provide comprehensible instruction to the English speakers in their second language while providing high quality input for the primary language development of the native speakers of the target language.

Case Studies Model

The Case Studies Curriculum was developed on the theory that academic success demands higher-order linguistic and cognitive skills which, once developed, will transfer from the primary language to English. Five basic principles form the backbone of this model:

1. For bilingual students, the development of proficiencies in both the native language and English has a positive effect on academic achievement.

2. Language proficiency is the ability to use language for both basic communicative tasks and academic purposes.

3. For limited English proficient students, reaching the threshold of native language skills necessary to complete academic tasks forms the basis for similar proficiency in English.

4. Acquisition of basic communicative competency in a
    second language is a function of comprehensible second
    language instruction and a supportive environment.

5. The perceived status of students affects the interaction
    between teachers and students and among students
    themselves.   In turn, student outcomes are affected.
    (Crawford, 1989, p. 129)

Figure 1 below represents the four phases of the Case Studies
Curriculum Model. Phase I generally lasts two years for LEP students
who start in kindergarten and includes primary language instruction in

Figure 1

THE CASE STUDIES CURRICULUM MODEL

Phase	Spanish	Sheltered English	Mainstream English
I. Non-English-Proficient (K-grade 1)* (SOLOM 5-11)	Language Arts Mathematics Science/Health Social Studies	ESL	Art Music Physical Education
II. Limited-English-Proficient (grade 2-3)* (SOLOM 12-18)	Language Arts Social Studies	ESL Mathematics Science/Health	Art Music Physical Education
III. Limited-English-Proficient (grades 3-4)* (SOLOM 19-25)	Language Arts	Transitional Language Arts Social Studies	Art Music Physical Education Mathematics Science/Health
IV. Fully-English-Proficient (grades 4-6)* (SOLOM 25 +)	Language Arts (extended Spanish activities)		Art Music Physical Education Mathematics Science/Health Social Studies Language Arts

*Typical grade level for each phase.
Source: Crawford, 1989

Spanish for language arts, mathematics, science/health, and social studies. Students study ESL and are mainstreamed for art, music, and physical education. In Phase II, Spanish continues as the medium of instruction for language arts and social studies, while the students take sheltered English instruction in mathematics and science/health.[4] Students continue to take ESL and are mixed with native English speakers for art, music, and physical education. In Phase III, typically designed for third and fourth graders, students continue Spanish language arts and take transitional English language arts and sheltered social studies classes. By this phase, students are also mainstreamed for mathematics and science/health. By Phase IV (grades 4-6), students are typically reclassified from LEP status. Classes in Spanish language arts and sometimes a social studies course are offered in Spanish.[5]

Bilingual Immersion

The Bilingual, or Two-Way, immersion model is enjoying widespread implementation both in California and across the U.S. As of the 1992-1993 school year, there were 156 schools with bilingual immersion programs, representing 87 school districts. By far, the bulk of the programs are in California and New York; however, bilingual immersion programs can be found in 15 other states as well. The majority of the programs take place at the elementary school level although there are several currently implemented in middle schools (12) and two at the secondary school level. The language of instruction in bilingual immersion programs is predominantly Spanish; however, programs exist in Cantonese, Korean, Russian, Portuguese, and Haitian Creole (Christian and Mahrer, 1991-1992; 1992-1993).

Key features of effective bilingual immersion are (Crawford, 1989; Lindholm, 1990):

- Long-term treatment (four to six years)

- Optimal input (comprehensible, relevant, sufficient, challenging) in two languages

---

[4] Sheltered English is defined as the use of special instructional techniques to teach content matter in English to language minority students. For a more detailed description, see the Crawford chapter in this volume; Chapter 10 of Richard-Amato and Snow (1992); and the Sasser and Winningham chapter in Peitzman and Gadda (1991).

[5] For a more detailed description of the Case Studies model, see Chapter 8 of Crawford (1989).

- Focus on academic subjects

- Integration of language arts with subject matter instruction

- Separation of languages for instruction

- Additive bilingual environment

- Balance of language groups (roughly equal proportions of English speakers to minority language speakers)

- Sufficient use of the minority language

- Opportunities for speech production in the minority language

- Administrative support

- Empowerment objective of instruction (in contrast to the "transmission model" in which teachers impart and students receive knowledge; in this approach teachers participate in genuine dialogue with students and facilitate rather than control student learning)

- High-quality instructional personnel

- Home-school collaboration

Clearly, other models that promote the use of the primary language exist. Such efforts as bilingual preschool programs and newcomer schools offering special one-year programs for LEP students at both the elementary and secondary levels constitute other attempts to prepare language minority students for the mainstream. Instruction beyond elementary school for language minority students, however, remains a major concern. Minicucci and Olsen (1992), for instance, found that access to content coverage for LEP students was spotty. In their survey, they found that regardless of the instructional approach (i.e., primary language instruction or sheltered English), fewer than one-fourth of the schools they surveyed offered full content programs for students learning English. More than half of the high schools and one-third of the intermediate schools had major gaps in their offerings or provided no content classes at all. Furthermore, they found that the pattern of course offerings appeared to be related to the nature of both district and school site leadership, staff availability and willingness to take training, and the decentralized nature of decision making in the departmentalized secondary school. The results of this study portray a worrisome picture of the realities beyond elementary school for language minority students whose future education career opportunities are dependent on access to quality content-area and English instruction.

Conclusion

Clark (1990) has identified 74 attitudes, knowledge types, and skills that teachers must possess to be effective in multicultural settings. The 33 proposed standards for the new (Bilingual) Crosscultural, Language, and Academic Development credential in California include many of these attitudes, knowledge types, and skills. Clearly, the job of the teacher of linguistically and culturally diverse students is a daunting one. Factors such as the shortage of bilingual teachers, the lack of models for providing primary language instruction for mixed linguistic and cultural populations, limited availability of suitable materials for the less commonly taught languages and the lack of time to develop appropriate materials and curricula, the dearth of appropriate instruments for assessing primary language, and the time constraints that the school system places on teachers to transition students to mainstream classes taught in English are among the many challenges facing today's teacher of language minority students. Moreover, we have seen a considerable effort focused on elementary bilingual programs and directed toward Spanish-speaking school populations given their critical mass in many regions of the country, but much remains to be learned about effective instruction at the intermediate and secondary levels and about the many other linguistic and cultural groups that constitute our language minority population.

The results of the research described in this chapter have powerful implications for the role of the primary language in the development of the literate behavior prerequisite to academic success. It implies a reconceptualization of the kind of instruction that promotes literacy. It is not a passive environment with limited opportunities for students to produce language and develop higher order thinking skills, but a dynamic, interactive setting. We know from the research reviewed in this chapter on effective instructional practices and the classroom-based research that the bridge to literacy is not crossed simply by the use of the primary language for instruction, but rather by primary language instruction in combination with interactive, cooperative, student-centered teaching that equips students with the academic literacy practices needed for success in school. In other words, primary language instruction must draw on effective techniques and strategies used in native, second, and foreign language teaching. Language minority students must be exposed to challenging subject matter instruction that exposes students to authentic literature and interdisciplinary topics, or what Yawkey and Prewitt-Diaz (1990) call "massed" experiences with the same concept from various themes and subject areas. This challenging instruction has students keep journals, learn writing as a process, take part in hands-on activities and experiments, produce plays, read for pleasure and for academic content, prepare semantic maps, learn to interpret time lines, charts, diagrams, and maps, guess the meaning of unfamiliar vocabulary from context, learn to use computers, to name just a few activities that will prepare language minority students for academic success.[6]

We also know from the research that monolingual teachers who do not speak their students' languages can still support primary languages in many valuable ways, both attitudinally and instructionally. Assigning students who speak the same language to work in pairs or small groups to assist one another, allowing students to use bilingual dictionaries, and using students as linguistic resources are some of the multitude of ways in which monolingual teachers can support the use of the primary language.

Finally, we know from the research that parents play a pivotal role in the academic success of their children. Virtually every study reviewed in this chapter identified home-school collaboration as an essential component of effective programs for language minority students. The parents of language minority students must be encouraged to provide a rich verbal environment at home in the native language despite the reluctance they often express. Teachers must help them to realize how vital their linguistic input is and to understand the rationale behind the use of the primary language. And, if the parents do not speak English well, teachers should discourage them from interacting in English at home in the mistaken notion that it will benefit their children.

Teachers can forge the link between the home and school in a variety of ways.[7] They can encourage parents and/or older siblings to read books aloud in the home language and tell stories, folk tales, riddles, and

---

[6] For many more suggestions for challenging, interactive teaching strategies, see Richard-Amato and Snow (1992); Perez and Torres-Guzman (1992); and Williams and Snipper (1990).

[7] These useful suggestions are taken from Legarreta-Marcaida (1981), p. 107.

sayings from the home culture. Cultural knowledge, traditional celebrations, music, dance, poetry, and artifacts such as photographs, records, and letters of the primary language culture can also be shared with the children and incorporated into class activities. Teachers can encourage participation in a home-school library program where children bring primary language stories, magazines, and books home for family use and, in turn, check out primary language materials from the school library for use at home. Encouraging parents to help their children with homework and class assignments is a critical home-school collaborative venture. Lastly, teachers can work with their school or district administrators to establish parent literacy programs. Assisting parents to learn to read and write in the home language or in English is yet another bridge to literacy for both them and their children.

Opportunity awaits us. By developing the primary language skills of our language minority students, we are creating a foundation of literate behaviors which will ultimately prepare them for the rigors of the mainstream classroom and for successsful entry into the English-speaking academic and work environment. Furthermore, we are pre-serving the vital natural resources our students possess upon arrival at school by promoting native language literacy. Heath and Mangiola (1991) remind us "that the students we are becoming accustomed to labeling 'at risk' are actually—like all our students—children of promise" (p. 11). Primary language instruction, a bridge to literacy, offers a compelling strategy for assisting our language minority students to reach this potential.

REFERENCES

Baker, K., & de Kanter, A. (1983). Federal policy and the effectiveness of bilingual education. In K. Baker & A. de Kanter (Eds.), *Bilingual education: A reappraisal of federal policy* (pp. 33-86). Lexington, MA: Lexington Books.

Berman, P., Chambers, J., Gandara, P., McLaughlin, B., Minicucci, C., Nelson, B., Olsen, L., & Parrish, T. (1992). *Meeting the challenge of cultural diversity.* Vols. I-V. Berkeley, CA: BW Associates.

Cazden, C. B. (1992). *Language minority education in the United States: Implications of the Ramirez report.* (Educational Practice Report: 1). Santa Cruz, CA: The National Center for Research on Cultural Diversity and Second Language Learning.

Cazden, C. B., & Snow, C. E. (Eds.). (1990). English plus: Issues in bilingual education. *The Annals of the American Academy of Political and Social Science, 508.*

Christian, D., & Mahrer, C. (1991-1992; 1992-1993). *Two-way bilingual programs in the United States; 1992-1993 Supplement.* Santa Cruz, CA: The National Center for Research on Cultural Diversity and Second Language Learning.

Clark, E. R. (1990). The state of the art in research on teacher training models with special reference to bilingual education teachers. In Office of Bilingual Education & Minority Languages Affairs (Ed.), *Proceedings of the first research symposium on limited English proficient students' issues* (pp. 361-391). Washington, DC: U.S. Department of Education.

Collier, V. P. (1987). Age and rate of acquisition of second language for academic purposes. *TESOL Quarterly, 21,* 617-641.

Collier, V. P. (1989). How long? A synthesis of research on academic achievement in a second language. *TESOL Quarterly, 23,* 509-531.

Crawford, J. (1989). *Bilingual education: History, politics, theory and practice.* NJ: Crane.

Crawford, J. (Ed.). (1992). *Language loyalties: A source book on the official English controversy.* Chicago: University of Chicago Press.

Darcy, N. T. (1953). A review of the literature on the effects of bilingualism upon the measurement of intelligence. *Journal of Genetic Psychology, 82,* 21-57.

Gale, K., McClay, D., Christie, M., & Harris, S. (1981). Academic achievement in the Milingimbi bilingual education program. *TESOL Quarterly, 15,* 297-314.

Garcia, E. (1991). *Education of linguistically and culturally diverse students: Effective instructional practices* (Educational Practice Report: 1). Santa Cruz, CA: The National Center for Research on Cultural Diversity and Second Language Learning.

Goldenberg, C. (1991). *Instructional conversations and their classroom application.* (Educational Practice Report: 2). Santa Cruz, CA: The National Center for Research on Cultural Diversity and Second Language Learning.

Hakuta, K. (1986). *Mirror of language: The debate on bilingualism.* New York: Basic Books.

Hawkins, B. (1988). *Scaffolded classroom interaction and its relation to second language acquisition.* Unpublished doctoral dissertation, University of California, Los Angeles.

Heath, S. B. (1986). Socio-cultural contexts of language development. In *Beyond language: Social and cultural factors in schooling language minority students* (pp. 143-186). Los Angeles: Evaluation, Dissemination and Assessment Center, California State University.

Heath, S. B., & Mangiola, L. (1991). *Children of promise: Literature activity in linguistically and culturally diverse classrooms.* Washington, DC: National Education Association.

Kagan, S. (1986). Cooperative learning and sociocultural factors in schooling. In *Beyond language: Social and cultural factors in schooling language minority students* (pp. 231-298). Los Angeles: Evaluation, Dissemination and Assessment Center, California State University.

Krashen, S., & Biber, D. (1988). *On course: Bilingual education's success in California.* Sacramento: California Association for Bilingual Education.

Lambert, W. E. (1980). The social psychology of language: A perspective for the 1980s. In H. Giles, W. P. Robinson, & P. M. Smith (Eds.), *Language: Social psychological perspectives* (pp. 415-424). Oxford: Pergamon Press.

Legarreta-Marcaida, D. (1981). Effective use of the primary language in the classroom. In California State Department of Education (Ed.), *Schooling and language minority students: A theoretical framework* (1st ed.) (pp. 83-116). Los Angeles: Evaluation, Dissemination and Assessment Center, California State University.

Lessow-Hurley, J. (1990). *The foundations of dual language instruction.* New York: Longman.

Lindholm, K. J. (1990). Bilingual immersion education: Criteria for program development. In A. M. Padilla, H. H. Fairchild & C. M. Valdez (Eds.), *Bilingual education: Issues and strategies* (pp. 91-105). Newbury Park, CA: Sage.

Long, M., & Porter, P. (1985). Group work, interlanguage talk, and second language acquisition. *TESOL Quarterly, 19,* 207-228.

Lucas, T., & Katz, A. (1991). *A contradiction or sound pedagogy? The roles of language minority students' native languages in exemplary English-based programs.* Paper presented at the annual meeting of the American Educational Research Association, Chicago.

Lucas, T., Henze, R., & Donato, R. (1990). Promoting the success of Latino language-minority students: An exploratory study of six high schools. *Harvard Educational Review, 60,* 315-340.

Macnamara, J. T. (1966). *Bilingualism and primary education: A study of Irish experience.* Edinburgh: Edinburgh University Press.

Minicucci, C., & Olsen, L. (1992). Programs for secondary limited English proficient students: A California study. *Focus,* Vol. 5, Washington DC: National Clearinghouse for Bilingual Education.

Padilla, A. M. (1990). Bilingual education: Issues and perspectives. In A. M. Padilla, H. H. Fairchild, & C. M. Valdez (Eds.), *Bilingual education: Issues and strategies* (pp. 15-26). Newbury Park, CA: Sage.

Peal, E., & Lambert, W. E. (1962). The relation of bilingualism to intelligence. *Psychological Monographs, 76.*

Peitzman, F., & Gadda, G., (Eds.). (1991). *With different eyes: Insights into teaching language minority students across the disciplines.* Los Angeles: UCLA Center for Academic Inter-institutional Programs.

Perez, B., & Torres-Guzman, M. E. (1992). *Learning in two worlds: An integrated Spanish/English biliteracy approach.* New York: Longman.

Ramirez, J. D., Yuen, S. D., & Ramey, D. R. (1991). *Longitudinal study of structured English immersion strategy, early-exit and late-exit transitional bilingual programs for language-minority children.* Final Report to the U.S. Department of Education. Executive Summary and Vols. I and II. San Mateo, CA: Aguirre International.

Richard-Amato, P. A., & Snow, M. A. (Eds.). (1992). *The multi-cultural classroom: Readings for content-area teachers.* New York: Longman.

Rosebery, A. S., Warren, V., & Conant, F. (1992). *Appropriating scientific discourse: Findings from language minority classrooms.* (Research Report: 3). Santa Cruz, CA: The National Center for Research on Cultural Diversity and Second Language Learning.

Saville-Troike, M. (1984). What *really* matters in second language learning for academic achievement? *TESOL Quarterly, 18,* 199-219.

Simon, P. (1980). *The tongue-tied American: Confronting the foreign language crisis.* New York: Continuum.

Snow, C. E. (1987). *Second language learners' formal definitions: An oral language correlate of school literacy.* Technical Report No. 5. Los Angeles: UCLA Center for Language Education and Research.

Snow, C. E. (1990). Rationales for native language instruction: Evidence from research. In A. M. Padilla, H. H. Fairchild, & C. M. Valdez (Eds.), *Bilingual education: Issues and strategies* (pp. 60-74). Newbury Park, CA: Sage.

Snow, M. A., Hyland, J., Kamhi-Stein, L., & Yu, J.H. (in press). U.S. language minority students: Voices from the junior high classroom. In K. M. Bailey & D. Nunan (Eds.), *Voices from the classroom: The lives of language learners and teachers.*

Tharp, R. G., & Gallimore, R. (1988). *Rousing minds to life: Teaching, learning, and schooling in social context.* New York: Cambridge University Press.

Thompson, G. G. (1952). *Child psychology.* Boston: Houghton Mifflin.

Thompson, L., Christian, D., Stansfield, C. W., & Rhodes, N. (1990). Foreign language instruction in the United States. In A. M. Padilla, H. H. Fairchild, & C. M. Valdez (Eds.), *Foreign language education: Issues and strategies* (pp. 22-35). Newbury Park, CA: Sage.

Tickunoff, W. J., & Vasquez-Faria, J. A. (1982). Successful instruction for bilingual schooling. *Peabody Journal of Education, 52.*

Tickunoff, W. J., Ward, B. A., van Broekhuizen, D., Romero, M., Castañeda, L. V., Lucas, T., & Katz, A. (1991). *Final report: A descriptive study of significant features of exemplary special alternative instructional programs.* Los Alamitos, CA: Southwest Regional Laboratory.

Tucker, G. R. (1984). Toward the development of a language-competent American society. *International Journal of the Sociology of Language, 45,* 153-160.

Tucker, G. R. (1990). Second-language education: Issues and perspectives. In A. M. Padilla, H. H. Fairchild, & C. M. Valdez (Eds.), *Foreign language education: Issues and strategies* (pp. 13-21). Newbury Park, CA: Sage.

UNESCO (1953). The use of vernacular languages in education. *Monographs on Fundamental Education* (No. 8). Paris: UNESCO.

Vygotsky, L.S. (1978). *Mind in society: The development of higher psychological processes.* Cambridge, MA: Harvard University Press.

Wells, G. (1981). *Learning through interaction.* Cambridge: Cambridge University Press.

Williams, J. D., & Snipper, G. C. (1990). *Literacy and Bilingualism.* New York: Longman.

Willig, A. C. (1985). A meta-analysis of selected studies on the effectiveness of bilingual education. *Review of Educational Research, 55,* 269-317.

Wong-Fillmore, L. (1992). Against our best interest: The attempt to sabotage bilingual education. In J. Crawford (Ed.), *Language loyalties: A source book on the official English controversy* (pp. 367-376). Chicago: University of Chicago Press.

Wong-Fillmore, L. (1985). When does teacher talk work as input? In S. Gass & C. Madden (Eds.), *Input in second language acquisition* (pp. 17-50). New York: Newbury House.

Wood, D. J. Bruner, J. S., & Ross, G. (1976). The role of tutoring in problem solving. *Journal of Child Psychology and Psychiatry, 17,* 89-100.

Yawkey, T. D., & Prewitt-Diaz, J. O. (1990). Early childhood: Theories, research and implications for bilingual education. In Office of Bilingual Education & Minority Language Affairs (Ed.), *Proceedings of the first research symposium on limited English proficient students' issues* (pp. 161-192). Washington, DC: U.S. Department of Education.

Reading Instruction for
Language Minority Students

Eleanor Wall Thonis

Introduction

A dozen years have passed since the publication of *Schooling and Language Minority Students: A Theoretical Framework.* The purpose in 1981 was to examine some of the issues related to the improvement of reading instruction for an ever-increasing number of such students. It was agreed that minority language groups, without question, face many challenges when they enroll in schools of the United States. They may possess few skills in English, the language of the instructional program. They may also have a limited awareness or a television-distorted understanding of American cultural expectations. They may encounter a totally different school environment among peers who do not speak their language. The 1981 collection of papers focused on topics of first language acquisition, second language learning, natural approaches, effective classroom strategies, and reading program alternatives. The views of the contributors, as expressed then, were drawn from the research and practices of the sixties and seventies. This revision of the chapter on reading restates some of the earlier constructs, affirms many of the previous intuitions, updates several of the findings from relevant research, and poses a few of the continuing questions in the quest for improving reading instruction.

This chapter is organized into seven sections as follows: the relevant constructs, the developmental nature of reading, the student background factors, the methods, the materials, the transferability of skills, and the best of biliteracy.

Relevant Constructs

Given the enormous complications implicit in designing reading instruction for language minority students, it seems prudent to suggest that there is no *single* solution applicable to all students who are not native

English speakers. Generally, if students cannot speak a language and use its vocabulary, syntax, and functional grammar at the approximate level of a six-and-one-half-year-old child, learning to read that language will be difficult. If they are not encouraged to develop at least *one* language fully across all four modalities of listening, speaking, reading, and writing, then a functional illiteracy may be the unfortunate result. If the natural course of language acquisition and language development has not been encouraged as students interact with an environment and use language as an organizer, then ability to mediate meaning at higher levels of cognition may be thwarted. Maturation, language, age and other variables must be considered. In addition, there are social, political, and economic factors that may support or militate against the best conditions for learning to read. These concerns have been the subject of research and argument among educators everywhere.

In American schools, the past debate has centered around English-speaking children who are struggling with the capricious nature of the English writing system. Children who speak Engish advance quite logically to the written language for which they have oral forms. For more than a century, despite voluminous literature in the field of reading instruction, the controversy continues over methods and materials best suited for ensuring literacy in English. For educators interested in the teaching of reading to language minority children, however, there is not such a long history of combat nor as impressive a number of combatants. Recognition of the unique literacy needs of language minority students in classrooms where English is the language of instruction is relatively recent. The research has been controversial and the recommendations, contradictory. Data from investigations of native language literacy as the introductory program have been overruled by data on the success of immersion in second language literacy plans (Bowen, 1977; Tucker, 1977). Findings suggesting early introduction to second language writing systems have been canceled by conclusions on the effectiveness of later introduction. Achievement levels in school subjects have been variously determined as better or worse when offered in native or second language. See Cummins's discussion of the length of time required for language minority students to develop proficiency in English in this volume.)

Well-developed speech, functional literacy, and adequate thinking ability are essential for success in school. Teachers at all levels agree that learning can best take place when students speak well, read easily, and think effectively. When all the students in a class are native English speakers, teachers are challenged to provide for *personalized* growth of listening and speaking abilities, for *individualized* literacy skills, and for the *unique* thinking strategies demonstrated by different students with diverse competencies in the *one* language. When students not native to English are in classrooms designed for English speakers, teachers are even more sorely pressed to adapt the educational offerings for students. Among the questions tormenting teachers are: Should the native language be used for instruction? Should reading and writing be introduced in the native language? How does language processing influence thinking? Partial answers to such questions may be found in an appraisal of the underlying assumptions that form the basis of available programs. Teachers should consider the various theoretical positions with a view to the influences each would exert in preserving the vital bond between speech and print and in promoting a unity between language (both oral and written) and thinking. If it can be argued that these three elements are essential requirements for optimum school achievement, then it follows that classroom practices must nurture the speech-print-thought triangle in consistent and appropriate ways. All normal human beings use language in their daily lives. This ability serves individuals in personal and social situations requiring communication.

Communicative Competence. There are several definitions of communicative competence: the ability to interact with other speakers (Savignon, 1991), the appropriate use of language in social contexts, and the sensitivity to sociocultural differences in the ways that students learn. (See Crawford's review of communicative approaches in this volume.)

The Functions of Teachers. Among the several attributes described by Berliner (1985) as the "executive functions of teacher" is the responsibility for creating a pleasant environment that emphasizes mutual respect, shared responsibility, politeness, and the valuing of social groups. Often, these aspects of teaching are thought to refer only to the control of deviant behavior and to the maintenance of a workplace where students attend to the business of learning. Yet, the value of a pleasant, respectful workplace for both students and adults is self-evident.

Learning Styles of Students. Archambeault (1992) has suggested that students' study styles may be identified in two areas: the students' preferences for strategies, and the environmental conditions in which students learn. She points out that the preferences for specific strategies may have already developed on the basis of the successes or failures of previously applied strategies. However, the learning environments may still contribute to effective or distracting habits, such as self-monitoring and self-awareness needed for metacognitive techniques.

Reflection in Learning. Reflection is the art of "turning inward" to consider thoughtfully ideas and responses beyond information that is provided through the senses. In classroom practice, there may be little time allowed for students to reflect silently so that communicative competence may be appreciated as *interpersonal* as well as *intrapersonal* characteristics of intelligent answers. Unfortunately, such limited opportunities for reflective thought may promote poor learning strategies and careless work habits (Tarvin and Al-Arishi, 1991).

The Developmental Nature of Reading

A very sensible definition of reading is given by Johnson and Myklebust (1967) who state that reading is a response to a visual symbol superimposed on auditory language. Beginning readers bring their experiences as encoded and stored to the page of print. They practice making accurate and speedy associations between auditory and visual language symbols. They grow to be efficient, rapid readers until they are scarely aware of the speech-print relationship. Capable students who are free from any serious learning problems read well, expand their real and imaginary worlds, and become literate. Accomplished readers have engaged in a process taking them through a sequence of activities as follows: (1) see print, (2) transform print into recognizable sounds and arrangements of sounds, (3) relate what has been recognized to experience, (4) construct meaning from prior knowledge and print, and (5) store print and the associations (meaning) for further use. This process moves the reader from the known to the unknown, from a reality represented by sounds to a new reality represented by symbols. Successful reading depends upon the number and quality of experiences stored; the general level of oral language development; the keenness of sensory-motor skills; the suitability of the instructional program for the reader; and the personal levels of interest, motivation, intelligence, and health. For all persons reading any language, reading is a process of seeing print, hearing speech, and associating whatever it is that has been seen and heard with stored and remembered experiences, called *referents.* When the reader sees the word *acrolith,* for example, this visual stimulus must be changed into an auditory one. The reader may decide, according to the word recognition strategies he or she uses, to say the word. If the reader doesn't know very much about Greek statues, the meaning of what has been seen and said will be unclear or completely lacking. Reading has not been accomplished until the meaning is constructed or discovered. Sometimes a reader can use context clues, picture clues, or other techniques that will help gather the meaning from material that may be unfamiliar. If reference to *acrolith* is within the subject matter content of Greek art, then the reader may be able to *reduce the uncertainties* in Smith's terms (1971) and gain an understanding of what has been read. The nature of the process itself calls to mind the "Vernacular Advantage Theory" (Modiano, 1968; Engle, 1975; Ramirez, 1991).

Oral language grows out of specific contacts with a particular environment. These experiences are mediated by the conventions of a specific speech community. Spoken language, as acquired, forms the basis for the specific conventions of the writing system of that same community. The mutuality, the interdependence between spoken and written language, can be perceived by the reader. There is little need to be reminded that many readers have difficulty learning to read their own language. Reading is more than a perceptual and a sensory-motor process; it is also a cognitive process. The successful reader must bring a background of concepts and ideas to a page of print. The amount and kind of comprehension the reader takes from that page is in direct proportion to what is brought. The reader must supply or infer the context. Unlike personal exchange in informal situations where meaning can be obtained from the contextual flavor of the situation, the exchange between reader and author may have a context that is known only to the writer. As Cummins (1980) has suggested, while language development of students may be adequate for situations in which the context is supplied informally, such language development may be quite inadequate for successful functioning in the decontextualized demands of formal schooling, particularly in the written language of textbooks. This statement could apply to both language majority and language minority students alike. The important difference for language minority students is one of distance from the context. They may have had far less exposure to the concepts represented by the vocabulary and may have not had the time to become familiar with the vocabulary and/or the grammatical and syntactical clues needed to predict meanings.

Human speech is graphically represented in a variety of forms that may be alphabetic, syllabic, logographic, or otherwise symbolic of the spoken word. Speech existed long before its graphic representation. Both oral and written forms of language are interdependent and share a mutual relationship. Well-developed speech provides the foundation for skill development in reading and writing. When students learn to read and write, they must organize the visual system of language in such a way as to make it meaningful according to the auditory system. They must make sense of writing by making a connection with the spoken language as represented. Words and their arrangements that students have learned to describe and explain their experiences become available to them in a visual form. The act of reading is a receptive one in which students see print, hear speech, and connect them to referents remembered and stored from their personal experiences (Thonis, 1976). Until the essential attachment to a meaningful referent has been accomplished, it cannot be said that students are reading.

In the usual course of human development, normal children learn to understand and to speak the language of the speech community into which they have been born. If the language has a written form, it is generally expected that the children will also learn to read and write that same language. In most parts of the world, this learning of the written forms of language is ordinarily provided during the years of middle childhood. Literacy is a task of the school-age years and is accomplished in a school setting. Thus, the students learn to listen, speak, read, and write the language that makes sense to them in the total environment in which they are living and growing. Reality has been interpreted and labeled by speech; speech is preserved through its representation in writing; and discrepancies that may exist between what is heard or said and what is read or written can be clarified and supplemented by the connections between reality, its oral label, and its written form. All writing systems are imperfect, but their imperfections can be managed and meaning can still come through when the students fill in any gaps in comprehension from their experiences and from their reservoir of oral language.

Students who speak Cantonese, Korean, Punjabi, Spanish, or one of the hundreds of languages other than English and who are learning to read and write in English, often have difficulty in supplying the needed information to obtain meaning. They may have a wealth of data stored, but their memories and concepts are not retrievable in response to English stimuli. The essential connections among speech, print, and referent cannot be formed. Smith (1971) has referred to reading comprehension as an act of "reducing the uncertainties" found in written language. When language minority students are attempting to deal with the uncertainties, they are (or may be) already burdened by the additional unknowns of the new visual forms, the unfamiliar structures, the strange vocabulary items, and the different view of reality. When these students see English print, hear their native speech, and seek meaningful referents drawn from their cultural heritage, they may fail to make connections. At best, their reading skill is stopped at the decoding level or, at worst, the written material may not make any sense to them at all. School districts with large numbers of language minority students only need to examine their own annual testing programs to discover the failure rates of these students.

There has been interest and excitement generated over the programs of reading instruction among select groups who have been introduced to reading by way of the second rather than the first language (Bowen, 1977; Tucker, 1977; Cohen, 1974). The "immersion" programs may take a variety of organizational models. The investigators take issue with the assumption that the speech-print connection is of primary importance and suggest that social-cultural factors may contribute more positively to the literacy skills of language minority students. English-speaking children placed in the Spanish language arts curriculum or French-speaking children assigned to English classes are two examples of immersion programs. The theorists have been careful to distinguish between immersion programs and submersion ones. Though they both represent a plan of instruction in which the child's home language is not used primarily, the important difference in programs of submersion may be found in the status of the school language, the continued valuing and use of the home language outside of school, the point at which all students begin in the school's language, and the attitudes of the school-community toward learning the language (Cohen and Swain, 1976). It has been suggested that language minority students immersed in a second language are given rewards and approval for each small increment of learning via that second language. This distinction becomes an important one for language minority students who are mixed in reading classes with English speakers. For these students, their submersion practically guarantees reading difficulties and limited achievement.

The Lambert and Tucker research (1972) suggested that English-speaking children immersed in French reading programs in Canada continued to achieve adequately in English reading without receiving instruction in it. Cohen (1975) found that English-speaking students who learned to read Spanish first, achieved grade level competence in English. These experiments and others of a similar type are generally cited as support for placing students from language minorities in English reading programs immediately. Immersed or submersed, the language minority students must keep afloat, learn to swim, or eventually sink. The data from studies on immersion and submersion point up the social and cultural determiners of successful school achievement, the potential for language skill transfer, and effective dimensions of learning. Setting aside for the moment the social and cultural factors, it appears reasonable to suggest that the advantage of dealing with one's experiences, speech, and written language all within the same common framework of the vernacular is undeniable. If the home language is absolutely unacceptable for political or social reasons or if the language has positively no economic value, then the speech-print connections must still be made in the second language. The language minority students from this group should have opportunities for extended readiness to read with rich and varied activities designed to promote oral language sufficient to support the print of English.

Student Background Factors

The language minority student is first a student and must be seen as a maturing, developing person. Students in elementary and secondary schools are normally en route to the expected developmental milestones in physical, social, emotional, and intellectual maturity according to the universal rules of human growth. Sometimes it is necessary to remind teachers and administrators of this ordinary fact when language minority students are under discussion. The descriptor *language minority* appears to take precedent over the word *student,* as educational plans are considered for them. Language minority students share the same needs as students of any language. Every serious professional in education knows what these common needs are. When it comes to identifying language and literacy needs, however, there is likely to be little agreement as to what those needs may be. One of the serious drawbacks of planning for minority language students stems from a lack of information about the language background. Often, all of the students are grouped together under one description: bilingual. The nature of the individual student's bilingualism is rarely identified with care and precision. In fact, the label *bilingual* often conceals more about the student than it reveals. Students may be at a serious disadvantage because once labeled bilingual, they may then be assumed to fit some predetermined category. Thus, their basic needs may be ignored and their language needs may be undifferentiated. The descriptive designation *bilingual* has been applied to students who come from another country, to students with certain physical characteristics, to students with ethnic surnames, and to students whose parents speak accented English. The criteria for using the term are often vague or misunderstood. To be bilingual suggests that students are capable of using two languages. Further, it is assumed that both languages can be used with relatively equal facility. To describe precisely what is meant by the term *bilingual student,* it is necessary to determine how the students can function in both oral and written language. There are sounds, structures, vocabulary, and meaning systems for both dimensions. When students are competent listeners, speakers, readers, and writers in one language, they control eight dimensions as native speakers. When the students add the sounds, structure, vocabulary, and meaning systems of the second language, eight more are added. Thus, bilingual persons are capable of managing sixteen separate and mutually supportive facets of both languages (proficient bilingualism). These students are rare, especially in United States' classrooms where monolingual, monoliterate education has inhibited or eradicated dual language opportunities.

If reading programs are to suit the varying degrees of language proficiency that language minority students bring to school, they must be designed on the basis of better information about language minority students and their functioning levels in the several dimensions. Language minority students may listen and understand but not speak, or speak but not read or write, or write and read but not speak. The combinations of possible competencies among the receptive and expressive phases of both oral and written language are many. The decision to assign a student to a reading class in the first language, to immerse the student in a second language reading group, to submerse the student in a particular reading program, or to offer two reading programs simultaneously could be improved by careful, thoughtful assessment of language strengths in all language functions.

The schooling opportunities that language minority students may have enjoyed in another setting may influence their abilities to cope with programs of reading instruction. Young students may not have had formal lessons in reading. They may still be at the prereading level of development and may only need to continue along the usual course of reading readiness. A few older students may also be found to be preliterate because they may have come from small towns and villages where they could not have attended school. Both of these groups of students share similar needs in getting ready to read. They need to coordinate eye and hand, refine motor responses, become aware of directionality and spatial factors of the written language, and sharpen their perceptual skills. These prerequisites for skillful reading apply across languages. There are specific background skills needed for different languages that must be addressed specific ways. At the prereading level, it is essential to consider the general factors that promote strong background abilities for literacy and the specific skills that must be nurtured within the context of a specific language. For example, the accuracy and speed with which students note differences in forms of written language is a general ability that promotes attention to fine visual details. This awareness can be applied in a global way to any writing system. But the distinction of detail between *b* and *d* or *w* and *m* would only be specific to forms of the Roman alphabet and would not necessarily apply to all alphabets.

Language minority students who have already learned to read their own language often amaze the reading teacher in a second language class. Adequate or better skills in the first language and good study habits may contribute to helping such students ease into the demands of the new writing system. If students are developmentally mature enough to have reached levels of thinking logically and abstractly, then they appear to be much better able to fit well into the new reading program. Such students call to mind the several constructs proposed to explain the apparent success of older students. Lambert (1975) writes of the *additive* effects of learning a second language while retaining the first. Majority language students who are immersed in a second language program have the opportunity to acquire the second language at no cost to the first. Older students already fluent and literate in one language may also enjoy this additive quality. On the other hand, it would appear that students with poorly developed language and literacy skills in the first language who are forced to take on another system prematurely or at the expense of the first may suffer *subtractive* effects. Cummins (1979) has considered these positive and negative influences in his *Threshold Hypothesis,* which posit that the level of language competence of language minority students may influence intellectual growth. Cummins (1980) also states that a *Developmental Interdependence Hypothesis,* which assumes that second language competence is partially a function of first language competence at the time of exposure to the second language, may account for the modest results of native language and literacy programs in the elementary grades. One obvious effect of such programs would be the time and opportunity provided to acquire concepts and to develop the vocabulary that explains them. Also, practice with more complex syntactical patterns and instruction in word formation and informal grammar improves the understanding of how a language system works and what generalizations about written forms can apply.

Many of the language minority students can be described as functionally illiterate. These are students who appear to have poorly developed language and literacy skills in two languages. They may not ever have learned to read and to write in their native language and may have had little success in learning to read the second one. These students are at a great disadvantage in the classroom because after the first or second grade, most of the school work is carried on in reading and in writing. Lambert (1975) would see these students as suffering from the subtractive effects of their language experiences. In Cummins's terms (1979), they would still be functioning below the first threshold. Language minority students who are failing to learn to read in school can easily be recognized in this group of underachievers. It would appear that the vital role of first language development in nurturing intellectual growth has been ignored, and most of these students have been struggling to organize school content in the second language. Both first and second language organizing fails because neither is fully developed. An unfortunate consequence is the loss of self-esteem and the deep sense of failure that may prevent students from becoming successful readers even when supportive programs are offered. Then students are likely to perceive their school problems as their own fault rather than the possible fault of an inappropriate program of reading instruction.

The Methods

Reading methods for language minority students are often debated from the viewpoint of whether the code or the meaning approach is the better. The synthetic method emphasizes the letters, sounds, syllables, and smaller segments of the written language. The analytic method in which whole words or utterances are presented stresses meaning at every level. How the parts of the writing system go together is not considered of great importance. Making sense of the written material and comprehending the ideas and events are the important goals of the reading instruction. For languages with many irregularities in the speech-print correspondence, like French or English, the analytic approach has worked well for some students. Eclectic methods offer the opportunities both to learn the code and to obtain meaning. Regardless of the method, to read is to comprehend and to comprehend is to think.

In the broadest sense, all methods may be grouped into three major categories: (1) synthetic approaches, (2) analytic approaches, or (3) approaches that combine both the synthetic and analytic. Synthetic methods stress part-whole relationships and give emphasis to building meaningful words or sentences as letters, sounds, and/or syllables are mastered. There is a heavy responsibility to learn how to "crack the code." Analytic methods focus on whole words and meaningful sentences which are examined further for their elements. A synthetic-analytic method may combine features that offer both the *code* and the *meaning* emphasis.

Synthetic Approaches

Several of the traditional reading methods used in learning to read those languages based upon an alphabetic writing principle are synthetic. For example, the onomatopoeic method in Spanish is one in which the students learn to make a single sound association for each visual symbol in order to remember the speech-print relationship that is represented. Each time the students see a symbol, they are to associate the letter with a familiar sound from the environment. For example, when learning the *u,* children are told to recall the sound of a train whistle; or when learning the *t,* they are reminded of the ticking of a clock. As they build a repertoire of such associations, they gradually accumulate enough of them to read at least at the level of decoding. The onomatopoeic method is frequently a delight to young learners. It *is* fun and it can be paced according to the rate at which students are making, storing, and retrieving connections between sounds and symbols. However, it can be a very artificial approach, one resulting in lessons that are very contrived and that contain stilted, unnatural language. It places such a strong emphasis on the recall of discrete elements that the *code* may emerge to detract from the *meaning.*

Another synthetic method is the alphabetic method. The pupil learns all the *names* of the letters of the alphabet. Unlike the onomatopoeic method, no attention is given to the sounds represented by the letters. The learner uses his/her knowledge of letter names to unlock words by spelling them, letter by letter. The method is easy to initiate and convenient for teachers, but it can be cumbersome and limiting. The students are blending *letters,* not *sounds,* and they may become confused when they are unable to unlock words that have been obscured by their spellings. Because the *whole* of anything is more than the sum of its parts, attention to small elements of written language may tend to create readers who fail to grasp the larger, more meaningful units.

The phonic method has many enthusiastic supporters. A phonic method is one in which the sound system of the language is primary. Students must hear speech sounds (the phonemes) and make accurate and rapid associations with the written symbols (the graphemes) representing them. Once they have the speech-print connections mastered, they are expected then to decode; that is, they can transform the written symbols back into the spoken ones. The phonic method has been very popular in languages where there is a good *fit* between speech and print, and when the written language is a fairly consistent, predictable representation of speech. The sound-symbol associations can be learned with relative ease by most students. There are in many languages what the linguists call a *poor fit* between speech and print. The same letter may represent different sounds, different letters may represent the same sound, or letters change their sounds in different word environments. There may be a very elaborate diphthong system or a system of diacritical marks to be learned in some languages. Speech-symbol relationships may be presented by means of picture-symbols, which require the learners to make an association with a picture, usually one representing an object in their world. The pictured object's name begins with the sound to be represented by the letter. The sound-symbol relationships may also be taught directly by presenting the letter name and the sound represented by the letter together with illustrations of the sounds in words familiar to the children. In Spanish, *el método fónico,* in its several variations, lends itself to a reasonable sequence with short units of speech-print understandings to be acquired and practiced as the program progresses. It can become boring and seem unrelated to the *total* act of reading unless the teacher adds the element of interest with tongue twisters *(trabalenguas),* rhymes *(rimas),* poems *(poesia),* and other language activities. Further, the method does focus on parts of words and may result in students learning to decode at the expense of gaining meaning. It is wise to remember that phonic skills in many languages may be great for unlocking unfamiliar words but, by themselves, contribute little to the comprehension of those words.

The syllabic method is another very traditional and time-honored method that depends heavily on the child's auditory memory. Part-whole approaches in small units of speech-print relationships can be offered to students as they are able to internalize and use them. Syllables may be organized and sequenced carefully to permit students to begin using them immediately in words and in sentences that provide meaning. The opportunity to apply the skills directly to the act of reading allows learners to feel that they are not merely acquiring some isolated information like letter names and letter sounds, which may often appear only peripherally related to *real reading*. Of this method it must be said, however, that it falls heir to the same criticism as other approaches that emphasize small units of speech sounds and their written representations in symbols.

Analytic Approaches

Among the analytic ways of teaching reading, the language experience approach has been used with some degree of success. The students are encouraged to respond to events in their experience by recalling what they have thought about and can put into words. The teacher or teacher aide then writes what has been said, reads it back, asks for several repetitions of it until the students, too, can read what has been written. Since the material comes from a meaningful experience in the students' own world, there is no question of comprehension. The students see the relationships among thinking, speaking, reading, and writing. They next learn the writing system and can create their own accounts of personal experiences. The teacher is responsible for maintaining a rich and interesting classroom environment that will elicit language and generate experiences about which talking, writing, and reading can be accomplished. For students from any language, the language experience approach can be a delight. They may draw upon culturally relevant and familiar topics that are near and dear to them. They are assimilating written language in whole phrases or sentences that make instant sense because they are their very own thoughts. The teacher enjoys the students' interest and motivation. However, this approach demands much of both teacher and learners. The teacher must manage an enormous amount of material, different for each child, since each student's language and experiences are unique. There is the ongoing requirement to change and to create new stimuli for more complex language and its written representation. In order to keep track of student progress, there is the considerable burden of recordkeeping so that the teacher will be able to follow individual development in the various reading skills. There is little or no control of vocabulary so that practice needed for mastery may not occur and words learned today may be forgotten tomorrow. The success or failure of such a reading approach depends in large measure upon many other classroom variables, one of which is how the teacher uses stories the students have produced.

The global method is one in which whole words and entire sentences are produced visually and the students are told what they are. They then memorize the words without ever taking them apart to look at their small elements. It is a *look-say* approach that stresses meanings and ignores the writing system as a code. Expressions such as *Today is Monday;* or customary classroom amenities such as *Good morning* are taught in their entirety. Theorists who support this method argue that dividing the words into syllables and learning the letters and sounds may create absurdities and destroy meaning, the heart of the reading process. The global method has its merits. It offers reading activities that students can readily understand *if the written material is prepared by the teacher at a level commensurate with students' experience.* It places a great burden on memory, however, and has been said to offer few or no opportunities to acquire basic awareness of how the writing system works. Expansion of the reading vocabulary and development of specific reading skills may not take place unless the teacher goes further with supplementary activities.

The generative word method operates much as the global method. Whole words and complete sentences are presented, illustrated, and pronounced by the students. After they have memorized the material and can read it, they *then* are taught how to analyze sentences and words into their component elements. Thus, they go from a meaningful emphasis to the code and analyze how the code has been put together to create the meanings for them. They may discover syllables, sounds, letters, punctuation marks, and capitalization. The students have finished the analysis, and they have a good grasp of both the *code* and the *meaning*. It has been said that one danger is the pitfall of passivity in the students. The teacher must do most of the analyzing; and once the students *know* what the written language represents, there is not much motivation for them to dig back into the *parts* that have created a meaningful *whole* for them already.

Eclecticism

The eclectic method is one that combines successful elements of both synthetic and analytic approaches in an attempt to offer students an effective reading program. It may include the presentation of whole sentences, identification of speech-print relationships by phonics, *look-say* practice with flash cards, use of the learner's own language, use of pictures for clues, and a variety of other features drawn from several methods.

It is prudent for teachers to consider *first* the student who is to be served by the reading approach and to recognize that no *one* method has a monopoly on success in the classroom. There are students with great visual memories, students with well-developed oral language, and students with good tactile-kinesthetic skills. There are *also* students who are weak in one or more of these areas. Add to this the fact that some students have long attention spans and some do not; some can persist in the completion of a task and some cannot; some are able to take direction and follow instructions and some are not. Yet all students have *something* the teacher may draw upon to ensure that they find a measure of success in learning to read.

Which of the methods are applicable to the teaching of both English and native language reading? Any method wisely used by a careful, knowledgeable teacher can be applied *if* it is suitable for the background and unique needs of students (Thonis, 1976, 1983). If students' auditory integrities are weak, a method that demands hearing and discriminating among fine speech differences (as required by the phonic method) would be a poor choice. If students have phenomenal visual strengths, a method that taps this ability to remember visually presented materials and arrange them in proper sequence (as the global method demands) may be an excellent alternative. Students with impressive command of oral language and rich stores of experiences may find an introduction to print that uses their language and experience an exciting encounter. The teacher is the one who must select the best methods to make the most of the reading opportunities. For language minority students, the language experience approach could be very effective in the teaching of *both* English and native language reading. A phonics method, one demanding the pupil to hear sounds and speech patterns, could be productive for native language reading and a disaster for English reading. Students could find it difficult if not impossible to hear accurately and to discriminate among the sounds of English. A method using whole words and sentences taken solely from an English-speaking cultural setting may be totally devoid of sensibility or interest for language minority students. Thus, the choice of methods certainly could be different for the *two* reading classes. It would be a grave error to assume that the *same* methods would necessarily apply to the teaching of both. It is essential to determine the method on the basis of first- and second-language readiness to read *each specific language* and the levels of language development in both native language and in English.

Lesson Design

Identifying a blueprint for lesson design, Merino (1991) outlines six principles as follows:

- Use of contextualized language (Krashen, 1982)
- Active student participation in high interest areas (Swain, 1983)
- Problem-solving activities, through joint negotiation (Long, 1990)
- Hierarchical presentation of concepts (Krashen, 1982)
- Recycling of concepts (Krashen, 1982)
- Cooperative grouping of limited and fluent English-speaking students (Kagan, 1986)

In summarizing the blueprint, Merino drew upon Krashen's construct of comprehensible input; the socio-affective filter; hierarchical presentation of concepts; and the recycling of concepts. They also use Kagan's cooperative groupings of limited and fluent students; Long's theory of negotiation of interaction; and Swain's theory of comprehensible output. Merino concludes by writing: "Simply put, we must have reasons for what we do."

Hiebert (1991) writes that some strategies have not been fully explored. For example, an examination of word-level strategies has become an unpopular topic because it is considered to be closely associated with traditional teaching skills. Hiebert also asks, "Can word-level strategies be revisited within the context of authentic reading and writing tasks?" These strategies may need different emphases for students who are discovering books and print for the first time in contrast to students who have enjoyed such experiences at home. Hiebert worked with small groups of students who, after shared reading, practiced writing on chalkboards or magnetic boards. Later, they had an opportunity to use these same words in their writing. Their shared reading had the advantage of allowing the students to see the text and read it along with the teacher and peers. It was important for the teacher to use the specific words as the highlight of the lessons. Hiebert points out that more study about the effectiveness of word-level practice in this manner should be carried out.

Social Context

The social context in which language is acquired has been addressed by several researchers. From these investigations such variables as cooperative learning, metalanguage communicative competence, groupings practices, and writing as a social act have been examined (Johnson, 1991; Savignon, 1991; Murphy, 1991; Bruder and Henderson, 1986; Hiebert, 1991; Hernandez-Chavez, 1984; Dolson, 1985; see also Snow's comments on the nature of the interactive classroom and the benefits that accrue to learners as they negotiate meanings in this volume).

Cooperative Learning

Encouraging students to work in small groups has been hailed as a great improvement over solitary, individual learners who struggle and compete in a classroom. Learning to work together collaboratively while pooling talents, knowledge, and skills has drastically altered the environment of many classrooms. Increased student achievement depends upon these variables: (1) individual responsibility and (2) the nature of the group goal. (See also Snow's description of the effectiveness of small group instruction in promoting classroom interaction among students in this volume.)

The natural processes of perceiving, thinking, and learning are receiving greater attention from the area of cognitive psychology and its related fields. Bransford and Vye (1989) and Beck (1989) ask the questions: (1) What do competent readers and writers know and do? (2) What is the initial (pre-instructional) state of the learner and how does this initial state match the goals of instruction? and (3) How do students *progress* from where they were initially and how do they develop more competence? Researchers remind the practitioners in classrooms that learners do not begin instruction as blank slates and may bring misconceptions to instruction. If the learner is full of misinformation, then a primary goal of the activities must be to clear up these misconceptions. Students then will be equipped to move on from factual knowledge to procedural knowledge. This viewpoint leads to the emphasis on "learning by doing," not merely providing additional practice in workbook-type exercises. One of the significant elements is "coached practice" in a social setting that emphasizes cooperative learning.

Palinscar and Brown (1989) recommend reciprocal teaching, an oral language activity, as a variant of cooperative learning. They note that reciprocal teaching in small groups of primary children has been an effective means of improving listening comprehension. Bermudez and Prater (1989) make a strong case for direct instruction to improve comprehension and retention. They think teachers cannot assume that ESL students will have the ability to solve and organize their ideas purely on the basis of opportunities to brainstorm, cluster, or summarize. They suggest that ESL students especially need to think, read, and write in "an integrated manner as they are acquiring communicative skills in English." They also believe that writing opportunities will enhance the students' abilities in higher-order thinking skills.

The Classroom Environment

Glatthorn (1989) asks the question: What kind of classroom environment will be most conducive to the development of writing and thinking skills? His view of the research summarizes these *traditional* teacher behaviors:

- Sets and enforces limits for behavior
- Sets reasonably high expectations for students

- Provides a clear structure for organizing verbal learning
- Provides guided and independent practice
- Monitors behavior and keeps students on task
- Provides feedback

These descriptions cover a task-oriented, highly *structured* environment. The fact that these teacher behaviors are described as *traditional* does not necessarily mean that they have no place in the contemporary classroom. Like many practices labeled as traditional, they have value in a classroom environment where there is a balance of structure and freedom.

Integration of skills

Adams (1990) in her summary of *Thinking and Learning About Print* asks the question: "With so much underlying agreement, why is there so much outward dispute?" Her conclusions are described in five categories as follows:

- Predictors of reading acquisition
- Before formal instruction begins
- Beginning to read
- Phonics instruction
- Beyond the basics

Considerations of each of these five areas include reminders that instruction is effective or ineffective only to the extent to which these pieces are "fitted together" to complement and to support the needs of the students. In each of them, there are strong statements relative to the importance of listening, speaking, reading, writing, and thinking in activities that encourage the integration of language and literacy skills in meaningful context. Adams makes a strong case for the maxim that the *whole* is certainly more than the *sum* of its parts.

Whole Language

Whole language principles in teaching reading and writing suggest the following (Goodman, 1987; Rigg, 1991):

- Knowledge is socially constructed.
- Language creates and communicates meaning.

- Functions of language must be authentic and make sense.
- Materials must be real.
- Writing must have a real and relevant purpose.
- Language is both social and individual.
- Literacy is a *part* of, not separate from, language.

These principles as implemented in a classroom mean that language instruction is student-centered; activities must have real, not contrived purposes; students may select from among activities offered; students and teachers both must enjoy the respect of their peers. (See Crawford's connection among sheltered English, whole language, and communicative approaches in this volume.)

Grammar

The formal teaching of grammar has been criticized by many theorists. Grammar has only a small influence on the acquisition of communicative competence according to Krashen (1985). There are some teachers and students, too, who may find explicit grammar task assignments boring. It appears that second language learners do not always have the *metalanguage* to talk about grammar as a subject. The present research does not fully address the effective formats for presenting grammar tasks. Formats that could enliven the social interaction have not been given much attention. Grammar "purists" are at times offended when told to ignore errors as a natural occurrence in the course of language growth (Fotos and Ellis, 1991).

Goldenberg (1990) suggests caution in selecting one method over another. He sees value in early opportunities for beginning readers to learn about letter-sound associations and the formation of syllables. He found that in his Spanish reading program, such practices were very successful. Goldenberg and the two very competent teachers with whom he worked found that it was more difficult to implement the listening experiences, dictation of stories, and other "top-down" approaches. Although this project of teaching Spanish-speaking children to read specifically examined the code emphasis versus the meaning emphasis in learning to read Spanish, the questions generated by the researchers are the same ones asked by those who explore early reading English. Goldenberg (1991) asks similar questions in his exploration of the balance of skills and meaning in the beginning literacy programs of New Zealand.

The Materials

When majority language students are learning to read, one of the joyous opportunities they have is their practice outside the classroom. They can take their readers and school library books home or go to the community libraries with their parents or family members. They are surrounded by signs, advertisements, newspaper, menus, and numerous written reminders that reading and writing are valued. Out-of-school practice reinforces the skills being developed in their daily lessons and results in improved learning. For language minority students, however, the practice depends on several conditions. Some language minority children learning to read the vernacular have parents who do not read. There are few library books in the home language on the shelves in the school and community libraries to challenge and delight them. The majority language surrounds them when they leave the classroom. Newspapers, magazines, restaurant lists, notices, and other written materials are offered in the language of the majority. Or, if language minority students are attempting to read in the second language, they may find it very difficult to handle the concept loading and speech-print connections of the media beyond the classroom. If they wish to share their second language literacy skills with their family, it may turn out that parents do not read the language. These are social and cultural factors discussed by Bowen (1977) and Tucker (1977) who feel that social and cultural considerations are more important than linguistic ones in deciding which literacy program is best for language minorities. The school is an institution created by society and is expected to reflect the values of that society. The expectations of the school and community certainly must be considered and weighed carefully.

An important issue is the selection of reading materials for language minority students. Both the suitability of the materials and their availability must be considered. If language minority students are being taught to read in their native language, it may be very disappointing for the students to find few or no books to read. When majority language students learn to read, they are likely to find the delight and wonder of stories, records, tapes, and other media for practice and for pleasure. Minority language students ordinarily do not find such treasures in school and community libraries of the United States. Like most skills, the skills of literacy are of little value if they are not used. If these students are to enjoy their hard-won skills, the school must consider seriously the addition of native language books and other materials to supplement the classroom instruction and to extend opportunities for growth in reading and thinking skills.

An appraisal of the suitability of materials is often a difficult task because there are so many elements involved in their selection. Minimally, teachers should take into account the appearance, the illustrations, the authenticity of language, the representative nature of the content, the relevance to the curriculum, and the cost. Materials should be attractive; the print should be an appropriate size; the quality of paper and binding should be adequate for the kind of use anticipated; the structures, vocabulary, sentence length, and concept loading should be suitable; and the political or religious content should be acceptable to the community. It is especially important that the materials not be hastily patched together translations of English. The cultural content should be interesting and relevant to the language minority students. The international literature of childhood and adolescence is stocked with charming stories that enchant students everywhere. Many classics from English have been lovingly translated into other languages with great care and with attention to idiomatic expressions, figurative language, vocabulary, and cultural detail. The concepts and values drawn from other cultural settings should be free from stereotyping. The views of various ways of living should be presented objectively. Reading materials should emphasize the commonalities among various groups as well as their differences. Reading materials carefully chosen on the basis of the language needs and developmental levels of minority students contribute greatly to learning success.

The Parents

It is noteworthy that successful reading programs, regardless of approach or language sequence, generally include strong support for reading at home. The literature describes the importance of the value given to reading. The reading interests of parents, the availability of reading materials, and many other family variables all may contribute or detract from students' learning to read. The traditional recommendations offered have been to invite parents to volunteer in classrooms; serve on school committees; read to their children at home; take them on visits to museums and places of historic interest; and other such suggestions requiring time, transportation, materials, money, and a knowledge of community resources that many minority language families lack. School personnel also have been fairly consistent in their recommendations that language minority families use the majority language in the home.

Parents who do attempt to follow this suggestion are likely to be providing poor language models and restricted language practice in the majority language while at the same time denying their children the richness and variety of their native language competence. It would appear that educators need to be more aware of the practical realities of language minority families and more knowledgeable about the impact of language on literacy before making suggestions that may not be in their students' best interests.

It is highly consistent with the research to encourage parents to continue using the native language at home. They should be urged to speak with and listen to their children. Both listening and speaking vocabularies can be increased and the background of concepts extended. Language development is part of total development. Children's home experiences can offer vital opportunities for learning about the family's history and heritage. The songs, dances, proverbs, poetry, recipes, games, and the hundreds of other remembrances from the childhoods of parents and grandparents offer not only a sense of self, but also a wealth of language skills. Legarreta-Marcaida (1981) has an exciting and practical list of suggested activities that enhance the parents' contribution to their children's reading potential.

In encouraging parents to continue using the home language, educators must take time to explain clearly their reasons for this recommendation. Often, parents do not appreciate the educational value of the home language in an English-speaking society. They need to be reassured that English language competence is a major instructional goal. They also need to be told that native language proficiency contributes to these second language skills. The school has a significant responsibility to foster understanding of the rationale that supports the sequence of language and literacy instruction. (See also Snow's practical suggestions for effective home-school collaboration in this volume.)

The Teacher

The teacher is the most important element in an instructional plan for minority students who are learning in a classroom designed for the language majority students. A competent and caring teacher can make the method and materials work. The teacher ideally should know and appreciate the language and culture of the students. The teacher should be skillful in assessing language, development, and achievement levels. The teacher needs to be flexible and creative in making adjustments to the plan of reading instruction to accommodate a variety of levels in language achievement. The teacher needs to be well-organized and well-informed about the availability of materials, personnel, and other resources to supplement classroom opportunities. The teacher should be strong in the conviction that language minority students are capable of learning to read and write at the same level of excellence as their majority language peers. The teacher needs to continue to search for improved methods of assessment and instruction as new research points the direction toward better reading programs for language minority students. The teacher must be willing to take the time necessary to bring these students along.

All instruction for all children should be intended to increase self-confidence and self-esteem. The school is only one source of nurturance of ego strengths; but it is a very powerful one for developing, maturing students. When the reading program alternatives are considered in relation to this sense of self-worth, it may be useful to consider first the status of the minority language in the school and outside of it. When the value of the minority language is rejected by the community, this message may diminish students' sense of self. There are certainly some social conditions over which the school has little or no control, and the societal rejection of a minority group and their language may be one of them. Within the school itself, however, everyone who works with language minority students should be made aware of the importance of the mother tongue in the enhancement of intellectual growth; the relevance of the speech-print connection in the improvement of literacy skills; and the role of first language development in the extension of second language competency. School-community contacts should be used to explain and describe the needs of language minority students from the framework of human development and learning theories. A climate of acceptance at school may serve the students well in supporting their self-esteem and in increasing their confidence in their abilities to succeed in language and literacy activities.

Keeping Records

What is the role of a management system in a bilingual reading program? It is always desirable to have *some* means of charting students' progress in reading. If they are learning to read in one language, *it is important;* if they are learning to read in *two* languages, *it is absolutely essential.* Yet, the teacher must guard against the management system taking over the program. The management system is a bookkeeping system only; it is not the reading program. To be useful, the system should be short and simple. It should be easy to use and convenient for the teacher who will use it. The system should contain some built-in flexibility to accommodate differential levels of students and the transiency rates in areas where students experience a high rate of school transfer. A management system should be neither too costly, in terms of a school's budget, nor too exacting in terms of the teachers' time, tears, and frustration. The system should be selected on the basis of its consistency with the established program within the district. If some provision for the students' checking of their own progress can be built into the system, it provides greater freedom from the paper chase that so often burdens teachers and teacher aides. Wise, experienced teachers have always had a management system of some kind. The system should work for the reading program and be supportive of it. Teachers and administrators must be cautious that the management system does not work against the program and does not become an end in itself.

Assessment of Student Progress

Evaluation has shifted from formal skills-based norm-referenced instruments to informal teacher and student assessments. Among the measures are teacher observations, conferences with students, prepared checklists, student-selected portfolios of work, and responses to questionnaires. The debate persists over the best way to evaluate student progress in general. When assessment of language minority students is considered, the argument increases in protestations and in volume. As schools change curriculum and instruction, they must also modify their evaluation methods. What is the importance of assessment? Assessment can be very important and can contribute greatly to the success of a program of reading two languages. The major problem lies in finding the most appropriate ways to assess the gains students are making and to redirect one's efforts if gains are not in evidence. Assessment may involve the administration of standardized tests, the observation of students, the application of informal measures, and other assessment techniques. It is wise to remember that assessment is an appraisal of the program; *it is not the program.* Therefore, assessment should be economical of both teacher and pupil time. The *use* of information obtained through assessment is of much greater value. As teachers appraise the progress of students, they may change objectives, edit materials, or alter timelines to improve students' chances for success. Assessment should be the servant, not the master, of the reading program.

Transferability of Skills

Transfer occurs when learning in one situation influences the potential for performance in a new situation. If it were not possible to draw upon previous experiences and information, human beings would be limited in the amount or kind of knowledge acquired in a lifetime. Transfer of learning is a significant element in the context of planning reading programs for non-native English speakers. Once students leave the primary grades, they are expected to read and write in almost every school subject. Therefore, the potential for transferability of skills from one system of written language to another should be seriously examined. Transfer takes place when there are elements in the new task similar to those in the task or skill previously acquired. For languages that share the same alphabet and have common features in the visual symbols, there are immediate transfer possibilities. For Asian languages with logographic writing systems, for other non-alphabet systems, or for different alphabetic writing such as the Armenian alphabet, transfer is not based on the similarity of elements but on the more general understanding that the visual symbols represent the auditory ones. This transfer is based on the application of principles and generalizations. The sensory-motor requirements of reading and writing involve the transfer of other skills. Students who have learned how to use pencils, pens, rulers, protractors, and other classroom tools do not have to develop fine muscle control or eye-hand coordination a second time. The tracking of the eye and hand in the direction required by the conventions of the writing system may vary (Chinese is read from top to bottom, Hebrew from right to left, Spanish from left to right, and Japanese from top to bottom and then from right to left), but the awareness that there is a directionality and that it is an arbitrary feature of the specific writing system is transferable. There are good reasons to believe that attitudes and habits transfer. Positive feelings about reading in one language are likely to carry over to another. The habits of attention, concentration, persistence, and task completion can transfer well to learning the new language.

Transfer of reading abilities from the first language to the second language can be identified in both general and specific terms for pre-reading, decoding, and comprehension skills. During the preparation for reading, students have been encouraged to develop good listening habits. Having learned how to listen for a sequence of events, immediate recall of facts, rhyming elements, discovery of relationships, and for other receptive language tasks, the students carry over their response set to the demands of the new, unfamiliar language. Visual-perceptual training transfers as well. When students have become skillful in observing the visual details of one form of written language, this observation of the visual symbol system's significant features is readily available for transfer to another form. If the writing system is one that uses diacritically marked forms, the attention to detail which is necessary to see differences in specific words as in *río, rio* or *papá, papa* (words whose meanings are significantly altered by the small detail of an accent mark or its placement), will transfer. Figure must be distinguished from ground in any language, and the background of page must be separated from the material written upon it. This visual-perceptual skill developed in one language transfers easily to another.

The visual-motor skills needed to track the eyes and hand in a specific direction to follow the sequence of written patterns, the coordination of eye and hand in writing and spelling those patterns, and the development of strength and motor control are abilities that need to be learned and practiced. The application of motor skills to any reading and writing system may be transferred without change or put to use in new language learning with modifications to accommodate the differences that may exist between the first and second language writing conventions. For languages that use a left-to-right direction such as English, Vietnamese, Spanish, and Portuguese, no change in eye or hand movement is needed. Farsi, Hebrew, or other languages that read from right to left, however, require the student to change direction. Yet the eye and the hand must still move smoothly together. Though preparation for reading and writing is *specific* to the language in the matter of oral vocabulary development, ear training for language sounds, and knowledge of word order, all the sensory-motor skills and visual perceptual abilities will transfer exactly as they have been learned or with modification that can be readily encouraged.

The act of making a connection between the sounds of a language (speech) and the graphic representation of that language (print, logograph, and ideograph) has been referred to as *decoding*. Developmental programs designed to introduce reading, writing, and spelling may stress the acquisition of techniques and strategies that assist students in making the speech-print associations needed to recognize the code. Using sound-symbol relationships, applying knowledge of word structures, and finding grammatical clues are examples of such skills that are encouraged in initial instruction. These are tools intended to help students recognize in written form what is known by the student in oral context. Thus, students begin to see what they have heard. The extent to which decoding skills transfer from one language to another depends upon the two writing systems. Those using a Roman alphabet may have greater potential for transfer according to the doctrine of identical elements. Languages written according to alphabetic principles may have common features that will transfer. Written languages vary; and transfer potential will also vary on the basis of the likenesses *and* the differences to be found among their alphabets, their syllabaries, and/or other arbitrary conventions of their written systems. Awareness of the rule-governed manner by which reading skills are learned, remembered, and practiced will transfer by generalization. There is little or no effective reading at the decoding level. Until students have made the meaning connection, they are not reading. Essentially, comprehension of written material requires the exercise of intellectual skills. Students must draw upon specific backgrounds of experience and concepts. They must use memory, reasoning, and creativity as they interpret and judge what has been read. Each comprehension task calls upon students to think. At the early levels, simple, literal comprehension is required; but as the reading material becomes more complex, the reader is expected to exercise interpretive and inferential abilities of a higher order. Reading comprehension demands thinking in *any* language. If students learn in the primary language to recognize a main idea, find supportive details, order a sequence of events, identify major characters, determine the existence of bias, or analyze emotional tone, then these *thinking* skills are abilities that do not ever have to be learned again. There is complete transfer of cognitive function to the new language. For the prereading, decoding, and comprehension levels, the power and potential of transferability cannot be underestimated.

It is reasonable to infer that the basis for language transfer in reading is found in the Cummins (1980) construct of cognitive academic language proficiency which undergirds the potential for literacy in general and contributes to the ultimate flowering of literacy skills specific to the instructional program. However, it is vital to recognize that only *strong* skills transfer and that the sequence of reading in any language may be arranged to make the most of the transfer possibilities between languages. This precept of transfer should give teachers in simultaneous reading programs in two languages or those in programs of premature introduction to the second language literacy pause for thought. Violations of learning principles could easily be responsible for the reading failure presently found among the minority language students.

Potential for L1 Reading Skill Transfer to L2

The Transfer Period. When is the best period during which the student is led from first to second language literacy in English? Reading teachers should develop their own criteria for placing their language minority students in the reading classes in English. Among these criteria are such considerations as the students' successful accomplishments in the native language reading class, their proficiency in oral English, their specific ear-training for the English sound system, and their expressed interest in discovering the content to be unlocked in English print. The most important consideration in these criteria is time. Students must be given sufficient time to establish strong literacy skills in their first language.

Once the decision is made that the students have met the standards set and that they could benefit from instruction in reading English, there are some additional factors to consider. The first concern is with the reading skill, whether the students will be able to transfer immediately from native language reading to English reading. The greatest transfer benefit, however, is the confidence of an already literate learner who has successfully managed the rigors of print and will face the second writing system with self-assurance. The second consideration is the recognition of potential phonological, lexical, or structural sources of interference from the writing system that need to be anticipated and minimized. The English reading teacher must watch for any problems and attempt to prevent them or to use them for learning. A third concern is to provide knowledge and opportunities to practice new skills specific to English reading. Word order patterns, punctuation rules, multi-semantic vocabulary items, and other features unique to written English must be learned in addition to those elements that have transfer possibilities. Thus, transition to English demands *at least* the following: (1) definitive criteria for assessing students' readiness to engage in reading English; (2) recognition of areas that do not have to be taught again; (3) clear understanding of skills that may transfer immediately; (4) keen sensitivity to interference problems and the expertise to deal effectively to minimize them; and (5) considerable competence in the contrastive sounds and structural systems of both the native language and English.

Good choices for the transfer stage might be the language experience approach supported by a cautious program of phonic skills based on sounds students can *hear* and *say*. Another method might be a *linguistic* program, which presents short written patterns on the basis of a regular sound-symbol correspondence *(man - Dan - ran - fan,* etc.*)* and supports this somewhat sterile, artificial written language by rich oral English in poems, storytelling, choral speaking, and dramatizations. Still another might be a carefully paced basal reader approach augmented by pictures, news events, and descriptions of life in the language minority community as written in English. In this manner, the content of the basal stories could be enlivened by content of cultural relevance to learners. The use of a variety of authentic stories in literacy and trade books presented through a whole language approach also could be appropriate, enjoyable, and effective. There are many combinations of methods that could well support the second language literacy plan in English. Teachers should be encouraged to sift among the many methods for the winning combination for their own students.

The Best of Biliteracy

Cummins (1980) has stated that cognitive academic language potential is strongly related to reading and writing skills. This potential permits readers to process written language and manipulate the content in reasoning and in dealing with abstractions. It is this ability that promotes effective reading comprehension skills. The question of the most appropriate reading program alternatives for the minority language student can then be considered from the multiple viewpoint of: (1) which language promotes cognitive development; (2) which writing system makes the best connection with language and cognition; (3) which reading program will be supported by social, political, and cultural factors; and (4) which alternative is best suited to the minority student's stage of development. There are doubtless other variables to consider in reviewing the many complexities of literacy and biliteracy in a country where the expected outcomes of the program in the past have been the creation of monolingual and monoliterate students. This goal has been in place for a long period of educational history in the United States.

The case for native language reading instruction for language minority students is strong. The rationale can be defended on logical grounds and empirical evidence. The perceptual, sensory-motor, and cognitive processes learned and practiced in any language have tremendous potential for transfer if developmental and learning principles are not violated. Once language minority students have learned to read well and have understood the strategies for obtaining meaning from print, these abilities provide a solid foundation for literacy skills in the second language. The essential characteristic of first language skills available for supporting the addition of the second language is *strength*. Only *strong* learnings transfer. Hasty, premature introduction to the second writing system may result in two weak sets of skills, neither of which serves well enough to be the carrier of content in school subjects.

Language minority students need access to content areas by way of the language and literacy which makes sense to them. Mathematics, social science, physical science, and other school subjects can be acquired and clarified in the stronger language and, once fully understood, can be labeled in the second language. Reading instruction is not an end in itself. The reason that the years of middle childhood are usually emphasized as the period for acquiring reading and writing skills may be found in the timetable of human development. These are the years for acquiring the basic instruments for lifelong learning. The growing complexities of subject matter after the fifth grade matches the students' increased abilities to manage abstractions and formal logic. Reasoning abilities, well-supported by language and literacy, allow students to expand their understanding of the world and the people in it. If students are not given the opportunity to learn and fully develop their native language, the subject areas must be taught at a slower pace and with as much nonverbal representation as possible. Sheltered English is one modification that has been effective. Even with this effort, language minority students may not be able to keep up with their language majority classmates. High achievement is possible when students are given textbooks for content areas in their stronger language and at the suitable level for their age and grade placement. If the students cannot read second language texts, alternative methods of presenting concepts must be identified.

There is no argument among language researchers, developmental psychologists, and reading theorists that written language is strongly related to some aspects of oral language. There is also agreement that language and literacy skills are mutually supportive and essential to cognitive growth. In the best possible conditions for learning, students would all read first the language which has made their world a meaningful place. They could come from the language of their families to the language of instruction with confidence and ease. With the addition of literacy, students could advance through the curriculum to the extent that good instruction and intellectual potential would permit. Language majority students do this and some are very successful; others are not. Yet, the difficulties when they do arise are not compounded by language differences as they are for minority students. With the growing numbers of these students in classrooms of the United States, there is a serious need to re-examine reading instruction alternatives for them. It is only reasonable to expect that not all communities can offer the advantages of vernacular reading for all language minority students. It is also very reasonable to expect consideration of initial and continuing native language reading instruction in communities where large numbers of the same language groups are found.

Regarding the differences existing between immersion and submersion programs, it may be useful to attempt to change some of the negative influences through a better exchange of information. The language majority group often fails to understand that the end in view is also excellence in English. There must be a continued effort to clarify the speech-print connection in literacy and to emphasize the important role that language and literacy skills play in the development of intelligence. A central purpose of the school is to teach students to think. Thinking includes, among other entities, problem solving, evaluating, creating, and reasoning. Well-developed speech and strong reading skills are instruments that nurture thinking. For language minority students, there is the rich potential for speaking, reading, writing, and thinking in two languages.

Transferability of first language skills, both oral and written, is important and possible. The potential for transfer of sensory-motor skills, identical elements, principles, patterns, and attitude must be recognized and promoted depending upon the languages involved. There should be a sequence of language and literacy skills that searches out transfer possibilities and watches carefully for potential interference. Exit criteria are *not* applied, as the central issue to consider is the *addition* of more formal second language instruction and the introduction of the written English forms. There must be the expectation that when English language skills are sufficiently strong they, too, will carry content in the subject areas. Self-esteem is promoted not only through the accomplishment of English but also by the advancement of native language abilities. The school personnel, rather than recommending use of English in the home, continues to encourage use of the native language in family activities, which enlarges the students' view of their environment and improves their background of information. The program is based on the *common underlying proficiency model,* which recognizes the value of stimulating general language growth by way of the native language channel. (See Cummins, in this volume, for a discussion of the two models—separate and common underlying proficiencies.) The common underlying proficiency model also makes sense in terms of stressing the use of the stronger language for instructional purposes. There is the logical assumption that first language strength contributes to second language acquisition and that second language achievement is not diminished by the development of the first language. Rather, excellence in the native language improves the chances of better second language functioning. It is reasonable to expect that students who talk well, read easily, think effectively in their own first language, and have developmentally reached the stage of abstract thinking will *also* talk well, read easily, and think effectively in the second language.

Glossary

Communicative Competence - The ability to interact with other speakers in social contexts with the appropriate use of language that is sensitive to cultural difference.

Learning Styles - The students' characteristic preferences for strategies and conditions through which students can best learn.

Functions of Teachers - The ways in which teachers create and control the values and responses of students in a learning environment.

Reflection - The thoughtful consideration of ideas in both interpersonal and intrapersonal responses.

Synthetic method - A method that emphasizes the parts of words and builds meaning through the learning of small elements of language.

Analytic method - A method that focuses on meaning through the learning of whole words and larger units of thought.

Eclectic method - A method that selects from both synthetic and analytic approaches to combine the optimum benefits for students.

Lesson Design - A plan for incorporating the relevant learning principles to support classroom practices.

Social Context - The setting in which language is acquired and expressed, including classroom groupings, cooperative learning activities, and shared learnings.

Cooperative Learning - The collaboration of students who work for a group purpose while pooling knowledge, talents, and skills.

Reciprocal Teaching - An oral language activity as a cooperative endeavor intended to improve listening, comprehension, and retention of material.

Integration of Skills - The skills of thinking, listening, speaking, reading, and writing, are practiced together in classroom instruction.

Transferability of Learning - The transfer that occurs when knowledge and skills acquired in one learning situation can be applied to the demands of a new or unfamiliar one.

Table

Skill Areas	Language Specific Transfer	Language General Transfer
I. Sensory Motor Transfer		
A. Visual Skills		
1. Eye-hand coordination		X
2. Fine muscle control		X
3. Visual attention to detail		X
4. Figure-ground awareness		X
5. Visual perception	X	X
6. Visual discrimination	X	X
7. Visual memory	X	X
8. Visual sequencing		X
B. Auditory skills		
1. Figure-ground awareness		X
2. Auditory perception	X	X
3. Auditory memory	X	X
4. Auditory discrimination	X	X
5. Auditory sequencing		X
C. Spatial skills		
1. Directional organization		X
2. Top-to-bottom orientation	X	X
3. Lateral orientation	X	X
4. Spatial integration		X
II. Transfer of Identical Elements		
A. The Common Features in Writing Systems		
1. Logographs, ideographs	X	
2. Alphabets	X	
3. Sound-symbol association	X	
4. Capitalization	X	X
5. Punctuation	X	X
6. Lines or other spatial constraints of the writing		X

Skill Areas	Language Specific Transfer	Language General Transfer
III. Transfer by Principles and Generalizations		
A. Reading as a Process		
1. Understanding speech-print relationships		X
2. Speech-print connections	X	X
3. Concepts of words, syllables, sentences, paragraphs		X
4. Comprehension (thinking skills)		
a. Main idea		X
b. Sequence of ideas		X
c. Supportive details		X
d. Inferencing		X
e. Predicting outcomes		X
f. Drawing conclusions		X
g. Recognizing emotions		X
h. Seeing cause and effect		X
i. Distinguishing fact from fiction		X
5. Rule-governed aspects of reading	X	X
6. Study skills		X
IV. Transfer of Habits and Attitudes		
A. Non-cognitive Transfer		
1. Attention		X
2. Listening skills		X
3. Concentration		X
4. Persistence		X
5. Task completion		X
B. Self-esteem Transfer		
1. Being literate		X
2. Feeling capable		X
3. Possessing specific competencies		X
4. Achieving		X
5. Believing in one's ability to learn		X

REFERENCES

Adams, M. (1990). *Beginning to read: Thinking and learning about print.* Urbana-Champaign, Illinois: Center for the Study of Reading.

Archambeault, B. (1992). Personalizing study skills in secondary students. *Journal of Reading, 35*(6), 468-472.

Beck, I. (1989). Improving practice through understanding reading. In *Toward a thinking curriculum: Current cognitive research.* Alexandria, VA: Association for Supervision and Curriculum Development.

Berliner, D. (1985). The executive functions of teaching. In J. Osbourne, P. T. Wilson, & R. C. Anderson (Eds.), *Reading education: Foundations for a literate America.* Lexington, MA: D. C. Heath.

Bermudez, A., & Prater, D. (1989). Evaluating the effectiveness of writing on the comprehension and retention of content reading. *NABE Annual Conference Journal,* 151-156.

Bowen, J. D. (1977). Linguistic perspectives on bilingual education. In B. Spolsky and R. Cooper (Eds.), *Frontiers of bilingual education.* Rowley, MA: Newbury House.

Bransford, J., & Vye, N. (1989). A perspective on cognitive research and its implications for instruction. In *Toward the thinking curriculum: Current cognitive research.* Alexandria, VA: Association for Supervision and Curriculum Development.

Bruder, M., & Henderson, R. (1986). *Beginning reading in English as a second language.* Washington, DC: Center for Applied Linguistics.

Cohen, A. (1974, March). The Culver City Spanish immersion program: The first two years. *The Modern Language Journal, 58*(3), 95-103.

Cohen, A. (1975). *A sociolinguistic approach to bilingual education: Experiments in the Southwest.* Rowley, MA: Newbury House.

Cohen, A., & Swain, M. (1976, March). Bilingual education: The "immersion" model in the North American context. *TESOL Quarterly, 10*(1), 45-53.

Cummins, J. (1979, September). Linguistic interdependence and the educational development of bilingual children. *Bilingual Education Paper Series.* Los Angeles, CA: National Dissemination and Assessment Center, California State University, Los Angeles.

Cummins, J. (1980, March). *The construct of language proficiency in bilingual education.* Paper presented at the Georgetown Roundtable of Language and Linguistics, Georgetown University.

Dolson, D. (1985). Bilingualism and scholastic performance: The literature revisited. *The NABE Journal, 10*(1), 1-35.

Engle, P. L. (1975). *The use of vernacular languages in education: Language medium in early school years for minority groups.* Papers in Linguistics Bilingual Education Series, 3. Arlington, VA: Center for Applied Linguistics.

Glatthorn, A. (1989). Thinking, writing, and reading: Making connections. In D. Lapp, J. Flood, and N. Farnam (Eds.), *Content area reading and learning* (pp. 283-296). Englewood Cliffs, NJ: Prentice-Hall.

Goldenberg, C. (1990). Research directions: Beginning literacy instruction for Spanish-speaking children. *Language Arts, 67,* 590-596.

Goldenberg, C. (1991). *Instructional conversations and their classroom application.* (Practice Report: II.) Santa Cruz, CA: The National Center for Research on Cultural Diversity and Second Language Learning.

Goodman, K. (1987). *What's whole in whole language?* Portsmouth, NH: Heinemann.

Fotos, S., & Ellis, R. (1991, Winter). Communicating about Grammar: A task-based approach. *TESOL Quarterly 25*(4).

Hernandez-Chavez, E. (1984). The inadequacy of English immersion education as an educational approach for language minority students in the United States. In *Studies on immersion.* Sacramento, CA: California State Department of Education.

Hiebert, E. (1991, March). The development of word-based strategies in authentic literacy task. *Language Arts, 68.*

Johnson, D. (1991). Some observations on progress in research in second language learning and teaching. In M. McGroaty and C. Faltis (Eds.), *Language in school and society: Politics and pedagogy.* Berlin: Mouton de Gruyter.

Johnson, D., & Myklebust, H. (1967). *Learning disabilities: Educational principles and practices.* New York: Grune and Stratton.

Kagan, S. (1986). Cooperative learning and sociocultural factors in schooling. In *Beyond language: Social and cultural factors in schooling language minority students.* Los Angeles: Evaluation, Dissemination and Assessment Center, California State University.

Krashen, S. (1982). *Principles and practice in second language acquisition.* New York: Pergamon Press.

Krashen, S. (1985). *Input in second language acquisition.* Oxford: Pergamon Press.

Lambert, W. E. (1975). Culture and language as factors in learning and education. In A. Wolfgang (Ed.), *Education of immigrant students.* Ontario, Canada: Ontario Institute of Studies in Education.

Lambert, W. E., & Tucker, C. R. (1972). *Bilingual education of children: The St. Lambert experiment.* Rowley, MA: Newbury House.

Legarreta-Marcaida, D. (1981). Effective use of the primary language in the classroom. *Schooling and language minority students: A theoretical framework.* (1st ed.) (pp. 83-116). Los Angeles: Evaluation, Dissemination and Assessment Center, California State University.

Long, M. (1990). The least a second language acquisition theory needs to explain. *TESOL Quarterly, 24,* 649-666.

Merino, C. (1991). Discourse processes in the second language classroom. In M. McGroaty and C. Faltis (Eds.), *Languages in school and society: Politics and pedagogy* Berlin: Mouton de Gruyter.

Modiano, N. (1968, Spring). National mother tongue in beginning reading: A comparative study. *Research in the Teaching of English, 11*(1), 32-43.

Murphy, J. (1991). Oral communication in TESOL: Integrating speaking, listening and pronunciation. *TESOL Quarterly, 25,* 51-74.

Palinscar, A., & Brown, A. (1989). Instruction for self-regulated reading. In *Toward the thinking curriculum: Current cognitive research.* Alexandria, VA: Association for Supervision and Curriculum Development.

Ramirez, A. (1991). Discourse processes in the second language classroom. In M. McGroaty and C. Faltis (Eds.), *Languages in school and society: Politics and pedagogy.* Berlin: Mouton de Gruyter.

Rigg, P. (1991, Autumn). Whole language in TESOL. *TESOL Quarterly, 25*(3), 521-542.

Savignon, S. (1991). Communicative language teaching: State of the art. *TESOL Quarterly, 25,* 261-277.

Smith, F. (1971). *Understanding reading: A psycholinguistic analysis of reading and learning to read.* New York: Holt, Rinehart, and Winston.

Swain, M. (1983). *Communicative competence: Some roles of comprehensible input and comprehensible output, in its development.* Paper presented at the 10th University of Michigan Conference on Applied Linguistics, Ann Arbor, MI.

Tarvin, W., & Al-Arishi, A. (1991, Spring). Rethinking communicative language teaching: Reflection and the EFL classroom. *TESOL Quarterly, 25,* 1.

Thonis, E. (1976). *Literacy for America's Spanish speaking children.* Newark, DE: International Reading Association.

Thonis, E. (1983). *The English-Spanish connection.* Compton, CA: Santillana.

Tucker, G. R. (1977). The linguistic perspective. In *Bilingual education current perspectives.* Arlington, VA: Center for Applied Linguistics.

RESEARCH-BASED CHECKLIST FOR DESIGNING AND MONITORING PROGRAM DELIVERY

DAVID P. DOLSON

In the first edition of **Schooling and Language Minority Students: A Theoretical Framework** (1981), the appendix contained a copy of the then current version of the **Bilingual Education Program Quality Review Instrument, Kindergarten Through Grade Six (Bilingual PQRI).** At the time, the **Bilingual PQRI** was used by the Bilingual Education Office of the California Department of Education to promote research-based standards for the design and implementation of bilingual education programs.

Gradually, school district personnel began to use the **Bilingual PQRI** as a resource document to design new programs and to review those currently in place. Since the items contained in the **Bilingual PQRI** were based on a synthesis of the most recent research and evaluation studies, the instrument was considered a useful way to compare the elements of a program against a set of standards which represented the best information available at the time.

Because of a continued need to assist school districts in the application of research knowledge, we have revised and updated the items in the **Bilingual PQRI** and recast the document into a more flexible and easier-to-use checklist format. The items of quality contained in the **Bilingual Program Delivery Checklist** are based primarily on the research reported in this volume and are consistent with other well-controlled research and evaluation studies on bilingual education published elsewhere.

The **Bilingual Program Delivery Checklist** is designed specifically for the review of full bilingual education programs, that is, programs organized to provide language minority students with instruction in and through English and the native language according to the educational needs of individual participants. At a minimum, full bilingual programs include instruction that (1) develops native-like proficiency in English and the minority language, (2) provides access to and sustains normal attainment in all courses required for grade level promotion and graduation, and (3) promotes the development of a positive self-concept and crosscultural knowledge and skills. Although the checklist is most closely aligned with the full bilingual education program model, most of the indicators of quality, with some minor adaptations, apply to other program approaches such as two-way bilingual, early-exit bilingual, and even structured immersion/sheltered instructional programs.

In the early planning stages, schools that enroll significant numbers of language minority students typically conduct a needs assessment of their student population and community. They also survey their teachers and other educational staff members. Based on the results of the needs assessment and deliberations concerning the goals and objectives of the proposed program, the school eventually selects a general direction or a program model for educating language minority students at the site. The items of quality found in the **Bilingual Program Delivery Checklist** collectively provide a framework for developing an instructional delivery system centered on effective program practices.

Even at this beginning stage, there are severe challenges to the maintenance of high levels of program quality. Invariably, schools are forced to design their bilingual programs in ways that accommodate local realities, especially in terms of competing priorities and the availability of the human and material resources needed for implementation.

Once implementation begins, there is a need for on-going monitoring to determine the degree to which the instructional treatment is actually being delivered as planned. Proper monitoring is also an appropriate safeguard against insidious encroachments of mediocrity which over time erode the overall quality of the program. The items contained in the **Bilingual Program Delivery Checklist** can be used to guide initial and enroute adjustments to both the program design and implementation practices. The items can also serve as a reminder to mend flaws in program delivery which develop over time as demands are made upon staff members to come up with interim but often "second best" solutions to pressing problems.

The **Bilingual Program Delivery Checklist** is divided into three sections. The first section contains the items of program quality organized by the major components of a bilingual education program:

I.   Spanish Language Development
II.   English Language Development
III.   Access to the Core Curriculum
IV.   Crosscultural Development
V.   Staffing and Professional Development
VI.   Home/School Communication and Collaboration

The degree and quality of implementation of each item is to be rated on a simple four-point scale as indicated below:

3 =   Superior
2 =   Satisfactory
1 =   Unsatisfactory
0 =   Not Implemented
X =   Not Observed

The "Not Observed" (X) rating is used only in instances where program reviewers do not obtain sufficient information on which to base a rating. The comments section is to be used by the program reviewers to clarify their findings.

Program reviewers should use a variety of strategies to collect data. The most obvious methods of investigation include: (1) review of program documents, reports, and student records; (2) interviews with teachers, paraprofessionals, administrators, parents, community, and students; and (3) observations of classroom and other instructional and instructional support activities.

The second section of the document consists of a list of several operational definitions provided to ensure a common understanding of key terminology used in the document. Whenever operational definitions are used in the text of the checklist, they appear in bold to alert the reader that a term with a specialized meaning has been encountered. Any item containing one or more operational definitions should conform to the specifications of the particular definitions in order for the item to be rated at "satisfactory" or "superior" levels.

The third and final section contains the bibliographic references. Only those references associated with the operational definitions are listed here. The actual references for the items of quality are drawn from the various articles contained in this volume and their corresponding bibliographies.

BILINGUAL EDUCATION PROGRAM DELIVERY CHECKLIST FOR FULL BILINGUAL EDUCATION PROGRAM, SPANISH/ENGLISH, KINDERGARTEN THROUGH GRADE SIX

This sample version of the **Bilingual Education Program Delivery Checklist** has been developed specifically for school sites enrolling Spanish-speaking students in a full, late-exit bilingual education program covering kindergarten through grade six.

To use this checklist to review programs serving students from other language groups, enrolled at grades 7-12, or being instructed in another program model (such as early-exit or sheltered/structured immersion), a number of relatively minor modifications would be needed. For example, each item should be reviewed for applicability to the alternative setting. In some cases revisions in terminology might be necessary. New and additional items should be added to fully address import programmatic features that are not adequately emphasized in this version. The process of revising the checklist will not only result in a customized and therefore more useful review instrument but also will serve as an excellent learning experience for the staff members involved in the program review, allowing them to gain further insights into the design and delivery of the program.

Items of Program Quality

I. Spanish Language Development

The program provides the instruction and instructional support services necessary to develop native-like proficiency in Spanish.

1. An assessment system is in place which provides information on the initial and current levels of Spanish language proficiency for individual students.

    ☐ Superior   ☐ Satisfactory   ☐ Unsatisfactory

        ☐ Not Implemented   ☐ Not Observed

Comments: _____

_____

_____

_____

2. Teachers can show a schedule or lesson plan indicating that students receive **planned instruction** in Spanish language arts.

    ☐ Superior   ☐ Satisfactory   ☐ Unsatisfactory

        ☐ Not Implemented   ☐ Not Observed

Comments: _____

_____

_____

_____

3. The teaching staff is knowledgeable of the main features of the methodology selected for Spanish language literacy instruction.

☐ Superior   ☐ Satisfactory   ☐ Unsatisfactory

☐ Not Implemented   ☐ Not Observed

Comments: _____

_____

_____

_____

4. Critical thinking skills are interwoven in the teaching of reading and writing through the use of strategies such as **Critical Literacy** and **Process Writing.**

☐ Superior   ☐ Satisfactory   ☐ Unsatisfactory

☐ Not Implemented   ☐ Not Observed

Comments: _____

_____

_____

_____

5. Students have access to a variety of reading materials in the Spanish language that are appropriate for their age and grade levels.

□ Superior   □ Satisfactory   □ Unsatisfactory

□ Not Implemented   □ Not Observed

Comments: _____

_____

_____

_____

6.   Children's literature books in Spanish represent proportionately the heritage background of the Latino students in the
program as well as other Spanish-speaking groups from other
parts of the world and other regions of the United States.

□ Superior   □ Satisfactory   □ Unsatisfactory

□ Not Implemented   □ Not Observed

Comments: _____

_____

_____

_____

II. English Language Development

*The program provides the instruction and instructional support
services necessary to develop native-like proficiency in the
English language.*

1. An assessment system is in place which provides information on the initial and current levels of English language abilities of individual students.

☐ Superior   ☐ Satisfactory   ☐ Unsatisfactory

☐ Not Implemented   ☐ Not Observed

Comments: _____

_____

_____

_____

2. Students are provided adequate exposure to acquire the English language through **planned instruction** using the following strategies:

    a.   communicative-based second language instruction;
    b.   content-based second language instruction;
    c.   opportunities to practice the second language at school;
    d.   opportunities to practice the second language outside of school.

☐ Superior   ☐ Satisfactory   ☐ Unsatisfactory

☐ Not Implemented   ☐ Not Observed

Comments: _____

_____

_____

_____

3. Students are provided with **planned instruction** in the English language in order to learn those aspects of the language most efficiently learned through direct instruction.

  ☐ Superior   ☐ Satisfactory   ☐ Unsatisfactory

        ☐ Not Implemented   ☐ Not Observed

Comments: _____

_____

_____

_____

4. Teachers providing English language development are knowledgeable of the main features of the second language teaching methodologies selected for use in the program.

  ☐ Superior   ☐ Satisfactory   ☐ Unsatisfactory

        ☐ Not Implemented   ☐ Not Observed

Comments: _____

_____

_____

_____

III. Access to the Core Curriculum
_____

The program ensures access to the core curriculum for every student by providing instruction in all courses required for grade

*level promotion and graduation in both Spanish and English,
depending on the individual needs of students.*

1. **Planned instruction** is provided through the Spanish language
in the following subject areas:

Social Science   Natural Science   Other:
Mathematics   Health/P.E.   Other:

☐ Superior   ☐ Satisfactory   ☐ Unsatisfactory

☐ Not Implemented   ☐ Not Observed

Comments: _____

_____

_____

_____

2. In most cases, Spanish medium instruction in the following
subject areas is conducted almost entirely in Spanish:

Social Science   Natural Science   Other:
Mathematics   Health/P.E.   Other:

☐ Superior   ☐ Satisfactory   ☐ Unsatisfactory

☐ Not Implemented   ☐ Not Observed

Comments: _____

_____

_____

_____

3. There are sufficient basic and supplementary materials in the Spanish language to support **planned instruction** in each of the following subject areas:

Social Science   Natural Science   Other:
Mathematics   Health/P.E.   Other:

☐ Superior   ☐ Satisfactory   ☐ Unsatisfactory

☐ Not Implemented   ☐ Not Observed

Comments: _____

_____

_____

_____

4. Spanish medium instruction is of sufficient scope and quality to sustain academic achievement. At least 50 percent of the students enrolled in Spanish medium instruction for a period of at least four years or more are at or above grade level in each of the following subject areas when assessed through Spanish:

Social Science   Natural Science   Other:
Mathematics   Health/P.E.   Other:

☐ Superior   ☐ Satisfactory   ☐ Unsatisfactory

☐ Not Implemented   ☐ Not Observed

Comments: _____

_____

_____

_____

5. As Spanish-speaking students acquire advanced levels of English proficiency, the amount and level of difficulty of English medium instruction increases accordingly. Designated students are enrolled in the following subject area courses in English using **specially designed academic instruction** or mainstream approaches, depending on the individual proficiency levels of the students:

Social Science   Natural Science   Other:
Mathematics   Health/P.E.   Other:

☐ Superior   ☐ Satisfactory   ☐ Unsatisfactory

☐ Not Implemented   ☐ Not Observed

Comments: _____

_____

_____

_____

6. English medium instruction is of sufficient scope and quality to sustain academic achievement. At least 50 percent of the students enrolled for a period of one year or more in English mainstream instruction are scoring at or above grade level in each of the following subject areas when assessed through English:

Social Science   Natural Science   Other:
Mathematics   Health/P.E.   Other:

☐ Superior   ☐ Satisfactory   ☐ Unsatisfactory

☐ Not Implemented   ☐ Not Observed

Comments: _____

_____

_____

_____

IV. Crosscultural Development

Children learn to respect and value their heritage language and culture as well as the heritage languages and cultures of others.

1.   The school has adopted and staff is manifesting a multicultural perspective with corresponding learning activities in all aspects of the curriculum.

☐ Superior   ☐ Satisfactory   ☐ Unsatisfactory

☐ Not Implemented   ☐ Not Observed

Comments: _____

_____

_____

_____

2.   Cross-ethnic experiences and friendships are fostered through the use of integrative strategies such as **cooperative learning.**

☐ Superior   ☐ Satisfactory   ☐ Unsatisfactory

☐ Not Implemented   ☐ Not Observed

Comments: _____

_____

_____

_____

3. There are a number of on-going activities at the school aimed at providing students with accurate information about their own heritage group as well as about the other cultural groups represented in the school, including:

    a.   library materials written by representatives of the respective groups;

    b.   presence of staff members who are role models;

    c.   visitations to community centers and other points of interest;

    d.   involvement of community members in regular and special school activities.

☐ Superior   ☐ Satisfactory   ☐ Unsatisfactory

☐ Not Implemented   ☐ Not Observed

Comments: _____

_____

_____

_____

4. As a result of inservice training programs such as **Teacher Expectations and Student Achievement** (TESA, and its gender equity counterpart GESA), staff members at the school have high achievement expectations for all students.

☐ Superior   ☐ Satisfactory   ☐ Unsatisfactory

☐ Not Implemented   ☐ Not Observed

Comments: _____

_____

_____

_____

5. The school is involved in a cultural and language exchange project with a sister school in a Spanish-speaking country similar to the **Orillas Computer Network Program.**

☐ Superior   ☐ Satisfactory   ☐ Unsatisfactory

☐ Not Implemented   ☐ Not Observed

Comments: _____

_____

_____

_____

6.   Through the use of a multicultural interventions such as **Antibias Curriculum,** students and staff develop a sense of empowerment and skills to act alone or in concert with others against social injustices generated by racism and prejudice.

☐ Superior   ☐ Satisfactory   ☐ Unsatisfactory

☐ Not Implemented   ☐ Not Observed

Comments: _____

_____

_____

_____

V. Staffing and Professional Development

Instruction in the program is provided by qualified teachers, who along with other colleagues at the school, are provided with opportunities for collaboration and inservice training.

1. There are a sufficient number of qualified teachers to provide instruction in and through Spanish.

☐ Superior   ☐ Satisfactory   ☐ Unsatisfactory

☐ Not Implemented   ☐ Not Observed

Comments: _____

_____

_____

_____

2. There are a sufficient number of qualified teachers to provide English language development and **specially designed academic instruction** in English.

☐ Superior   ☐ Satisfactory   ☐ Unsatisfactory

☐ Not Implemented   ☐ Not Observed

Comments: _____

_____

_____

_____

3. Teachers and other staff members hold regularly scheduled meetings to share information, review program implementation practices, and plan activities.

☐ Superior   ☐ Satisfactory   ☐ Unsatisfactory

☐ Not Implemented   ☐ Not Observed

Comments: _____

_____

_____

_____

4. The training needs of each teacher and other staff members are assessed at least annually.

☐ Superior   ☐ Satisfactory   ☐ Unsatisfactory

☐ Not Implemented   ☐ Not Observed

Comments: _____

_____

_____

_____

5. The program provides regularly scheduled training sessions that are based on the individual needs of teachers and other staff members.

☐ Superior   ☐ Satisfactory   ☐ Unsatisfactory

☐ Not Implemented   ☐ Not Observed

Comments: _____

_____

_____

_____

VI. Home/School Communication and Collaboration

Parents and community members are aware of the purposes and major features of the bilingual education program. They are knowledgeable of various ways that they can assist their own children with the academic and social demands of school.

1. The school provides parents and community members with a **bilingual education program orientation guide,** available in both English and Spanish versions.

☐ Superior   ☐ Satisfactory   ☐ Unsatisfactory

☐ Not Implemented   ☐ Not Observed

Comments: _____

_____

_____

_____

2. Staff members employ a variety of strategies to disseminate and explain the contents of the **bilingual education program orientation guide,** including at least three of the following:

    a.   Sent home with students or mailed;
    b.   Presented as topic at parent meeting;
    c.   Explained at parent/teacher conference;
    d.   Explained during home visits;
    e.   Other:

☐ Superior   ☐ Satisfactory   ☐ Unsatisfactory

☐ Not Implemented   ☐ Not Observed

Comments: _____

_____

_____

_____

3. The school encourages and assists parents to become involved in the education of their children by sponsoring activities such as:

    a.   Dissemination of a parent/student activity guide;
    b.   Home/school learning projects such as the **Pajaro Valley Family Literacy Experience;**
    c.   Child development training.

☐ Superior   ☐ Satisfactory   ☐ Unsatisfactory

    ☐ Not Implemented   ☐ Not Observed

Comments: _____

_____

_____

_____

Operational Definitions

1. **Antibias Curriculum** is an integrated multicultural approach developed by early childhood educators to enable young children of various racial, ethnic and class backgrounds, and physical abilities to develop positive concepts of self and of others in a diverse world (Derman-Sparks, 1989).

2. **Bilingual Education Program Orientation Guide** is a written document that describes the intent and content of the bilingual education program. Information included in the guide addresses the following topics:

    a.   individualized instruction based on language and academic needs;

    b.   desired individual pupil and program outcomes;

    c.   student identification, assessment, and placement procedures;

    d.   nature of the curriculum;

    e.   staff characteristics and staffing arrangements;

    f.   parent and community involvement and educational opportunities.

3. **Cooperative Learning** is the structuring of classrooms so that students from diverse backgrounds study and work together in small groups in ways that (1) stimulate academic achievement, especially for language minority students, (2) create positive intergroup relations, and (3) socialize students toward prosocial values and behaviors (Kagan, 1986).

4. **Critical Literacy** is an approach to reading instruction based on Freire's (1973) pedgogical approach which organizes lessons into four phases: (1) descriptive reading, (2) interpretive reading, (3) critical analysis, and (4) creative response, that is, relating the reading to one's own context and selecting possible resolutions or appropriate courses of action. This process integrates the development of critical thinking skills with fundamental literacy instruction (Ada, 1986).

5. **Orillas Computer Network Program** is a project that promotes Spanish literacy development through a computer information exchange between sister schools. For example, schools in Connecticut, California, and Mexico formed a network to share student writings on issues of mutual interest. (Sayers and Brown, 1987).

6. **Pajaro Valley Family Literacy Experience** is a home/school literacy program conducted in Spanish. Parents and their children select books and works together using the **Critical Literacy** approach described in operational definition No. 4. School personnel conduct orientation sessions in which parents learn how to discuss the books with their children. Follow up sessions are held to cover other subjects such as questioning strategies and writing projects (Ada, 1988).

7. **Planned Instruction** means at least three organized lessons totaling at least 120 minutes per week.

8. **Process Writing** is an approach where students are allowed to acquire writing skills by engaging in writing activities that are creative and intrinsically interesting. Beginning writers, when they realize that they have something to say, become confident that they can communicate through the written form of the language. Traditional approaches to writing instruction which stress correctness of surface forms of language are de-emphasized initially (Graves, 1983).

9. **Specially Designed Academic Instruction** is an instructional approach which uses English as a medium of instruction for subject matter classes such as mathematics, science, and social science. This type of instruction is sometimes used with Spanish-speaking students at intermediate or advanced levels of English proficiency when these students are initially introduced to English medium subject matter instruction. Various techniques are employed to make the English academic input comprehensible to the Spanish speakers:

    a.   a focus on content rather than surface language;
    b.   use of concrete contextualized referents (realia);

c.   no restrictions on Spanish use by pupils;

d.   grouping students by English proficiency levels;

e.   no overt correction of language form errors;

f.   frequent comprehension checks;

g.   overriding concern to always negotiate meaning.

10. **Teacher Expectations and Student Achievement (TESA)** is a professional development program in which teachers learn to identify specific teaching behaviors, which when used in an equitable manner with so-called "underachievers" (i.e., language minority students), stimulate scholastic performance. Examples of teacher behaviors include listening attentively to students; providing students opportunities to respond; giving individual attention to students; personalizing the students' participation in the class; and using expressions of courtesy (Kerman et al., 1980).

REFERENCES

Ada, A. F. (1986). Creative education for bilingual teachers. *Harvard Educational Review, 56,* 386-394.

Ada, A. F. (1988). The Pajaro Valley experience, working with Spanish-speaking parents to develop children's reading and writing skills in the home through the use of children's literature. In T. Skutnabb-Kangas and J. Cummins (Eds.), *Minority education: From shame to struggle.* Clevedon, England: Multilingual Matters.

Derman-Sparks, L. (1989). *Antibias curriculum: Tools for empowering young children.* Washington, DC: National Association for the Education of Young People.

Freire, P. (1973). *Education for critical consciousness.* New York: Seabury.

Graves, D. (1983). *Writing: Children and teachers at work.* Exeter, NH: Heinemann.

Kagan, S. (1986). Cooperative learning and sociocultural factors in schools. In *Beyond language: Social and cultural factors in schooling language minority students.* Los Angeles: Evaluation, Dissemination and Assessment Center, California State University, Los Angeles.

Kerman S. et al. (1980). *Teacher expectations and student achievement.* Downey, CA: Office of the Los Angeles County Superintendent of Schools.

Sayers, D., & Brown, K. (1987). Bilingual education and telecommunications: A perfect fit. *The Computing Teacher, 17,* 23-24.